# RESTRUCTURING
## THE
# MIDDLE LEVEL SCHOOL

SUNY Series, Middle Schools and Early Adolescents
Jan Streitmatter, editor

# RESTRUCTURING THE MIDDLE LEVEL SCHOOL

## Implications for School Leaders

by
Sally N. Clark
and
Donald C. Clark

STATE UNIVERSITY OF NEW YORK PRESS

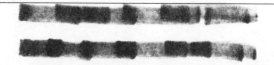

Published by
State University of New York Press, Albany

For information, address the State University of New York Press,
State University Plaza, Albany, NY 12246

**Library of Congress Cataloging-in-Publication Data**

Clark, Sally N., 1951-
    Restructuring the middle level school : implications for school
leaders / by Sally N. Clark and Donald C. Clark.
        p.    cm. — (SUNY series, middle schools and early adolescents)
    Includes bibliographical references and index.
    ISBN 0-7914-1921-5 (alk. paper). — ISBN 0-7914-1922-3 (pbk. :
alk. paper)
    1. Middle schools—United States.  2. Middle schools—United
States—Administration.  3. School management and organization-
-United States.  4. Educational change—United States.  I. Clark,
Donald C.  II. Title.  III. Series.
LB1623.5.C53  1994
373.2'36'0973—dc20                                          93-26782
                                                                CIP
                                                                Rev

10  9  8  7  6  5  4  3  2  1

# CONTENTS

SECTION IV. RESTRUCTURING THE
MIDDLE LEVEL SCHOOL: DEVELOPING, IMPLEMENTING,
AND EVALUATING THE STRATEGIC PLAN

# LIST OF FIGURES

# FOREWORD

If this book had been written to sell in mall book stores it would have been entitled *Everything You've Always Wanted to Know About Middle Schools and How to Put That Knowledge to Use.* Among popular paperbacks, such a broadly enticing claim might simply be a rhetorical exaggeration, but in this case it could be a valid summary of the volume. This book is that comprehensive, although it is not designed for the reader looking for easy answers. Its messages are not rhetorical but reality-based. The Clarks have put together in this publication a truly complete and thorough review of middle level education, its historical development, and its present status. Then they have gone beyond that to show how educational leaders can implement what is known about developmentally responsive programs for young adolescents. It is a treatise worthy of close attention by any serious middle level educator.

With conscientious scholarship that comes through with passion, this book provides a solid knowledge base and a sound philosophy. Its prose is direct but not pedantic. Sally and Don Clark have produced a remarkable book. While other reviews of the past and present are available and books on leadership and administration are in ample supply, no other work so effectively combines middle school theory and reality with strategies for providing leadership in program implementation. The book includes a substantial section on building a knowledge base—a matter too often slighted in books that assess educational status and offer recommendations. As the movement to restructure American education continues to gain momentum, this book will be an important tool. For those in positions of middle level administrative responsibility, it is essential.

Don and Sally Clark, with three decades of practical experience in middle level education, speak with authority that is undergirded by impeccable scholarship. They know both the literature and the classroom, as is evident from the careful citations and the illustrations from the field. Early junior high school sources, reflecting an awareness of and appreciation for an historical context, are present along with contemporary studies and research findings to present the most detailed and scholarly treatment of middle level education and leadership available.

This book clarifies a grand vision and then gives structure to processes and procedures that ought to be used to achieve that vision. They make it clear that restructuring is not a matter of organizing new programs but is rather a process of institutionalizing a new vision. Sound theory is followed by practical guidelines. This is not a book to be read casually and put aside with the comment, "very interesting." It challenges and impels readers to consider how they could more effectively tackle the important task of bringing about developmentally responsive middle level programs. *Restructuring the Middle Level School: Implications for School Leaders* combines information, analysis, vision, and structure in an uncommon but excellent way. The profession owes much to these two educators.

*John H. Lounsbury*
*Dean Emeritus, School of Education,*
*Georgia College and Publications Editor,*
*National Middle School Association*

# PREFACE

The development of a successful middle level school involves many important factors. It is, however, middle level school leaders and the vision they hold for their schools that drives the restructuring process. We recently came across a statement from a New England building contractor who restores old homes. She stated, "Anything I can visualize, I can do." This statement, we believe, is also applicable to middle level school restructuring. While "visioning" what a developmentally responsive middle level school should be is a critical first step in starting the restructuring process, several questions become apparent. What should the vision be? Whose vision is it? On what foundation do educators, parents, and community leaders build their vision? Do school leaders really believe they can achieve what they visualize? What steps, processes, and strategies should be used to achieve the vision?

The answers to these questions form the basis of our beliefs about middle level schools and the strategies that are used to begin and maintain successful restructuring. We believe, for example, that the development of an appropriate vision for the middle level school and the decisions about the restructuring process should be the responsibility of those who are the closest to young adolescents—their principals, their teachers, and their parents. In addition, we believe that middle level school restructuring must be done by educators, parents, and community members who believe in their vision and are *informed* decision makers.

These beliefs have evolved over the years based on our work with middle level educators, parents, and community members who are successfully restructuring schooling for young adolescents, on our study of middle level and educational reform literature, and through our participation in numerous research studies. From this background of experience and study it has become increasingly apparent to us that successful middle level school restructuring is built on school-based decision making dependent on several factors:

1.  Leadership - opportunities for administrators, teachers, students, staff, parents, and community members to exercise leadership in school restructuring.
2.  Collaboration - opportunities to work together, plan together, teach together, make decisions together, and evaluate together.
3.  Involvement - opportunities for members of all stakeholder groups to participate in meaningful ways in the governance and operation of the school.
4.  Information - opportunities to build comprehensive knowledge bases about students and parental and community expectancies, about successful middle level programs and practices, and about responsive leadership and the restructuring process.
5.  Inquiry - opportunities for continuous inquiry and reflection about successes and failures.
6.  Strategic Planning - opportunities to determine mission, goals, programs, professional development, implementation strategies, and assessment through the process of systematic long-range planning.

It has also become increasingly apparent that teachers and administrators, while encouraged to reform or restructure their schools, are often getting few opportunities to expand their knowledge base about middle level schools and successful practices, to acquire the skills necessary for school restructuring, to learn strategies for effective collaboration, or to gain expertise in the organization of leadership for school-based decision making.

The challenge for us was to create a book that would assist school, parent, and community leaders in acquiring the skills to be successful in the comprehensive and complex task of restructuring middle level schools. *Restructuring the Middle Level School: Implications for School Leaders* is designed to meet that challenge. With its emphasis on important elements of school restructuring, the book is intended to provide educators with the information they need to build a knowledge base about appropriate programs and practices. It is also designed to assist in the acquisition of the skills and processes necessary for the successful and systematic implementation of school change. We envision that this book will provide teachers, principals, parents, central office administrators, community members, and graduate students with many of the skills, knowledge, and processes to begin or to sustain their efforts to successfully restructure middle level schools. It is also our intention that the book's careful description of the literature and documentation of current research will contribute to the body of knowledge on middle school leadership and restructuring.

## ORGANIZATION OF THE BOOK

Organized around the six factors identified earlier, the major sections of the book include middle level school perspectives past and present; building a knowledge base; restructuring, leadership, and collaboration; strategic planning; and maintaining the climate for change.

In Chapter One, we define middle level education and describe the forces that shaped and continue to shape middle level education, the evolution of middle level schools to what they are today, and current middle level school organization and practice. The rhetoric and research about how middle level schools should be organized, what successful middle level schools should look like, and why they need to change are the major issues examined in Chapter Two.

Building a comprehensive knowledge base for planning and decision making is the focus of Chapters Three through Six. In Chapter Three we examine the developmental characteristics of young adolescents from the vantage point of John Hill's framework. In addition to the description of these characteristics, implications for appropriate programs and practice are presented.

Chapter Four begins with David Elkind's definition of developmental appropriateness. We then identify the components of the middle level curriculum, including the core or basic curriculum, the exploratory curriculum, the social curriculum, and the integrated curriculum. The chapter concludes with a section on curriculum and student assessment as it relates to developmental appropriateness.

In Chapters Five and Six, we review successful middle level school programs. Chapter Five examines interdisciplinary teaming, teacher advisory, and student activity programs while in Chapter Six we describe parent involvement programs and youth service programs. Rationale, descriptions, examples from practice, and research on program effectiveness are provided in both chapters.

Restructuring, leadership, and collaboration are the topics of Chapters Seven and Eight. Restructuring is defined in Chapter Seven, the tasks of successful restructuring are identified, and critical factors which support successful restructuring are discussed. Also highlighted is the crucial role that leadership must play in bringing about school change. Collaboration, including approaches to teacher leadership and decision making, structuring successful school involvement, and organizing participation for strategic planning are reviewed in Chapter Eight.

The processes of strategic planning (planning, implementing, and evaluating) provide the focuses for Chapters Nine, Ten, and Eleven. In Chapter Nine we define strategic planning, identify specific steps in the strategic planning process, and present several examples. We offer a plan for organizing staff development in Chapter Ten which includes the rationale for staff development and specific procedures for planning and implementing viable programs. The importance of leadership in supporting staff development is emphasized. In Chapter Eleven we examine the purposes and functions of program evaluation and describe four specific programs that can be used to assess program success and goal accomplishment.

In Chapter Twelve, the concluding chapter of the book, we emphasize that successful middle level schools are always in the process of restructuring. We also stress the importance of continuing the inquiry and reflection process. Maintaining a climate of change is a leadership challenge that must be met if schools are to continue to be developmentally responsive to young adolescent learners.

## ACKNOWLEDGMENTS

*Restructuring the Middle Level School: Implications for School Leaders* reflects many of the ideas, concepts, and understandings we have gained from our associations with middle level leaders and scholars throughout the United States. We are especially indebted to Dr. John Lounsbury for writing the foreword, and for his friendship, advice, and encouragement over the years.

This book also reflects our years of association with middle level principals and teachers and our many graduate students with whom we have engaged in stimulating discussions and problem solving. We would especially like to thank southern Arizona middle level principals Bob Hamil, Jud Jones, Susan Masek, Mary Scheetz, and Bob Smith. They have shared their joys and frustrations and their ideas and innovations. They have welcomed our students, both undergraduate and graduate, and they have made their schools available to use for study. Many of the ideas incorporated in this book come from their schools.

We would also like to thank reviewers Dr. Laurel Martin Kanthak, Associate Executive Director and Director of Middle Level Education, National Association of Secondary School Principals, and Dr. John Swaim, Professor of Middle School Education, University of Northern Colorado. Their comments and those of reviewers not identified provided valuable information in improving the quality of the book. Also, our thanks to Dr. Janice Streitmatter, Series Editor, and our colleague at the University of Arizona, for suggesting that we write this book and for providing us with encouragement along the way; and to Priscilla Ross, State University of New York Press Editor, for her suggestions and insights during the writing process.

*Sally N. Clark*
*Donald C. Clark*
*Tucson, Arizona*
*August 1993*

# COPYRIGHT ACKNOWLEDGMENTS

Levine, D. U. (1991). Creating effective schools: Findings and implications from research and practice. *Phi Delta Kappan, 72*(5), 389-393.

Lieberman, A., & Miller, L. (1990). Restructuring schools: What matters and what works. *Phi Delta Kappan, 71*(10), 759-764.

Wiggins, G. (1989). A true test: Toward more authentic and equitable assessment. *Phi Delta Kappan, 70*(9), 703-713.

Quotations and adapted material from the following articles and books are reprinted by permission of the National Association of Secondary School Principals. These materials are copyrighted by NASSP—all rights reserved.

Clark, S. N., & Clark, D. C. (1984). Creating a responsive middle level school through systematic long-range planning. *NASSP Bulletin, 68*(473), 42-51.

Clark, S. N., & Clark, D. C. (1990, December). Restructuring middle schools: Strategies for using Turning Points. In *Schools in the middle: Theory into practice.* Reston, VA: National Association of Secondary School Principals.

Clark, D. C., & Valentine, J. W. (1981, June). Middle level programs: Making the ideal a reality. *NASSP schools in the middle: A report on trends and practices.* Reston, VA: National Association of Secondary School Principals.

Howard, E. R., & Keefe, J. W. (1991). *The CASE-IMS school improvement process.* Reston, VA: National Association of Secondary School Principals.

Johnston, J. H. (1985, January). Four climates of effective middle level schools. *NASSP schools in the middle: A report on trends and practices.* Reston, VA: National Association of Secondary School Principals.

Lounsbury, J. H., & Clark, D. C. (1990). *Inside grade eight: From apathy to excitement.* Reston, VA: National Association of Secondary School Principals.

NASSP Council on Middle Level Education. (1985). *An agenda for excellence at the middle level.* Reston, VA: National Association of Secondary School Principals.

Winton, J. J. (1988, October). Interdisciplinary studies at the Shelburne Middle School. *NASSP schools in the middle: A report on trends and practices.* Reston, VA: National Association of Secondary School Principals.

# SECTION I

Perspectives on the Middle Level
School: Past, Present, and Future

# 1

# Perspectives on Middle Level Education Past and Present

"... the junior high school is not at present a definite institution, but rather a state of mind, or a striving to achieve a vision, either limited or extensive."

Thomas H. Briggs

Striving to achieve a vision of what education for young adolescents should be has been the goal of administrators, teachers, scholars and researchers for almost 100 years. This century-long struggle for identity and purpose is significant to current middle level administrators and teachers who, drawing on the experience and wisdom of past leaders, can create new visions for the future. While much has changed in middle level education over the past 100 years, one is impressed by the number of forces, functions, and purposes that remain similar.

Understanding the complexities of middle level education as it exists in the late twentieth century is based upon four important factors:

1. The definition of a middle level school
2. Knowledge of the forces that led to the establishment and rapid growth of the junior high school
3. Knowledge of how middle level schools have evolved during the past three decades
4. Knowledge of current middle level school organization and practice

## WHAT IS A MIDDLE LEVEL SCHOOL?

Defining middle level schools and middle level education is a complex process that requires the consideration of several perspectives. These perspectives include **purposes, separation, organization, curriculum,** and **program** (Figure 1-1).

**Figure 1-1**
Middle Level Schools - Some Perspectives

*Purpose*
To be developmentally responsive to the
special needs of young adolescents

*Uniqueness*
A unique, autonomous unit, separate from the elementary school
that precedes it and the high school that follows it

*Organization*
The inclusion of the grade levels with the largest
number of students who are beginning the process
of becoming adolescents (any combination of grades 5-9)

*Curriculum and Instruction*
Content that connects with the everyday lives of students
and instruction that actively involves them in the learning process

*Program*
Programs that are developmentally appropriate
and include but are not limited to interdisciplinary teaming,
teacher advisories, cocurricular activities and youth service

Most scholars and practitioners agree that middle level schools should exist for one **purpose**, and one purpose only, to be developmentally responsive to the special needs of the early adolescent learner. This purpose has an historic precedent that began in the early twentieth century (Briggs, 1920; Koos, 1927; Pringle, 1937) and continues to the present time (Clark and Clark, 1987; Lounsbury, 1991; Lounsbury and Clark, 1990; NASSP, 1985).

Most middle level educators suggest also that middle level schools must be a **separate** school—a unique, autonomous unit—separate from the elementary school that precedes it and the high school that follows it. Separation in this context not only means a separate school facility where special accommodation can be made for early adolescent needs and characteristics, it also means a separate and unique program and curriculum.

The **organization** of middle level schools is based upon the inclusion of the grade levels that have the largest number of students who are beginning the process of becoming adolescents. Over the past seventy years the grade levels included in middle level schools have varied from the 7 through 9 configuration of the original junior high schools, to 5 through 8 or 6 through 8 of today's middle schools. Currently among the more than 12,000 middle level schools in the United States, the 6 through 8 grade level configuration is the most frequently found organization (Alexander and McEwin, 1989; Cawelti, 1988). This shift to include the lower grade is largely attributable to the early onset of puberty which begins 18 to 24 months earlier than it did at the turn of the century (Thornburg, 1981). Other factors such as enrollment and desegregation have also contributed to the differing grade level structures in middle level schools (Alexander, 1968; Valentine, Clark, Nickerson, and Keefe, 1981).

Meeting the needs of young adolescents requires a special **curriculum**, a curriculum that features content that connects with the everyday lives of students as well as instruction that actively involves them in the learning process. Opportunities for young adolescents to explore interests has been a unique part of middle level education since its inception. The concept of exploratory experiences, long a cornerstone of middle level education, was originally intended to include every program and activity in the school curriculum. More recently, the concept of "exploratory" curriculum has been considerably narrowed, and currently it is defined primarily as courses and activities not normally included in the core subjects. In the last decade of the twentieth century, many middle level educators are calling for the return to the original concept of exploration as a major component of every content area and activity in the school (Lounsbury, 1991).

**Program** is also an important part of the definition of "a middle level school." Through the development of a variety of different programs and organizational patterns such as interdisciplinary teaming, teacher advisories, alternative instructional strategies, grouping, student activities, career education, and youth service, middle level educators have attempted to make their schools developmentally responsive. During the decades of the sixties, seventies, and eighties, some middle level educators tried to use program to define the differences between junior high schools and middle schools (e.g., middle schools had team teaching and teacher advisories; junior highs had traditional single subject schedules and counselors, etc.). Classifying developmental responsiveness by program was erroneous for two reasons: (1) middle level schools are too complex to be defined by only one element, and (2) research on middle level schools found that developmentally responsive programs were found in schools regardless of their grade level configurations or their name (Alexander and McEwin, 1989; Cawelti, 1988; Lounsbury and Clark, 1990; Mac Iver, 1990; Valentine, Clark, Nickerson, and Keefe, 1981).

Defining junior high schools and middle schools would not be complete without addressing the terms "middle level schools" and "middle level education." Seeking to find a term which would describe schools that served young adolescents was an issue of concern and debate among middle level educators during the late 1970s. The terms "middle level schools" and "middle level education" were first used extensively by the Research Team of the Dodge Foundation/National Association of Secondary School Principals (NASSP) National Study of Schools in the Middle in their two Volumes—*The Middle Level Principalship—Volume I: A Survey of Middle Level Principals and Programs* (Valentine, Clark, Nickerson, and Keefe, 1981) and *The Middle Level Principalship—Volume II: The Effective Middle Level Principal* (Keefe, Clark, Nickerson, and Valentine, 1983). These terms, however, gained general acceptance among junior high and middle school educators largely through the energetic efforts of George Melton, Deputy Executive Director of NASSP, who popularized the terms through his work with schools throughout the nation and his numerous presentations at state, regional, and national conferences and conventions. By the end of the 1980s the terms "middle level school" and "middle level education" had gained wide acceptance and were the terms used by middle level educators to describe their schools in the educational hierarchy (Lounsbury, 1991).

What is a middle level school? Considering the elements previously described, a middle level school can be defined as:

> A separate school designed to meet the special needs of young adolescents in an organizational structure that encompasses any combination of grades five through nine, wherein developmentally appropriate curricula and programs are used to create learning experiences that are both relevant and interactive.

## FORCES THAT LED TO THE ESTABLISHMENT AND RAPID GROWTH OF THE JUNIOR HIGH SCHOOL

Most middle level scholars generally agree that the first junior high schools were opened during the 1909-10 school year when Columbus, Ohio and Berkeley, California established junior high schools. The origins of the concept, however, are found in the late 19th century and early 20th century and involve some of the leading scholars and educators of the time.

The idea of a separate school for young adolescents evolved slowly, based primarily on concerns about the perceived failure of the 8-4 organization of schools. As one examines the historical development of middle level education, it becomes increasingly apparent that the initial impetus was to solve major problems that existed in the current school structure rather than to create a new organization. Hansen and Hern suggest that:

> The history of the first middle school, the junior high school, indicates that it was conceived not as a movement to introduce something new into American education but as an expedient endeavor to ease several supposed deficiencies (1971; 4).

Thomas H. Briggs (1920), a professor at Columbia University and a leading scholar in junior high school education, identified several critical conditions in elementary and secondary schools in the late 19th century that influenced major criticisms of the 8-4 school organizational system. The conditions described by Briggs (1920) included the tremendous increase in the number of high schools, changes in social and industrial life, an "unparalleled" increase in the number of children continuing beyond elementary school, the necessity of a more highly differentiated curriculum, demands for increased budget to support programs, and the indefiniteness of function and of purpose of schools.

During the same period of time Briggs was describing conditions in American schools that influenced educational change, Leonard Koos (1927), another leading early junior high school educator, was examining what he called the forces responsible for the establishment of junior high schools. "Many forces . . . ," he stated, "are responsible for the movement for educational reorganization finding expression in the present widespread establishment of 'junior high schools' or 'intermediate schools'" (1927; 1). These forces identified by Koos (1927) included:

(1) economy of time, (2) concern for high student mortality—drop-out rates, (3) wide variations in learners, and (4) needs of young adolescents.

## Economy of Time

The issue of economy of time was the factor that received the most attention in early attempts to reorganize America's educational system. For forty years (1873-1913), educators, primarily college presidents such as Charles Eliot of Harvard, were concerned because students spent too much time in elementary school leaving little time for them to be exposed to the more difficult subjects important for success in college. Eliot became the leading spokesperson for college presidents throughout the United States in advocating for compression of elementary and secondary education, thus allowing students to enter college at an earlier age. As chair of the Committee of Ten on Secondary Studies, appointed in 1892, Eliot recommended that several subjects reserved for high school (algebra, geometry, natural science, and foreign languages) be taught earlier. The committee also recommended that secondary school education should begin at the seventh grade (two years earlier than the present), thus leaving six years instead of eight of elementary education (NEA, 1894).

The Committee on College Entrance Requirements (1895-1899) supported the concept of the six-year secondary school and recommended it in their report (NEA, 1899). This committee, which was composed of an equal number of public secondary school educators and college/university presidents, recommended the six-year secondary school for a somewhat different reason than did Eliot's Committee of Ten. Van Til, Vars, and Lounsbury (1961) report:

> The Committee on College Entrance Requirements pointed out that "the seventh grade, rather than the ninth, is the natural turning-point in the pupil's life, as the age of adolescence demands new methods and wiser direction." The members believed that the 6-6 division would make transition to adolescence easier, and would tend to close the gap between the elementary and high school, and would retain more students in school. In other words, the Committee argued that the proposed change would be good for the young people of the stage involved, early adolescence. (p. 9).

In drawing conclusions about the importance of the Committee on College Entrance Requirements Van Til, Vars, and Lounsbury state:

The Committee was more concerned for the best program here and now for children entering early adolescence and less concerned for President Eliot's major interest in sending students to college earlier. But the college presidents still stressed economy of time and earlier study of college subjects (p. 9).

Eight years later another committee was appointed to again specifically address *economy of time issues*. Appropriately named the Committee on Economy of Time in Education, it began its work in 1907 and issued preliminary reports during the period of 1908-1911. For middle level educators the most significant part of the Report of the Committee on the Economy of Time in Education was an individual member's report which suggested that the secondary school be reorganized into junior high and high school divisions—a reorganization which at the time of the report was already being implemented in a number of school systems.

For the first time a major report had given attention to the importance of dividing the six year high school into junior and senior high schools (Van Til, Vars, and Lounsbury, 1961). The innovative nature of the Committee on Economy of Time's recommendations was further demonstrated by the committee's conception of reorganization to include provision for accommodating vocational needs and interests of adolescents. The call for economy of time continued to be an issue in the reorganization of schools, but it received less attention as the junior high movement matured. During the years of careful study, the focus of economy of time went from one of emphasis on preparing those who wished to go on to college to an emphasis on the preparation of all of America's youth.

## Pupil Mortality—Retentions and Dropouts

The second force that influenced the establishment of the junior high school was the concern for the high number of students who at early ages were dropping out of school. The "fulfillment" of the dream of equality of educational opportunity for all of America's youth was being seriously questioned as the nation moved into the twentieth century. New studies directed by Thorndike (1907), Ayers (1909), and Strayer (1911) showed that an alarming number of students were leaving school prior to the start of ninth grade. Their studies, which were based on data collected from schools in cities across the United States, indicated that a high percentage of pupils dropped out after fifth grade, only one-third of the students reached ninth grade, and only slightly more than one in ten students completed high school.

Briggs (1920) in discussing findings reported, "The amount of elimination from all our schools between the sixth and the beginning of the tenth is roughly speaking, about seventy pupils out of every hundred" (p. 18). He attributed this high student mortality rate partly to the lack of compulsory attendance laws and partly to the lack of articulation between elementary and secondary schools. He also believed that the dramatic break between elementary and high school created marked differences in program and teaching, differences that were so difficult for many students that they chose to drop out. These differences as identified by both Briggs (1920) and Koos (1927) included (1) a major change in subjects studied, (2) differences in school organization, (3) differences in behavioral expectations (discipline), and (4) differences in school atmosphere and environment.

Creating an additional barrier was the fact that there was a sharp break between elementary and high school, often giving a sense of completion. This break in the continuity of educational experience and the lack of articulation between elementary and secondary school when combined with the "release" from compulsory attendance laws often led to the decision of many pupils to drop out of school. Briggs contended that, "There is considerable evidence showing that if a pupil before being released by the law has entered upon secondary-school work, he tends to persist somewhat longer than if still in elementary school" (1920; 19).

Pupil mortality was also influenced by the high rate of student failure and the number of "left-backs" or students repeating a grade level.

> About one third of the school children in the early twentieth century were left back some time during the few years they spent in school. About one out of every six children in any grade was a repeater in that grade (Van Til, Vars, and Lounsbury, 1961; 15).

"No one enjoys failure," stated Van Til, Vars, and Lounsbury (1961). "Left-backs very often become drop-outs. American educators became increasingly critical of conditions which led to so many left-backs and drop-outs. They argued that we could do better in democratic America. Consequently, when the new proposal for a junior high school was advanced, many educators were ready to approve. They hoped that the new seventh-through ninth-grade organization with improved methods and content more related to the learner's life might better serve education by reducing drop-outs" (Van Til, Vars, and Lounsbury, 1961; 15).

## Student Learning Differences

Another contributing factor to the high rate of drop-outs and left-backs was the failure of schools to recognize and provide for individual differences. Traditional notions about the homogeneity of pupils were being challenged during the first decade of the twentieth century. Thorndike, Cattell, and other leading psychologists of the day were calling attention to the importance of individual differences. For the most part schools in the early twentieth century appeared to be based on the assumption that all pupils were very much alike. And perhaps they were. Van Til, Vars, and Lounsbury (1961) suggest that the schools' clientele were drawn from only the able students and the others, unsuccessful pupils, dropped out. As a result, the remaining students, in fact, were very much alike. Failure to recognize individual differences in schools led to erroneous beliefs about student learning. It was a common belief that if a pupil did not learn it was the pupil's fault. All one had to do to be successful was to practice good study habits and to work hard. Students who failed lacked commitment, did not apply themselves, or were considered to be lazy.

Psychologists at the turn of the century were reporting data that refuted the validity of these assumptions. Briggs referred his readers to Thorndike's book entitled *Individuality*, which he characterized as a "succinct and sound summary of some facts about individual differences" (1920; 17).

Koos (1927) believed that there was abundant evidence of the fact of learning variation in the school and of the need to recognize it in the instruction and administration of the nation's schools. He cited research that supported differences among seventh, eighth, and ninth grade students in the following categories (Koos, 1927; 36-50):

1. Variation in Age of Students
2. Differences in Physique
3. Differences in Sexual Maturation
4. Differences in Mental/Intellectual Capacity

5.   Differences in Academic Work
6.   Expanding Range of Differences
7.   Differences in Interest

With the increasing awareness of the number of differences among school children, educators and psychologists began to explore the factors that led to these variations.

This recognition of the wide variations among adolescent learners in grades seven, eight, and nine, and the factors that contributed to them, supported the efforts for school reorganization. It was imperative that educators consider seriously strategies with which to deal effectively with these differences, and many believed that the junior high school was the most suitable place for this to happen. Koos suggested that the junior high school was especially well suited to recognize individual differences by providing for "differentiation of work through partially variable curricula, groups moving at differing rates, promotion by subject, permitting brighter pupils to carry more courses, and supervised study" (1927; 50).

The new emphasis on individual differences was enhanced by the report of the Commission on the Reorganization of Secondary Education of the National Education Association (1918) (Figure 1-2). The most famous of all the reports during the early years of the twentieth century, this report published in 1918 became known as the "Cardinal Principles of Secondary Education." Although the Commission recommended and endorsed the junior

**Figure 1-2**
The Cardinal Principles of Secondary Education

---

Health

Command of Fundamental Processes

Worthy Home Membership

Vocation

Citizenship

Worthy Use of Leisure Time

Ethical Character

---

Commission on the Reorganization of Secondary Education. (1918). *Cardinal principles of secondary education* [Bulletin 1918, No. 35]. Washington, D.C.: U.S. Department of Interior, Bureau of Education.

high school and suggested organizational and programmatic components, the significance of the report lies in it emphases on the larger purposes of American secondary education, purposes that recognized the importance of creating educational experiences relevant to all of America's youth. The "Seven Cardinal Principles" broadened the scope of educational aims beyond subject mastery and expanded them to include citizenship, vocation, family membership, and leisure activities. These new principles were very much in tune with the purposes of the new school for young adolescents, the junior high school. Without doubt, the "Seven Cardinal Principles" fueled the momentum to establish junior high schools, a movement that was by 1918 sweeping the country.

## The Unique Needs of Young Adolescents

The last major force identified by Koos (1927) was the recognition that early adolescence was a unique time in the life span. It was the work of G. Stanley Hall that brought attention to the special needs of adolescents. His "recapitulation" or "cultural epoch theory," whether valid or not, provided the impetus needed for educators to begin to address the special needs of adolescent youth. Hall believed that adolescence was a time of abrupt and radical changes and that these changes took place in all phases of a child's life, emotional, physical, mental, and social. He suggested that the responsibility for these changes were the physiological phases of puberty.

His writings, which gave new importance to adolescence as a distinct and unique period in life, encouraged educators to examine current educational practice, practice that was giving no special consideration for this unique age group. His followers sought to establish new schools that were separate from both elementary and high schools. They believed that these schools should be organized differently, use different instructional methods, and make provisions for the special needs of their young adolescents.

Many adolescent psychologists have since disagreed with Hall's theories, but to his credit it must be said that he heavily influenced educational programs for adolescents. Because of him and his work, junior high and middle school educators have developed a tradition and a commitment to assist children and youth to successfully make the difficult transition through the early adolescent years.

These four forces described by Koos and reinforced by other early scholars and educators provide a framework for examining the changes that took place in American education, changes that eventually led to the establishment of the junior high school and its rapid growth during the first half of the twentieth century. These forces, along with other elements, continue to be influential in current efforts to reform American education, particularly the middle level school.

## THE EVOLUTION OF MIDDLE LEVEL SCHOOLS

The evolution of middle level education is a complex and ongoing process, a process that continues to be influenced by those forces identified by the early writers in junior high education (Briggs, 1920; Cox, 1929; Davis, 1924; Koos, 1927; and Smith, 1927). Using the four categories of forces as identified by Koos (1927), the evolution of middle level education will be described.

### Economy of Time

The economy of time issue, originally conceived by Eliot and others as a way to allow students to enter college at a younger age, soon took on a much broader focus. That focus was school reorganization. School reorganization issues in the early 1900s were centered, much as they are now, around grade level organization, compression of time spent in school, pressures to push "high school" coursework to lower grades, and departmentalization and specialization.

**Grade Level Organization.** The junior high school, with its grade level configuration of grades 7-9, was created to replace the 8-4 system of schooling in existence at the beginning of the twentieth century. Reformers justified the change by claiming that such a reorganization would provide better educational opportunities for students and a better transition between elementary and high school. For almost fifty years education for young adolescents was defined by the term "junior high school" with grade level organizations of 7-8 or 7-9.

In the early 1960s some educators began to challenge the effectiveness of the junior high school in meeting the special needs of their students. Many of these educators, who claimed that the junior high school had become nothing more than a "junior edition" of high school, called for the development of a new school. Believing that the junior high school had failed, they advocated the organization of middle schools. These schools, which would reflect the earlier onset of puberty, would push the grade levels further into the elementary school grades to include grade six and in some cases, grade five. Just as reformers had done more than fifty years earlier, middle level educators of the 1960s had taken the initial steps to reorganize the grade levels of schooling for young adolescents.

The advocates of the new middle school, particularly William Alexander and Donald Eichhorn, sought to define this new school in terms of developmental appropriateness and responsiveness rather than by grade level. Alexander (1968), then active in the Association for Supervision and Curriculum Development, was an early promoter of the "middle level concept." It was, however, Donald Eichhorn who, through his publication *The Middle School* (1966), established the legitimacy of the new middle school. His descriptions of the philosophy, purposes, and programs of middle level schools made his book the "cornerstone" on which middle level schools have been built.

Paralleling the earlier junior high movement, the grades of a school defined what it was. Some educators began to draw distinctions between grade level organizations, characterizing schools with grades 6-8 as responsive student-centered middle schools and schools with grades 7-9 as unresponsive subject-centered junior high schools. Despite these distinctions, the "first comparative studies and surveys revealed that the new middle schools and the old junior high schools were surprisingly alike in actual practice" (Lounsbury, 1991; 68).

As middle level educators became more knowledgeable about young adolescents, their efforts focused more on the development of programs to meet the specific needs of their students regardless of the grade level organization of their schools. In spite of this renewed effort for being more developmentally responsive, the issue of grade level organization still remains an important force in American middle level schools.

**Compression of Time in School.** While the Committee on Economy of Time's (Baker, 1913) recommendation for reducing schooling by two years was never implemented, finding ways to effect economy of time continues to be a major force in American education. In 1984, John Goodlad, in his book *A Place Called School*, advocated better use of instructional time. He also suggested that American schooling be reorganized into a 4-4-4 grade level pattern and that pupils complete their public schooling by age sixteen. Unlike Eliot and Conant (1960), who were seeking economy of time for the benefit of college students, Goodlad was seeking more effective, efficient educational systems for all of America's youth.

**Pressure to Push "High School" Coursework into Lower Grades.** From the early days of the junior high school movement through its evolution to the middle level school of today, the issue of "high school type" courses at the middle level has reemerged periodically. In the late 1950s former Harvard president James B. Conant made a major impact on American secondary education. Following his comprehensive study of American high schools, *The American High School Today* (1959), Conant turned his attention to the study of junior high schools. *In a Memorandum to School Boards: Recommendations for Education in the Junior High School Years* (1960), Conant, among other recommendations, supported effecting economy of time through earlier college preparation. With this recommendation and other specific recommendations for courses that should be included in the junior high curriculum, Conant was reflecting the views of an earlier Harvard president, Charles Eliot, who was also concerned primarily with economy of time and earlier college preparation.

A *Nation at Risk* (1983), while not mentioning middle level schools specifically, in advocating more rigorous coursework at the high school level implied that the same rigorous type of coursework should be pushed into middle level schools. This was particularly true of foreign language, the sciences, and mathematics. The writers of *A Nation At Risk*, as were the reformers in the early twentieth century, were greatly concerned about unfavorable comparisons of American schools to schools in other countries.

While the "pushing down of content" to lower grade levels was a significant force in the development of the junior high, the influence it exerts on middle level schools today has been, for the most part, detrimental to the continuing efforts to make middle level schools more developmentally responsive (Clark and Clark, 1986).

**Departmentalization/Specialization.** The early reformers believed that with secondary education beginning at the seventh grade young adolescents would have the advantage of receiving their instruction from teachers specially prepared to teach a specific content area. This departmental organization, which was designed to expose young adolescents to experts in the subject matter areas, became and has remained the predominate form of curriculum organization in middle level schools. In spite of attempts over the last two decades to develop interdisciplinary curricula, departmentalization has remained firmly entrenched in middle level schools.

## Pupil Mortality—Retentions and Dropouts

The low number of students who completed high school during the early twentieth century was of great concern to educators of that time. They thought that by reorganizing the schools steps could be taken that would increase the number of young people who would stay in school. There is reason to believe that in some instances they were right, for the percentages of students remaining in school districts with junior high schools did appear to be higher than those who maintained the 8-4 pattern of organization (Briggs, 1920). Closely aligned with high drop-out rates was a concern about the high number of students (left-backs) who were "repeating" a grade level for a second or third time. Several important issues evolved from these early concerns over pupil mortality and grade repetition, including provision for educational opportunity for all students, repeating courses—rather than an entire grade, a more relevant curriculum, and better instructional strategies.

**Educational Opportunity.** Early scholars such as Briggs and Koos saw American schools as being narrowly focused on the preparation of students for college. Because of that focus a high percentage of students dropped out of school. These advocates of the junior high school called for schools that would be more democratic, schools that would give opportunities for learning and success to all students. The junior high school was the way to "democratize" education (Koos, 1927).

Middle level educators of today "dream the same dream." While the drop-out rate is not as high as it was when the first junior high schools were established, dropping out is still a serious problem. Unlike the early 1900s when a school dropout could be absorbed into the work force and become a contributing member of society, a high percentage of today's dropouts face an uncertain future of low paying jobs and unemployment. Offering equal educational opportunity to all students continues to be a major concern of middle level and high school educators.

**Repeating Courses rather than Repeating a Grade Level.**
Repeating a grade was generally acknowledged as a contributor
to pupil mortality. With the introduction of departmentalization
to the junior high school, students no longer failed the entire
grade, they failed individual courses. The hypothesis, of course,
was that failing a course had less of a stigma attached to it and
students could make up the work in that course without having
to repeat all of the other courses. Success or failure in each
course thus became an integral part of the junior high and middle school.

While the number of students in middle level schools who are
repeating a grade is much fewer, there are still a significant
number of students who are either failing courses or achieving at
very low levels. Lack of academic success is recognized by many
as a contributing factor in dropping out (Mac Iver, 1990). Middle
level educators of today share this concern with educators of
the past, and they are continuing to address this issue through
curricular relevancy and instructional strategies.

**Curriculum Relevancy and Instructional Strategies.** Making
the curriculum relevant to the needs of young adolescents and
using instructional strategies that actively involved learners were
also important issues to the developers of the first junior high
schools. These issues of curriculum and instruction, which also
are important when dealing with individual differences of students and the special needs of young adolescents, continue to be
forces in the modern middle level school. Participatory learning
and connecting content with students' lives are more important
now than at any time in the twentieth century.

## Student Learning Differences

The work of Thorndike and other researchers gave solid evidence
of the differences among learners in the typical classroom. As
educational opportunity has broadened, the range of diversity
has expanded. Not only must schools deal with the variations in
learning ability and achievement, they must provide for the needs
of youth from a variety of socioeconomic levels, family settings,
and primary language backgrounds. While Thorndike and others
did increase the awareness of educators about individual differences and sparked efforts to provide for these differences in the
classroom, the impact of their work was not altogether positive.
Two major issues which became popular in the early years of

the twentieth century and which are of great concern to middle level educators of today are the legitimacy and importance of standardized testing and homogeneous grouping (ability grouping, tracking).

**Ability and Achievement Testing.** Americans believe in tests as valid measures of student achievement. Although ability and intelligence testing do not enjoy the degree of popularity they did two decades ago, achievement testing is considered by many as the only "appropriate" way to measure student learning. Many middle level educators, as well as educators from elementary and high schools, are concerned that so much credibility is given to the results of a multiple choice test when they know that the test measures so few of the goals of the school. Middle level educators are also greatly concerned that the general public is so willing to categorize schools as good schools or poor schools based upon school test scores published in the newspaper.

Current efforts to find alternative ways of assessing student progress, assessments that are more correlated with school, district, state, and national purposes, are being implemented throughout the nation. Middle level schools, with their emphasis on developmental appropriateness, are particularly "in tune" with alternative assessment. Evaluation procedures, such as portfolios, projects, and demonstrations, correlate well with curriculum relevance and student involvement in learning.

**Homogeneous Grouping/Ability Grouping/Tracking.** It seemed logical to the early reformers that one of the best ways to meet individual differences was to place all children who were alike together in the same classroom or same course. As a result, along with a departmentalized curriculum, most junior and senior high schools began the practice of tracking. This practice grew in popularity and was almost universally supported by educators and the general public. Conant (1960), in his report on junior high schools, strongly endorsed ability grouping and recommended that early differentiation of program begin in the junior high school (e.g., college preparatory, vocational).

About three decades ago, some educators and sociologists began to question the practice of ability grouping; and in recent years, the evidence has mounted as to the deleterious effects of grouping practices among children and youth, particularly among minority and low income youth (Braddock, 1990; Oakes,

1985). Middle level educators have been particularly outspoken about the negative effects of tracking on young adolescents, yet the practice continues in the vast majority of America's middle level schools (Braddock, 1990; George, 1988; Lounsbury and Clark, 1990).

It is ironic that an idea that was originally developed to provide for individual student differences would sixty years later become a practice that has been found by many researchers to be harmful to the achievement and self-concept development of middle level students.

## The Unique Needs of Young Adolescents

Ever since G. Stanley Hall first called attention to the unique needs of adolescent youth, the junior high school and the middle school have attempted to serve those special needs. Examination of the development of middle level education demonstrates that while "meeting the needs of young adolescents" has always been a major goal, goal accomplishment leaves much to be desired. Although there were many programs and activities that were adopted in the early junior high schools that focused on the needs of young adolescents, the issues that have remained the most important over the years are content relevancy, student involvement in learning, and guidance. These three important areas are, perhaps, most appropriately considered as functions of "exploration."

**Exploratory Experiences.** Exploration, identified by the early junior high school leaders (Briggs, 1920; Koos, 1927; Smith, 1927), was a concept that permeated every aspect of the early junior high school. Briggs stressed the importance of exploration by incorporating the concept into almost all of his original five statements of purpose for the junior high school (Lounsbury, 1991). Koos (1927) identified "exploration for guidance" (p. 18), and Smith (1927) listed as two of his purposes of junior high schools the exploration "of interests, abilities, and aptitudes of children. . ." and the exploration of "the major fields of human endeavor" (pp. 196-197).

Although "exploratory" has remained a truly middle level concept, its definition has changed over the years. From being a concept that permeated the entire program, it changed (largely due to downward pressures from the high schools) to become a collection of courses which commonly include art, music, shop, and home economics. As middle level educators begin again to refocus on the needs of the young adolescents in their schools, the concept of "exploration" is being integrated again into the entire school program. In reflecting this new definition, middle level educators are implementing exploratory experiences that include specialized courses, independent study and projects, and involvement in clubs and activities. The concept of exploratory is also being integrated into the content and instructional strategies in all content areas, and it has become an integral part of advisory programs where teachers encourage pupils to explore feelings, attitudes, and values.

## Other Elements Influencing Change

From the earliest days of the junior high school to the current decade three additional elements have influenced the development of middle level schools. Identified by Koos in 1927, these elements of overcrowding, momentum, and "jumping on the bandwagon" have continued to be factors in the growth of middle level education.

**Overcrowding.** The first element described by Koos deals with creation of middle level schools to solve the problem of "overcrowding" at high schools. "By removing pupils of the ninth grade from the high school building," he states, "and housing them with those in the seventh and eighth grades in some older buildings, the problem is solved" (1927; 3). Koos continues:

> This easy emancipation from a housing difficulty has sometimes been the primary cause of a superficial reorganization; it has also sometimes been used to effect genuine reorganization where otherwise there might be too great opposition to a change for which the populace was not yet prepared (1927; 3).

In addition to Koos, the existence of this element in the early junior high movement has been confirmed by many other junior high school historians and scholars. Hansen and Hern (1971) quote from D. W. Lenz:

> It is apparent that . . . it [the junior high school] was established not because of any strong and proved educational values, but as an expedient, usually to solve a housing problem; in many cases because it was the thing to do in educational circles . . . (Hansen and Hern, 1971; 6-7).

Throughout the evolution of middle level education school districts have continued to view their middle level schools as the "wild card" for solving enrollment problems (Alexander, 1967; Valentine, Clark, Nickerson, and Keefe, 1981). In many cases when elementary schools are overcrowded, the sixth grade is moved to the middle level school; when high schools are over- crowded, the ninth grade is moved to the middle level school. Unfortunately, in most instances little or no attempt is made to develop programs that are developmentally appropriate for the students in the newly configured school. As a result, when sixth graders are placed in a 7-8 or 7-9 school, a high school type program is often being pushed down one more grade level.

**Momentum.** A second element identified by Koos (1927) was "momentum." He believed that to the forces of economy of time, the problem with dropouts, the need to recognize individual dif- ferences, and the unique needs of young adolescents should be added the influence of momentum on the change process. He states:

> . . . the momentum of the history of the [junior high] move- ment . . . [is] responsible for the vast array of reorganization with which we are now surrounded (Koos, 1927; 7-8).

The first two decades of the junior high school (1910-1930) were marked by high levels of visibility that included books, articles, reports, and conference presentations. This high vis- ibility, fueled by rhetoric and research, initiated and sustained the momentum that led many educators to consider and establish junior high schools in their districts. This same type of "momentum" has reemerged in American middle level schools during the past two decades. As a result of the lead- ership of the National Association of Secondary School Principals, the National Middle School Association, and fund- ing from the U. S. Department of Education and private foun- dations, middle level education has begun to gain recognition as a separate entity in the educational hierarchy. Of particular importance to this recognition is the work of the Carnegie Task Force on Education of Young Adolescents (1989). Their report, *Turning Points: Preparing American Youth for the 21st Century*, has refueled the "momentum" for change in middle level edu- cation.

**Jumping on the Bandwagon.** A third element identified by Koos (1927) as being important to the development of junior high schools was "jumping on the bandwagon." He suggested that in examining the "broad sweep of the movement for reorganization" that one of the most influential factors was the "desire of some school authorities to be progressive" (1927; 4).

> This factor is not unlike the force of a fad. It often operates without any clear understanding of the purposes of reorganization and it not uncommonly results in change which, rather than being fundamental, restricts itself to such a superficiality as the mere regrouping of grades (Koos, 1927; 4).

As in the early years of the junior high school, there is a strong desire by many educators to be on the "cutting edge" of innovations. Often times this is manifested by "jumping on the bandwagon." Although it is generally recognized that the grade levels contained in a school do not necessarily make the school more responsive, some school districts have reorganized the grade level configurations of their junior high and/or intermediate schools and changed the name to "middle school." In this process, little has been done to change school environments to ensure that the programs of these schools are developmentally appropriate.

In responding to the issues/forces discussed in this chapter, junior high and middle school scholars and practitioners with vision, concern, and hard work have created in less than ninety years a school in the middle that is commonly accepted as the appropriate place for the education of young adolescents. John Lounsbury, writing in *As I See It* (1991), gives a good overview of this evolution of middle level education during the twentieth century. He states:

> **Eighty years ago** the idea of a junior high school was not yet clearly formed.

> **Seventy years ago** it was just an infrequent experiment.

> **Sixty years ago** the junior high school was the coming thing in American education.

> **Fifty years ago** it had achieved considerable status and become a regular part of our educational system.

> **Forty years ago** criticism concerning the junior high began to mount. Most frequently cited was its tendency to merely mimic the high school in program and policies, to be simply a downward extension of secondary education.

**Thirty years ago** the middle school, composed of grades 6-8 or sometimes 5-8, was being touted as an alternative and solution to the failures of the junior high school.

**Twenty years ago** the first comparative studies and surveys revealed that new middle schools and old junior high schools were surprisingly alike in actual practice.

**Ten years ago**, after many needless rounds in the literature of junior high *vs* middle school, junior high and middle school proponents and practitioners began to coalesce into a single cause—the cause of improving early adolescent education.

**Today**, the phrase middle level education has gained acceptance as the best term to refer to a distinctive level in the continuum of public eduction however it may be housed in a particular school district (1991; 67-68).

## CURRENT MIDDLE LEVEL SCHOOL ORGANIZATION AND PRACTICE

From the early discussions about school reform that began in the 1870s and led to the establishment of the first junior high schools in 1910, middle level education has grown to include more than 12,000 middle level schools. Almost universally middle level school educators recognize the importance of schools that are developmentally responsive to the needs of young adolescents. While there is agreement on the general purpose of middle level schools, middle level educators, drawing from tradition, practice, rhetoric, and research, organize their schools and programs in a variety of ways. What do these middle level schools of the 1980s and 1990s look like? How are they organized? What programs do they offer?

Descriptions of middle level schools of the eighties and early nineties is drawn from the following studies: The Dodge Foundation/NASSP National Study of Schools in the Middle (Valentine, Clark, Nickerson, and Keefe, 1981), ASCD Study of Middle Schools (Cawelti, 1988), Schools in the Middle: Progress 1968-1988 (Alexander and McEwin, 1989), Middle Grades: A National Survey of Practices and Trends—Center for Research in Elementary and Middle Schools—Johns Hopkins University (Epstein and Mac Iver, 1990), A Survey of Arizona Middle Level

Schools (Clark and Clark, 1990), and the NASSP National Eighth Grade Shadow Study (Lounsbury and Clark, 1990).

## School Organization

**Grade Level Configurations.** By the 1960s the 7-9 junior high school had become firmly entrenched as the "school in the middle." With four out of five high school graduates having attended the school systems organized around the 6-3-3 grade level configuration, the junior high school had clearly reversed the statistic from 1920 that indicated that four out of every five students had gone through the 8-4 elementary-high school plan (Alexander and McEwin, 1989).

Over the next 25 years, dissatisfaction with the junior high school and recognition of earlier maturation among young adolescents led to the increasing popularity of 6-8 and 5-8 middle level schools. Although the 1981 Report of the Dodge Foundation/NASSP National Study of Schools in the Middle (Valentine, Clark, Nickerson, and Keefe, 1981) found that the 7-9 configuration was still the most frequently used grade level organization used by middle level schools, they also reported the increased popularity of the 6-8 grade level configuration. By the mid to late 1980s the 6-8 configuration had become the most frequently used pattern of grades in middle level schools (Alexander and McEwin, 1989). Young adolescents today are most likely to be enrolled in middle level schools with grades 6-8, followed by 7-8 and 7-9.

**School Size.** Although enrollments vary with school grade level configurations, a majority of middle level school pupils will receive their education in schools that have enrollments between 400-800 students. Junior high schools (7-9) tend to have higher enrollments, with an average size of 733 students, while the average size for 6-8 schools is 557 students, and the average size for 7-8 schools is 491 (Epstein and Mac Iver, 1990; Valentine, Clark, Irvin, Keefe, and Melton, 1993; Valentine, Clark, Nickerson, and Keefe, 1981; ).

## School Programs

While it is generally recognized that one of the important features of responsive middle level schools is flexible scheduling, the single subject (traditional, high school schedule) schedule is still the predominate method of allocating instructional time in middle level schools. Depending on the study, **interdisciplinary teaming** in middle level schools ranged from a low of 16 percent of the schools in the ASCD study (Cawelti, 1988) to 42 percent of the students who received instruction in interdisciplinary teams sometime between grades 5-9 as indicated by Mac Iver (1990). Alexander and McEwin (1989) indicated that between 35 and 40 percent of the schools in their study had interdisciplinary teaming programs and Clark and Clark (1990) reported 39 percent of Arizona schools with teaming programs.

The presence of interdisciplinary teams in schools does not necessarily mean that teams are functioning effectively or in ways that have a positive impact on young adolescents. Alexander and McEwin (1989) were concerned that some schools in their study were not taking full advantage of the possibilities of interdisciplinary teaming, and Lounsbury and Clark (1990) reported in their Shadow Study that teaming seemed to have very little impact on the classroom instruction of eighth graders.

**Guidance**, another important function of middle level education, was examined in several of the studies. Particular interest was placed on the concept of **teacher advisories**. The ASCD study (Cawelti, 1988) found teacher advisory programs, in conjunction with a counselor, in 29 percent of the schools. Thirty-nine percent of the schools reported teacher advisories in Alexander's and McEwin's (1989) study, and while Mac Iver (1990) reported that 66 percent of the schools in the CREMS study indicated teacher advisory programs, only 28 percent of the schools indicated the use of support type activities at least once a month.

The evidence is mounting about the importance of teacher advisory programs in reducing dropouts and increasing self-concept, yet schools are slow to implement this program and when they do, many of them are not functioning in the ways necessary to accomplish intended goals (Lounsbury and Clark, 1990; Mac Iver, 1990).

The **core curriculum** of middle level schools, in almost all cases, consists of English/language arts, social studies, mathematics, and science (Alexander and McEwin, 1989; Clark and Clark, 1990; Valentine, Clark, Nickerson, and Keefe, 1981). Concern was expressed by Cawelti (1988) who characterized the middle level curriculum as being "extensively affected" by state department of education mandates and requirements. Lounsbury's and Clark's curricular concerns dealt mainly with the lack of relevancy of the curriculum to early adolescent lifestyles. They urged that efforts be taken to connect school content with the everyday lives of its pupils (1990).

The **exploratory curriculum**, a unique feature of middle level education since the first junior high schools, continues to be an important, though somewhat restricted, element of middle level schools. More narrowly defined in recent years as "exploratory courses, fine and practical arts, and mini-courses," exploratory experiences have been reduced due to pressures by reformers for "higher academic achievement" and the resultant increase in the number of required courses (Cawelti, 1988). State mandates calling for minimum competency testing in basic skills may also be playing an important role in restricting the opportunities of students to be exposed to skills and experiences that might prove useful (Becker, 1990).

The **instruction** in middle level schools is, for the most part, teacher-dominated direct instruction. Based upon shadow studies of eighth graders, Lounsbury and Clark (1990) reported that students spend period after period sitting passively in classrooms listening to teachers, reading textbooks, filling in ditto sheets, and taking tests, with little active learning taking place. Although Epstein and Mac Iver (1990) were a little more optimistic in characterizing instructional experiences in middle level schools, they concluded that all schools "have hard work ahead to make instruction engaging and compelling for all students" (p. 44). Direct instruction (teacher lecture, drill, practice, etc.) was regularly used in 98 percent of the schools in the ASCD (Cawelti, 1988) study. Less than half of the schools indicated the use of inquiry teaching (41%), cooperative learning (40%), independent study (30%), and consideration for teaching/learning styles (26%).

## Grouping Practices

Ability/homogeneous grouping and tracking are practiced in a vast majority of American middle level schools. Lounsbury and Clark (1990) found that 89 percent of the schools in their shadow study used some form of ability or achievement grouping. Braddock reported:

> The number of students who experience at least some homogeneous grouping increases across the grades from about 70% of fifth-graders, to 80% of sixth-graders and 85% of seventh-, eighth-, and ninth-graders. The proportion of students who are

in fully "tracked" programs, in which all classes are grouped by ability, increases from 12% of fifth-graders to about 25% of sixth- through ninth-graders (1990; 447).

Students are most likely to be grouped in mathematics, reading, and English and least likely to be grouped in science and social studies (Braddock, 1990).

To summarize, based upon the research on the status of middle level schools in the 1980s and early 1990s, middle level schools of today can most likely be characterized as schools where:

1.  The grade level configuration is 6-8 or 7-8 with an enrollment between 400 and 800 students,
2.  A traditional single subject schedule is followed by most teachers and students,
3.  The guidance program is primarily the responsibility of a counselor or counselors,
4.  The core curriculum consists of English-language arts, social studies, science, and mathematics and a limited exploratory program,
5.  The instruction is largely teacher dominated and student "passiveness" is a predominate element, and
6.  Most students are ability grouped for some subjects, and some students are "tracked" for the entire day.

In these middle level schools there is about a 40 percent chance that some form of interdisciplinary teaming will exist and about a 30 percent chance of the existence of a teacher advisory program that features academic and social support activities.

## SUMMARY

The examination of middle level education, its definition, the forces that led to its establishment, and its evolution to what it is today are important endeavors for any middle level educator involved in school restructuring. This knowledge provides the foundation on which schools can be "revisioned" and "restructured."

It is evident that as middle level educators move their schools into the twenty-first century they must do so from a clear understanding of the past. The perspectives gained from the lessons of the past provide guidance for the decisions and actions of the future. The study of the evolution of middle level schools makes it clear that the efforts of middle level leaders past and present have made a difference in the lives of some young adolescents. It is equally clear that in many ways middle level schools have not lived up to their promise and that much work needs to be done in the continuing struggle to provide all young adolescents with developmentally responsive environments in which to learn, flourish, and experience success.

Unlike its predecessor, the junior high school as described in Briggs's quote, middle level schools are a "definite institution." But, like Briggs's junior high school, developmentally responsive middle level schools are still "a state of mind, or a striving to achieve a vision, either limited or extensive." Expanding the vision of middle level education is dependent on educators who are not only knowledgeable of the past but who are conversant with successful practice, who understand what middle level schools can be, and who know why middle level schools must be restructured. The remainder of this book will focus on the restructuring process: current research and practice, the developmental needs and characteristics of young adolescents, appropriate curriculum structures, successful programs and practices, elements of leadership and change, developing and implementing the plan, providing needed staff development, and choosing appropriate methods of program assessment and evaluation.

## REFERENCES

Alexander, W. M. (1968). *The emergent middle school.* New York: Holt, Rinehart and Winston.

Alexander, W. M., & McEwin, C. K. (1989, September). Schools in the middle: Progress 1968-1988. *Schools in the middle: A report on trends and practices.* Reston, VA: National Association of Secondary School Principals.

Ayers, L. P. (1909). *Laggards in our schools.* New York: Russell Sage Foundation, Survey Associates, Inc.

Baker, J. H. (1913). *Report of the committee of the national council of education on economy of time in education* [Bulletin 1913, No. 38]. Washington, D.C.: Department of Interior, Bureau of Education.

Becker, H. J. (1990). Curriculum and instruction in middle grade schools. *Phi Delta Kappan, 71*(6), 450-457.

Braddock, J. H., II. (1990). Tracking in the middle grades: National patterns of grouping for instruction. *Phi Delta Kappan, 71*(6), 445-449.

Briggs, T. H. (1920). *The junior high school.* Boston, MA: Houghton Mifflin Company.

Carnegie Task Force on Education of Young Adolescents. (1989). *Turning points: Preparing American youth for the 21st century.* Washington, D.C.: Carnegie Council on Adolescent Development.

Cawelti, G. (1988, November). Middle schools, a better match with early adolescent needs, ASCD survey finds. *ASCD Curriculum Update.* Alexandria, VA: Association for Supervision and Curriculum Development.

Clark, S. N., & Clark, D. C. (1986, September). Middle level programs: More than academics. *Schools in the middle: A report on trends and practices.* Reston, VA: National Association of Secondary School Principals.

Clark, S. N., & Clark, D. C. (1987, October). Interdisciplinary teaming programs: Organization, rationale, and implementation. *Schools in the middle: A report on trends and practices.* Reston, VA: National Association of Secondary School Principals.

Clark, S. N., & Clark, D. C. (1990). *Arizona middle schools: A survey report.* Phoenix, AZ: Arizona Department of Education.

Commission on the Reorganization of Secondary Education. (1918). Cardinal principles of secondary education [Bulletin 1918, No. 35]. Washington, D.C.: U. S. Department of the Interior, Bureau of Education.

Conant, J. B. (1959). *The American high school today.* New York: McGraw Hill Book Company.

Conant, J. B. (1960). *A memorandum to school boards: Recommendations for education in the junior high school years.* Princeton, NJ: The Educational Testing Service.

Cox, P. W. L. (1929). *The junior high school and its curriculum.* New York: Charles Scribner's Sons.

Davis, C. O. (1924). *Junior high school education.* Yonkers-on-Hudson, New York: World Book Company.

Eichhorn, D. H. (1966). *The middle school.* New York: The Center for Applied Research in Education, Inc.

Epstein, J., & Mac Iver, D. (1990). *Education in the middle grades.* Columbus, OH: National Middle School Association.

George, P. S. (1988). Tracking and ability grouping. *Middle School Journal, 20*(1), 21-28.

Goodlad, J. (1984). *A place called school: Prospects for the future.* New York: McGraw-Hill Book Company.

Hansen, J. H., & Hern, A. C. (1971). *The middle school program.* Chicago, IL: Rand McNally and Co.

Keefe, J. W., Clark, D. C., Nickerson, N. C., & Valentine, J. W. (1983). *The middle level principalship—Volume II: The effective middle level principal.* Reston, VA: National Association of Secondary School Principals.

Koos, L. V. (1927). *The junior high school.* Boston, MA: Ginn and Company.

Lounsbury, J. (1991). *As I see it.* Columbus, OH: National Middle Level Association.

Lounsbury, J. H., & Clark, D. C. (1990). *Inside grade eight: From apathy to excitement.* Reston, VA: National Association of Secondary School Principals.

Mac Iver, D. (1990). Meeting the needs of young adolescents: Advisory groups, interdisciplinary teaching teams, and school transition programs. *Phi Delta Kappan, 71*(6), 458-464.

NASSP Council on Middle Level Education. (1985). *An agenda for excellence at the middle level.* Reston, VA: National Association of Secondary School Principals.

National Commission on Excellence in Education. (1982). *A nation at risk: The imperative for educational reform.* Washington, D.C.: U. S. Department of Education.

National Education Association. (1894). *Report of the committee of ten on secondary school studies.* New York: American Book Company.

National Education Association. (1899). *Journal of proceedings and addresses.* Denver, CO: National Education Association.

Oakes, J. (1985). *Keeping track: How schools structure inequality.* New Haven, CT: Yale University Press.

Pringle, R. W. (1937). *The junior high school: A psychological approach.* New York: McGraw-Hill Book Company.

Smith, W. A. (1927). *The junior high school.* New York: The Macmillan Company.

Strayer, G. D. (1911). *Age and grade census of our schools and colleges* [Bulletin 1911, No. 5]. Washington, D.C.: U. S. Department of the Interior, Bureau of Education.

Thornburg, H. (1980). Early Adolescents: Their developmental characteristics. *The High School Journal, 63*(6), 215-221.

Thorndike, E. L. (1907). *The elimination of pupils from schools* [Bulletin 1907, No. 4]. Washington, D.C.: U. S. Department of Interior, Bureau of Education.

Valentine, J. W., Clark, D. C., Nickerson, N. C., & Keefe, J. W. (1981). *The middle level principalship—Volume I: A survey of middle level principals and programs.* Reston, VA: National Association of Secondary School Principals.

Valentine, J., Clark, D., Irvin, J., Keefe, J., and Melton, G. (1993). *Leadership in middle level education, Vol. I: A national survey of middle level leaders and schools.* Reston, VA: National Association of Secondary School Principals.

Van Til, W., Vars, G. F., & Lounsbury, J. H. (1961). *Modern education for the junior high school years.* Indianapolis: Bobbs-Merrill Company, Inc.

# 2

## Middle Level Schools:
## The Rhetoric of Today as the
## Foundation for Tomorrow

> "Middle grade schools—junior high,
> intermediate, and middle schools—
> are potentially society's most pow-
> erful force to recapture millions of
> youth adrift, and help every young
> person thrive during early adoles-
> cence."
>
> *Turning Points*

In Chapter One a middle level school was defined as "A separate
school designed to meet the special needs of young adolescents,
in an organizational structure that encompasses any combination of grades five through nine, and where developmentally
appropriate curricula and programs are used to create learning
experiences that are both relevant and interactive." While a definition is an important first step in describing middle level
schools, it leaves many questions unanswered. What are developmentally responsive middle level schools and how should they
be organized? What do successful middle level schools look like?
Why do most middle level schools need to be restructured? These
three questions will provide the focus for this chapter.

### HOW SHOULD MIDDLE LEVEL SCHOOLS
### BE ORGANIZED?

In the mid 1960s William Alexander and Emmett Williams (1965)
and Donald Eichhorn (1966), leading advocates of the middle

school, began to clarify the goals and purposes of middle level schools. These middle school leaders, in addition to supporting the reorganization of grade levels, also examined ways in which middle school programs could be developmentally appropriate. Alexander and Williams (1965) recommended programs such as homeroom groups of 25 students directed by teacher counselors, each with a subject area specialty in language arts, social studies, mathematics, or science. These four teachers would jointly plan curriculum and serve as team teachers for their 100 students. Each team (called the wing unit) would join with "wing units" from other grade levels to form "a school within a school." The curricular focus of these teams would fall into three areas, learning skills, general studies, and personal development (Alexander and Williams, 1965).

Eichhorn (1966), who focused more heavily on the developmental needs of young adolescents, developed the "Socio-Psychological Model" (p. 65). The model featured two integrated curricula: Analytical which included Language, Mathematics, Social Studies, and Science; and Physical/Cultural which included Fine Arts, Practical Arts, Physical Education, and Cultural Studies. In Eichhorn's model instruction was integrated and was delivered in a variety of organizational arrangements including blocking and flexible scheduling.

The rhetoric on middle level schools during the late 1960s and early 1970s, while supporting the work of Alexander and Williams and Eichhorn, became more focused on organizational and programmatic structures of middle level education. Grooms (1967) called for middle level school programs that would feature a non-graded structure wherein students could progress on a continuous learning basis without recognized grade levels or grade classification. Gatewood (1973) believed that one of the major goals of middle level schools should be the development of an instructional system focused on individualized learning, with many curricular options and appropriate opportunities for individualized instruction.

Other middle level educators, while placing the emphases of the curriculum on the early adolescent learner rather than on structure, advocated program goals that featured flexibility of time and group size, individualized/personalized instruction, a variety of learning experiences, alternative evaluation procedures, and new roles for teachers and administrators (Eichhorn, 1973; Sale, 1979).

In summarizing the ideal goals, purposes, and characteristics of middle level schools of the 1970s, Educational Research Services (Robinson, 1975) listed the following items:

- Emphasis on guidance and human relations
- De-emphasis on sophisticated social activities
- Individualized instruction
- Exploratory courses and activities
- Interdisciplinary teaching teams
- Home-base teachers
- Diversity in teacher certification
- Flexible scheduling
- Gradual transition from elementary to secondary education

Alexander and George (1981) listed the essential features of middle level schools as: (1) Guidance, (2) Transition/Articulation, (3) Block Time Schedule/Interdisciplinary Teams, (4) Appropriate Teaching Strategies, (5) Exploratory, and (6) Appropriate Core Curriculum/Learning Skills. These essential features supplemented the earlier purposes identified by Gruhn and Douglass (1947) and reflected the current rhetoric of middle level scholars (Figure 2-1).

**Figure 2-1**
Six Functions of the Junior High School*

1. *Integration* of learnings in ways that they will become coordinated into effective and wholesome behavior;

2. Discovery and *exploration* opportunities for all pupils that are based on their specialized interests, aptitudes, and abilities;

3. *Guidance* to assist pupils in making wise choices educationally, vocationally, and in their personal and social living;

4. *Differentiation* of educational facilities and opportunities that accommodate the varied backgrounds and needs of pupils;

5. *Socialization* experiences that prepare pupils to participate in the present social order and to contribute to future changes; and

6. *Articulation* through provision for a gradual transition from preadolescent education to educational programs suited to the needs and interests of adolescent youth.

---

* Adapted from: Gruhn, W. T., & Douglass, H. (1947). *The modern junior high school*. New York: Ronald Press.

Drawing on the literature and research of the 1970s, Clark and Valentine (1981) organized middle level programs into three major areas: environmental (organizational structure), content (scope and sequence), and strategies (processes, methods, and materials of instruction). These areas included the following items:

## Program Environment

A. Schedule that includes provision for both interdisciplinary blocks and single-subject courses.

B. Co-curricular activities as part of the regular school day.

C. Opportunity for all students to participate in intramural and, when appropriate, interscholastic programs.

D. Provision for community involvement in the educational program. (This includes bringing community members into the schools and involving students in the community).

E. Opportunities to learn through interdisciplinary teams where students can interact with a variety of teachers in a wide range of subject areas.

## Program Content

A. Emphasis on the acquisition of basic skills (language arts, mathematics, social studies, and science).

B. Availability of required exploratory courses (music, art, home economics, and industrial arts, etc.).

C. Opportunity to participate in elective classes.

D. Provision for both remediation and enrichment.

E. Required reading instruction.

F. Provision for daily physical education.

G. Opportunity for instruction in both health and sex education.

## Program Strategies

A. Availability of multi-media (print and nonprint) resources.

B. Provision for a variety of teacher-student teaching and learning styles.

C. Provision for flexible learning group size.

D. Adaption of the curriculum to concrete/formal learning needs of students.

E. Availability of a teacher-adviser program.

F. Provision for individualized grade reporting based on each student's ability and including parent conferences.

G. Opportunities for each student to explore and clarify values (self, community, and national).

H.   Provision for individualized/personalized programs that include diagnosis (skills and learning style), prescription, and evaluation.

I.   Organization of content into a continuous progress sequence that allows students to progress at their individual rates (Clark and Valentine, 1981; 2-3).

Additional efforts to identify organizational and programmatic structures of middle level schools were undertaken by the National Middle School Association and the National Association of Secondary School Principals. In 1982 a task force commissioned by the National Middle School Association identified what they believed to be the essential elements of a "true" middle level school. In *This We Believe* (1982, 1992) the following elements were identified:

1.   Educators knowledgeable about and committed to young adolescents
2.   A balanced curriculum based on young adolescent needs
3.   A range of organizational arrangements
4.   Varied instructional strategies
5.   A full exploratory program
6.   Comprehensive advising and counseling
7.   Continuous progress for students
8.   Evaluation procedures compatible with young adolescent needs
9.   Cooperative planning
10.  Positive school climate

The NASSP Council on Middle Level Education's *An Agenda for Excellence at the Middle Level* (1985) examined 12 dimensions of middle level schooling that they believed to be essential for success (Figure 2-2). Incorporating many of the elements identified by others, a comprehensive listing was presented that included among other elements the identification of core values, a focus on instruction, a description of effective teachers, and the importance of transition. Of particular importance, *An Agenda for Excellence* placed major emphasis on the elements of culture and climate, connections, and client centeredness.

The Council believed that improvement of middle level schools was dependent on a change in the school's **culture** and **climate**, not on the addition of certain program elements that appeared to be

**Figure 2-2**
An Agenda for Excellence at the Middle Level*

1. **Core Values.** Everyone involved must be committed to clearly articulated core values that guide both individual behavior and institutional practices and policies.

2. **Culture and Climate.** School improvement depends on a change in the culture and climate of the institution. Specific attention must be given to altering the culture/climate of the school so that it supports excellence and achievement.

3. **Student Development.** Success in school and adjustment to adult life depend, to a large degree, on personal attributes and behaviors.

4. **Curriculum.** The middle level school curriculum must develop in young adolescents the intellectual skills and an understanding of humankind that will permit them to gather information, organize it, evaluate its veracity and utility, form reasonable conclusions about it, and plan for individual and collective action.

5. **Learning and Instruction.** The quality of any young adolescent's educational experience is determined by the nature of instruction provided in the classroom.

6. **School Organization.** School organization should encourage the smooth operation of the academic program, clear communication among teachers and administrators, and maximum teacher and student control over the quality of the learning environment.

7. **Technology.** Young adolescents should be educated to use technology competently and thoughtfully in their study of specific subjects and in their approach to complex problems.

8. **Teachers.** Teachers require special preparation and certification which must include the study of human development, counseling, differentiated instruction, classroom management, and home-school cooperation.

9. **Transition.** One of the main responsibilities of the middle level school is to assure a smooth transition for students from elementary school to high school.

10. **Principals.** Successful schools enjoy strong administrative leadership, a clear sense of mission, and confidence in the capacity of administrators to handle problems that interfere with the learning program of the school.

11. **Connections.** The success of any school is determined by the extent to which it is supported and valued in the community and by the parents of the young adolescents who attend.

12. **Client Centeredness.** Successful schools are those that understand the unique needs of their clients and fill those needs quickly and effectively.

---

* Adapted from NASSP Council on Middle Level Education. (1985). *An agenda for excellence at the middle level*. Reston, VA: National Association of Secondary School Principals.

effective. The school's culture and climate must be altered so "that it supports excellence and achievement rather than intellectual conformity and mediocrity" (p. 3). **Connections** with the home and the community are important to middle level school success. Since fewer households have children in school, the public "no longer has the 'child's eye view' of school that was common for so long. This means that the school has to work harder to maintain good relations with its constituent community" (pp. 18-19).

The final element and perhaps the most important element suggested by the Council was **client centeredness**. *The Agenda for Excellence* states:

> The most successful schools are those that understand the unique needs of their clients and fill those needs quickly and effectively. Most important, effective schools understand the relationship of development to learning so that students are not asked to violate the dictates of their development in order to fully participate in the educational program (1985; 20).

James Garvin (1987), in interviews with more than 1,000 parents, offered a different perspective on what middle level schools should be like. Although Garvin's listing does not specifically address organizational structures of middle level schools, it does offer insight on parents' expectations, expectations that have implications for school organization.

Parents were asked: "What would you like for the middle level school to provide for your child?" (Garvin, 1987; 3). The answers are listed in rank order.

1. When my child goes to school, more than anything else I want to know that he/she is safe!
2. I want to know that when my child is in school that he/she knows at least one adult well enough to go to if support is needed.
3. I want to know that the school is concerned about helping my youngster develop constructive friends.
4. I expect that school will provide my youngster with opportunities to be involved in activities.
5. When my youngster comes home from school, I want to know that he/she has had enough good experiences to want to return the next day.
6. While my child is in school, I want to know that the school is teaching him/her what he/she will need to be prepared for high school.

7.  While my youngster is in school, I want teachers to keep me informed on his/her progress.
8.  When I visit the school, I want to feel welcomed by teachers and administrators.
9.  I'd like to know that the school is making every effort to provide opportunities for parents to be informed about what to expect from youngsters over these years (1987; 3-4).

No listing of how middle level schools should be organized would be complete without mention of the Carnegie Task Force on Education of Young Adolescents report (1989). Entitled *Turning Points: Preparing American Youth for the 21st Century*, the report suggests that a vast majority of American middle level schools are failing to meet the needs of young adolescents.

The Carnegie Task Force on Education of Young Adolescents provides educators with guidelines for establishing a purpose for middle level schools. Their study was guided by the following questions:

> What qualities do we envision in the 15-year-old who has been well served in the middle years of schooling? What do we want every young adolescent to know, to feel, to be able to do upon emerging from that educational and school-related experience (1989; 15)?

They go on to say:

> Our answer is embodied in five characteristics associated with being an effective human being. Our 15-year-old will be:
> An intellectually reflective person;
> A person enroute to a lifetime of meaningful work;
> A good citizen;
> A caring and ethical individual; and
> A healthy person (Carnegie Task Force, 1989; 15).

By establishing this purpose, the Carnegie Task Force on Education of Young Adolescents instituted a national purpose for middle level education.

Integrating current research with "considered and wise practice," the Task Force suggested that the transformation of education for young adolescents involved eight essential principles. These principles are:

•  Large middle grade schools are divided into smaller communities for learning.

- Middle grade schools transmit a core of common knowledge to all students.
- Middle grade schools are organized to ensure success for all students.
- Teachers and principals have the major responsibility and power to transform middle grade schools.
- Teachers for the middle grades are specifically prepared to teach young adolescents.
- Schools promote good health; the education and health of young adolescents are inextricably linked.
- Families are allied with school staff through mutual respect, trust, and communication.
- Schools and communities are partners in educating young adolescents (Carnegie Task Force, 1989; 36).

Numerous states have also addressed middle level school organization and structure. Most notable among these are California's *Caught in the Middle* (1987) and New York's *Regents Policy Statement on Middle-Level Education and Schools with Middle Grades* (1989). Among the 22 principles of middle level education listed in *Caught in the Middle*, seven (school culture, extracurricular and intramural activities, student accountability, transition, structure, scheduling, and assessment) deal with school organization and structure.

The New York Regents Policy on Middle Grade Organization and Structure (*Regents Policy Statement on Middle-Level Education and Schools with Middle Grades*, 1989) suggests 13 elements for school organization. These include:

- Middle level schools with at least three grade levels
- Small student enrollments
- Organization of houses, teams, or families to reduce the feeling of isolation
- Multiyear assignment of teacher advisors, classroom teachers, and teaching teams
- Grouping strategies that maintain heterogeneous classrooms but group for specific experiences of a short term
- Teaching teams that share the responsibilities for a common group of students
- Common planning time for teaching teams
- Flexible schedules within blocks of time that facilitate interdisciplinary curriculum
- Gradual transition from elementary to high school

- Cocurricular and extracurricular activities
- Participation of special needs students in cocurricular and extracurricular activities
- Integration of special needs students into the regular programs of the school
- Support services such as guidance, counseling, health-related services available to all students

## WHAT DO SUCCESSFUL MIDDLE LEVEL SCHOOLS LOOK LIKE?

There is widespread agreement about how middle level schools should be organized and structured. While the literature on middle level schools has consistently identified a number of common elements essential to developmentally responsive schools, the research of the last decade reports that a vast number of middle level schools are falling short of meeting the expectations described by scholars, researchers, and practitioners (Lounsbury and Clark, 1990; Mac Iver, 1990).

There have been, however, some notable exceptions, instances where researchers have found "outstanding middle level schools" and then described them. Lipsitz (1984), in her study of successful schools for young adolescents, examined four successful middle level schools. Her purpose was to describe how and why these schools were successful in meeting the needs of young adolescents.

What she found in these schools was a strong sense of purpose centered around making every practice in the school appropriate to the needs of their particular students. Lipsitz stated that "The most striking feature of the four schools is their willingness and ability to adapt all school practices to the individual differences in intellectual, biological, and social maturation of their students" (1984; 167). She goes on to say:

> The four schools set out from the beginning to be positive environments for early adolescent personal and social development, not only because such environments contribute to academic achievement, but because they are intrinsically valued, stemming from a belief in positive school climate as a goal, not a process toward a goal (1984; 168).

It was evident to Lipsitz that a major factor in these schools' success was not only their commitment to the needs of their students but the clarity they had achieved about the purposes of their school and the children they teach.

Leadership was also an important factor in the success of these schools. Lipsitz found principals at each of the four schools with "driving visions," principals who imbue "decisions and practices with meaning, placing powerful emphasis on why and how things are done" (1984; 174). Decisions were being made not on the basis of expediency, but for reasons of principle.

Another factor of importance to middle level school success was positive school climate. Critical factors which shaped the positive climate in these schools as identified by Lipsitz were "the physical setting, the means by which order is achieved, teachers' working conditions, their beliefs and expectations, and the acknowledgement of reciprocity in human relations" (1984; 179). Important contributors to the positive climate were the "strikingly high level of caring in the schools," a commonly accepted group of norms, the lack of adult isolation, and daily positive experiences for teachers.

Lipsitz describes the development of school organization and structure as being "organic and evolving." The four principals had a vision of what schooling should be for young adolescents, a vision, interestingly, that need not include the concept of teams or houses. Decisions to implement these and other organizational arrangements in their schools resulted from the school philosophy, a "school philosophy that was deeply influenced by sensitivity to the age group" (p. 193).

Despite the differences in the four schools, they were all responsive to their particular constituencies. It is this responsiveness that contributes to their success. "Successful schools," says Lipsitz, "are responsive to particular social contexts. They contribute, as a result, to greater diversity rather than homogenization in American schooling" (1984; 198).

Middle level schools should be different to be responsive to differing needs of the students they serve and the community contexts where they exist. There appears, however, to be little disagreement with Lipsitz when she suggests that:

> . . . schools responsive to early adolescent development will reduce the size of the focus groups, personalize the quality of adult student relationships, give ample room for peer groups to flourish, acknowledge diverse areas of competence, involve students in participatory activities, emphasize self-exploration and physical activity, and encompass all these in a clearly defined, structured environment (p. 199).

Paul George and Lynn Oldaker (1985) surveyed 130 reputedly successful middle level schools to determine the degree to which the programs of these schools could be perceived as effective. Eighty-one percent of the schools responded and reported the following information:

- 90 percent organized teachers and students into interdisciplinary teams—rather than self-contained or departmentalized instruction
- 94 percent used flexible scheduling during the school day—often with some type of block scheduling
- 93 percent included a home base period and a teacher advisor for every student
- 99 percent focused curriculum on students' personal development and skills for continued learning, and a wide range of exploratory activities
- All reported that administrators and faculty members collaborated on decisions that shaped school policy (p. 79)

Analysis of the data showed that a majority of the schools described consistent academic achievement, 80 percent noted a significant reduction in discipline problems, 80 percent indicated that student emotional health, creativity, and confidence in self-directed learning was positively affected, and 90 percent of the schools believed that student self-concept and social development benefited from the programs.

The schools also reported improvement in the school learning climate, faculty morale, and parental involvement and support. Staff development was also reported as being effective in improving classroom management and instruction.

The nature of their findings led George and Oldaker (1985) to draw the following conclusions:

> Results indicate that middle schools which manage to receive a reputation as highly successful are very similar in terms of the components of the program. The programs common to these exemplary middle schools do tend to conform to the recommendations in the literature of middle level education in the last half century. Such programs, too, are distinctly different from those common to elementary and high schools. Furthermore, when implemented in this way, the results are dramatically positive. Academic achievement, student behavior, school learning climate, faculty morale, and staff development, and a number of other factors are affected in positive ways (1985; 36).

The findings of George and Oldaker are highly supportive of the efficacy of the elements of organization and structure reported earlier. The findings, particularly those dealing with school climate, emphasis on meeting the needs of young adolescents, and collaborative decision making, are congruent with the findings of Lipsitz (1984).

J. Howard Johnston (1985), using data collected from middle level schools who were recognized as outstanding schools by the U.S. Department of Education's Secondary School Recognition Program, concluded that in these outstanding schools four types of climate existed: Physical, Academic, Social-Emotional, and Organizational (1985; 2).

The following examples of **physical climate**, perhaps the least important of the four, were commonly found in all of the recognition schools visited by Johnston:

- The schools, despite their age, were well-lit and bright
- The buildings were well-maintained; no plaster was loose, no broken tiles, no broken lockers, or other damaged equipment were evident
- The buildings were uniformly clean
- There were no graffiti in or on any of the schools (p. 2)

Johnston characterized the **academic climate** of these schools by five features:

- People in the schools talk about academics
- Academic achievements are recognized and rewarded
- Academics form the basis for leisure pursuits
- Expectations are high but reasonable, and failure is tolerated
- Teachers use time wisely (pp. 3-4)

Four characteristics of **organizational climate** were especially evident in these schools. They included:

- These schools have few rules, but those that exist are clear, and, on their face, reasonable
- Student council has a dual role in the school—advisory and service
- Students know how to influence school policy and believe they can
- Teachers make major decisions (pp. 5-6)

"The **social-emotional climate** of effective schools I visited," reports Johnston, "was in some ways the most striking and in others the most difficult to detect. Clearly, though, this climate has a profound effect on the school, the academic quality of its programs, and the effectiveness with which students and teachers perform" (p. 6). The following factors of social-emotional climate were observed at the schools:

- The schools are encouraging, welcoming, supporting places
- The schools are secure places
- The schools anticipate student needs and fill them without fanfare
- The best schools are trusting places
- The schools are civil places (pp. 6-8).

In examining the effect of climates on the quality of schooling, Johnston suggests that the characteristics so often associated with school effectiveness actually stem from the culture of that school. He asks:

> How can these conditions be influenced? I will venture one tentative conclusion. The creation of a school culture is more dependent upon the behavior of adults in the school than on characteristics of students, economic climates of the community in which the school is located, per pupil expenditure, physical facilities, or a host of other demographic-environmental variables.
>
> That's the good news. We can do something as professionals to make schools more effective. Now we must be sure that the things we do are the things that make schools effective—not just the things that make them look effective (Johnston, 1985; 8).

Clearly, the data from Johnston's study on school climate in excellent middle level schools support the findings of Lipsitz and George and Oldaker. Their organizational structures support warm, supporting, caring climates for both teachers and students; they are developmentally responsive to needs of the students they serve; they have norms and expectancies for young adolescents that are developmentally appropriate; and they provide extensive opportunities for collaborative decision making.

## WHY MIDDLE LEVEL SCHOOLS MUST CHANGE

There are several compelling reasons why middle level schools must change. First, the needs of young adolescents and the society demand that middle level schools be more developmentally responsive. Second, despite the research and literature supporting significant change in the way middle level schools are organized and structured, most middle level schools remain unchanged. Third, successful, developmentally responsive middle level schools have the potential to provide successful intellectual, physical, social, and emotional experiences for all middle level students.

Recent studies have confirmed that many young adolescents are in fact "losing themselves." In *Turning Points*, the report of the Carnegie Task Force on Education of Young Adolescents, the authors state:

> Unfortunately, by age 15, substantial numbers of American youth are at risk of reaching adulthood unable to meet adequately the requirements of the workplace, the commitments of relationships in families and with friends, and the responsibilities of participation in a democratic society. These youth are among the estimated 7 million young people—one in four adolescents—who are extremely vulnerable to multiple high-risk behaviors and school failure. Another 7 million may be at moderate risk, but remain a cause for serious concern (1989; 8).

In the *National Educational Longitudinal Study of 1988—A Profile of The American Eighth Grader* (Hafner, et. al., 1990), researchers report that one-third of all eighth graders are age 15 or over and 18 percent have already repeated at least one grade. The authors also report that the typical eighth grader spends four times as many hours watching television per week than s/he spends on homework—21.4 hours *vs* 5.6 hours.

The NELS Eighth Grade Study also reports that only 19 percent of the eighth graders are proficient at advanced math levels (simple problem solving and conceptual understanding) and that only 34 percent are proficient at advanced levels of reading (able to make inferences beyond author's main thought, to summarize, to make generalizations).

In describing "At Risk" factors, the NELS Study states:

> "At Risk" status refers to possessing certain characteristics which have been found to be associated with educational disadvantage, or with school failure (Hafner, et. al., 1990; 77).

The study found that 53 percent of the sample had no risk factors, 26 percent had one risk factor, and 20 percent had two or more risk factors (Figure 2-3). Students with two or more risk

**Figure 2-3**
Factors Which Place Young Adolescents At Risk*

| Factor | Percentage of Students Affected |
|---|---|
| Single Parent Family | 22 |
| Family Income Less than $15,000 | 21 |
| Home Alone for More than 3 Hours a Day | 14 |
| Parents Have No High School Diploma | 11 |
| Sibling Dropped Out | 10 |
| Limited English Proficiency | 02 |

* Hafner, A., Ingels, S., Schneider, B., Stevenson, D., & Owings, J. (1990). *National educational longitudinal study of 1988: A profile of the American eighth grader.* Washington, D.C.: U.S. Department of Education, Office of Educational Research and Implementation.

factors were **six times** as likely as those students with no risk factors to not graduate from high school. These students are also twice as likely to be in the lowest grade and achievement test quartile. Hispanic eighth grade students are more likely than other students to have parents who did not finish high school, and students whose parents never finished high school are **three times** as likely to repeat a grade as students whose parents are college graduates.

Certain combinations of risk factors were shown to be particularly detrimental to success. These include single parent home with a low income and parents with limited English proficiency who have no high school diploma. The study also found no difference in the impact of "At Risk" factors on males and females, but found differences varied greatly by race/ethnicity. Blacks, Native Americans, and Hispanics are twice as likely to have two or more risk factors.

Many middle level students go home to unsupervised environments at the end of the school day (latchkey kids). Being home alone for more than three hours a day is another risk factor identified by the NELS Study. In contrast to other "at risk" factors which were most likely to affect low socioeconomic and minority students, eighth graders with the highest socioeconomic status (SES) are twice as likely to have no one home while whites and blacks are more likely than Hispanics to have no one home.

In addition to the previously identified "at risk" factors, many of which significantly impact minority students, there is considerable evidence that adolescent girls are also "at risk." A recent report of the American Association of University Women (1992) contends that "as girls mature they confront a culture that both idealizes and exploits the sexuality of young women while assigning them roles that are clearly less valued than male roles" (p. 2). Drawing from a broad spectrum of research the report declares that America's educational system is not meeting the needs of girls. The report cites research that shows girls falling behind males in mathematics and self-esteem measures; receiving less classroom attention than boys; emerging from school with less confidence; and being subjected to increasing sexual harassment (from innuendo to actual assault) (AAUW Educational Foundation, 1992; 1).

Information from other national data bases offer equally compelling reasons for restructuring schools for young adolescents (Carnegie Task Force, 1989; Hodgkinson, 1985; Hodgkinson, 1991; Wiles and Bondi, 1986). The following is a compilation from these reports.

**Dramatic Shifts in the Ethnic Composition of Schools**
- By the year 2020 nearly half of all school age children will be nonwhite.
- Minority youth of low economic status are traditionally the group least well served by American schools.
- Typically, minority children are more likely to be retained in grade level; as a result, they are much more likely to drop out.

**Changing Status of Families.** The "so called" typical American family, which includes a working father, a mother who stays at home and two children, now constitutes less than 10 percent of American families.

- More than half of school age children will live in a single parent family by age 18.
- Over 4 million children are living with a mother who has never married.
- Children raised by single mothers (15 million in 1990) will have about one-third as much money spent on them as children being raised by two parents.
- More than 2 million children spend two to three hours daily without adult supervision. Another 2 million are not being reared by either parent.
- One in four families moves every year.

**Adolescents At-Risk.** Hodgkinson (1991) reports that when compared to children in other developed nations a U. S. Census Bureau study found that American children were the most "vulnerable in most of the dimensions covered in the study, particularly in the following areas: number of children affected by divorce, youth homicide rate, number (and percentage) of youngsters living in poverty, infant mortality rate, and teenage pregnancy rate" (Hodgkinson, 1991; 13-14).

- Four out of five **adolescent deaths** are linked to accidents, homicides, and suicides. Many of these deaths are related to high risk-taking behaviors. Accidents are the leading killer of youths 10 to 14 years of age.
- **Suicide** is a major killer of teens 15-19 years of age—10.3 per 100,000—triple the rate of the 1950s. Between 1980 and 1985 the suicide rate of 10 to 14 year olds more than doubled.
- More and more teens under the age of 16 are becoming **sexually active** leading to extremely high risks of pregnancy.
    - Every day 40 teenage girls give birth to their third child, and the proportion of pregnant teenage girls under the age of 15 is beginning to exceed that of girls over 15.
    - White teenagers are 2 times as likely to give birth outside of marriage as in other developed nations.
    - Teenage mothers tend to give birth to children who are premature. Prematurity leads to low birth weight, a good predictor of major learning difficulties when a child reaches school.
    - One-fourth of all sexually active teenagers will become infected with a sexually transmitted disease before they graduate from high school.
- **Alcohol** is the most prevalent drug problem among U. S. students. Of those in the high school class of 1987 who began drinking before leaving high school, 56 percent began drinking in grades six through nine.
- Of high school students who **smoke**, 51 percent began in grades six to nine; of those who use **illicit drugs**, 29 percent began during the middle grade years (6-9). The average age of beginning smokers dropped from age 14 to age 10 in the last decade.

Clearly, young adolescents live in a society that places them at risk. The opportunities for making choices in today's society are abundant, and it is readily apparent that many young people are making poor choices, choices that will severely diminish their chances for success. While it is obvious that many of the problems facing young people are caused by factors outside the control of the school, it is equally obvious that these factors will have a major impact on the way schools are organized and structured.

While it is easy to assume that schools would be the first to respond to the increasing demands of adolescent youth for successful school experiences, it is evident that many middle level schools are slow to change. Anthony Jackson (1990), Project Director, Carnegie Task Force on Education of Young Adolescents, reports the response to *Turning Points* by the education community all over the country "has been overwhelmingly positive" (1990; 1). He goes on to say:

> Nevertheless, some educators have commented that there is very little that is new in the report. "We are already doing that" is a common response to many of the recommendations in *Turning Points* from schools across the nation.
>
> Despite such perceptions, recent studies show that few of the recommended actions, though frequently proposed, are actually practiced in schools (1990; 1).

Jackson's comments are confirmed by numerous studies in the late 1980s. In spite of the evidence that many of the common elements identified by Alexander and George (1981), Clark and Valentine (1981), Lipsitz (1984), and the NASSP Council (1985) are successful in creating more developmentally appropriate environments for young adolescents (George and Oldaker, 1985; Lipsitz, 1984; Mac Iver, 1990), these elements are not found in a majority of this country's middle level schools. National studies conducted by the Association for Supervision and Curriculum Development (Cawelti, 1988), Alexander and McEwin (1989), and the Center for Research on Elementary and Middle Schools at Johns Hopkins University (Mac Iver, 1990) give evidence that most programs commonly recommended by middle level educators and the Carnegie Council on Adolescent Development are not being widely implemented.

While *Turning Points* confirms the importance of many of the programs middle level educators have been advocating for their schools, the Carnegie Task Force also indicted middle level schools for their failure to provide appropriate learning environments for their students. Nowhere is this indictment more clear than in the introduction of the report when the Task Force (Carnegie Task Force, 1989) states:

> A volatile mismatch exists between the organization and curriculum of middle grade schools and the intellectual and emotional needs of young adolescents. Caught in a vortex of changing demands, the engagement of many youth in learning diminishes, and their rates of alienation, substance abuse, absenteeism, and dropping out of school begin to rise (pp. 8-9).

In calling for major structural and organizational changes in middle level schools, the Carnegie Task Force on Education of Young Adolescents not only reconfirms the importance of middle level schools but challenges educators to restructure their schools to provide every young adolescent with an opportunity to be successful. The urgency for middle level school change is also echoed by Lounsbury and Clark (1990) who, based on their findings in the NASSP National Study of Eighth Grade, offered eleven recommendations which they hoped would give direction to middle level educators who are in the process of restructuring their schools. These recommendations (Lounsbury and Clark, 1990; 134-139), which are organized into the categories of *school organization*, *developmental appropriateness*, and *personnel*, are as follows.

## School Organization

In the area of school organization the following recommendations were made:

**1.    Interdisciplinary instruction must be vigorously pursued and integration of content must become an important part of teaming.**

Even in those schools who reported interdisciplinary teaming, examples of interdisciplinary instruction were all but nonexistent. The shadow study results indicate that much fragmentation of instruction still exists and that interdisciplinary teaming is still having little impact on the instructional experiences of eighth graders.

**2.    Teacher advisory programs should be more fully implemented.**

Programs that focus on social and academic support have been found to reduce drop-out rates (Mac Iver, 1990). This is a difficult component to implement because many middle level educators do not yet accept working with early adolescent social needs as an equal part of the curriculum.

### 3.    Reduce the use of homogeneous grouping.

The full implementation of the middle level concept will require a drastic reduction in the amount and degree of tracking and homogeneous grouping. At this developmental stage, labels and accompanying assumptions about ability have serious and long lasting negative effects on students (Braddock, 1990; Oakes, 1985).

## Developmental Responsiveness

The following recommendations relate to the area of developmental responsiveness:

### 4.    Developmentally responsive programs for eighth-graders must be implemented. Students must experience success now!

Developmental responsiveness carries with it major implications for school restructuring. Restructuring demands that middle level educators create new visions of what schooling for middle level students can be and move beyond the mere form and structure of middle level programs and become more increasingly concerned with the substance of these programs. What counts is how these programs are functioning daily in classrooms with young adolescents.

### 5.    Schools must be freed of developmentally inappropriate requirements.

Inappropriate requirements must be eliminated. Often teachers feel constrained and frustrated by expectations and requirements that are regarded as developmentally inappropriate. To meet the academic, social, emotional, and physical developmental needs of young adolescents, teachers and administrators must be allowed to develop curricula and programs that are responsive to the needs of their students.

### 6.    The social needs of middle level students must be recognized.

Schools that are serious about meeting the developmental needs of this age group will organize activities and schedules in such a way that the youngsters will be able to interact in legitimately appropriate ways. Young adolescents need opportunities to work together in cooperative learning groups and participate in peer tutoring, peer mediation, community projects, and youth service.

### 7. Students must be actively involved in the learning process.

While students seem willing enough to do what they are told to do, their lack of ownership was an effective barrier to effective learning. The absence of adequate involvement of students and the resulting dominance of passive learning was commented on by observers and analysts alike as much as any other concern.

### 8. Critical thinking should be a priority goal.

The relatively low level of intellectualism so painfully evident in most eighth grade classrooms is damaging to those youngsters who are able to think hypothetically and to those who need to be enticed to think analytically. While some eighth graders have not yet arrived at this necessary level of intellectual maturity, they need to be stimulated and encouraged to think analytically and critically.

### 9. Curriculum content must be relevant.

Students see the school's curriculum as a thing apart—something to be tolerated but of no real help to them in their daily lives. Only when students sense the value of content and activities to their "world" will they make quality efforts.

### 10. Early adolescents' expectations of school must be raised.

Students accept what they get too readily; they expect very little from school, and they resign themselves to classes that are boring. At this vibrant, exciting time of life when new vistas and new relationships are opening up to youth, middle level schools are not capitalizing on that excitement.

## Personnel

In a final recommendation Lounsbury and Clark commended the teachers and administrators in this study who really cared for "kids" but were overwhelmed by the requirements of the bureaucracy. They sensed a feeling in these educators of a lack of efficacy and a frustration caused by having to do things they truly believed to be developmentally inappropriate. The following recommendation was made:

## 11.    The ultimate importance of the teacher must be recognized.

When all is said and done, the quality and character of the individual teacher personality is of more importance in facilitating learning than the content, the materials, or the organizational arrangement. Therefore, if middle level schools are to become truly developmentally responsive, "educational improvement must deal directly with teachers as persons, with their understandings, attitudes, and abilities. It is naive to assume significant changes can be made simply by changing schedules, textbooks, or courses, and bypassing the personal growth of teachers" (Lounsbury and Clark, 1990; 139).

## SUMMARY

From the very beginning of the junior high school movement, scholars and practitioners have called for significant changes in the way middle level schools have been organized and structured. During the last three decades, the literature has been considerable and specific in describing the kinds of changes needed to make middle level schools developmentally responsive to the needs of the young adolescents they serve. Even more significant, the research of the 1980s has supported the organizational and structural reforms called for in the rhetoric of middle level education.

Middle level schools, for the most part, have not responded to these calls for reform, and remain primarily the traditionally oriented schools that they have always been. It becomes increasingly evident that schools must undergo major reorganization if they are to meet the continuing developmental needs of their students and the society in which they live.

The literature and research on middle level schools provides an excellent foundation on which middle level educators can build their programs. To what degree, however, are middle level educators knowledgeable or aware of this literature and research? What is their knowledge base about early adolescent needs and characteristics? How cognizant are middle level educators of appropriate curriculum and instructional organization?

What is their knowledge base about successful programs and practices?

Successful middle level restructuring is built on a foundation of knowledge. School restructuring requires that middle level educators be well informed in two major categories:

1.  Specific knowledge about early adolescent needs and characteristics
2.  Extensive knowledge about successful middle level school organization, curriculum and instruction, and programs and practices

The most crucial and perhaps the most neglected area of knowledge needed for school restructuring is that area of knowledge dealing with the developmental characteristics of young adolescents. Middle level schools exist to be special places where students can learn and grow, can prosper, and can be successful. Issues such as intellectual development, social characteristics, emotional needs, and physical growth patterns must be studied and well understood before developmentally appropriate curriculum, programs, and practices can be implemented.

A knowledge of successful middle level structures and practice is also important in the decision-making process. Middle level "restructurers" must be aware of successful programs for middle level schools, programs that make provision for teaming, teacher advisories, appropriate activities, parent and community involvement, and youth service. Middle level leaders must also be knowledgeable of developmentally responsive curricular approaches and be cognizant of the broad range of instructional strategies available to facilitate student learning. Knowledge of appropriate assessment tools is also important information for those involved in middle level school restructuring.

These, the specific knowledge bases of middle level education, will be the basis for the second section of this book. Emphasis will be placed on young adolescents and their unique characteristics and needs (Chapter 3), developmentally appropriate curricular organization, instructional strategies, and appropriate assessment (Chapter 4), successful organizational structures and programs such as interdisciplinary teaming, teacher advisory programs, and student activities (Chapter 5), and parental and community involvement programs (Chapter 6).

# REFERENCES

Alexander, W. M., & George, P. S. (1981). *The exemplary middle school.* New York: Holt, Reinhart, and Winston.

Alexander, W. M., & McEwin, C. K. (1989, September). Schools in the middle: Progress 1968-1988. *NASSP schools in the middle: A report on trends and practices.* Reston, VA: National Association of Secondary School Principals.

Alexander, W. M., & Williams, E. L. (1965). Schools for the middle years. *Educational Leadership, 23*(3), 217-223.

American Association of University Women Educational Foundation. (1992). *The AAUW report: How schools shortchange girls (Executive summary).* Washington, D.C.: American Association of University Women Educational Foundation.

Braddock, J. H., II. (1990). Tracking in the middle grades: National patterns of grouping for instruction. *Phi Delta Kappan, 71*(6), 445-449.

Carnegie Task Force on Education of Young Adolescents. (1989). *Turning points: Preparing American youth for the 21st century.* Washington, D.C.: Carnegie Council on Adolescent Development.

Cawelti, G. (1988, November). Middle schools, a better match with early adolescent needs, ASCD survey finds. *ASCD Curriculum Update.* Alexandria, VA: Association for Supervision and Curriculum Development.

Clark, D. C., & Valentine, J. W. (1981, June). Middle level programs: Making the ideal a reality. *NASSP schools in the middle: A report on trends and practices.* Reston, VA: National Association of Secondary School Principals.

Eichhorn, D. H. (1966). *The middle school.* New York: The Center for Applied Research in Education, Inc.

Eichhorn, D. H. (1973). Middle school in the making. *Educational Leadership, 31*(3), 195-197.

Garvin, J. (1987). What do parents expect from middle level schools? *Middle School Journal, 19*(1), 3-4.

Gatewood, T. E. (1973). What research says about the middle school. *Educational Leadership, 31*(3), 221-224.

George, P. S., & Oldaker, L. L. (1985). *Evidence for the middle school.* Columbus, OH: National Middle School Association.

Grooms, M. A. (1967). *Perspectives on the middle school.* Columbus, OH: Charles E. Merrill Books, Inc.

Gruhn, W. T., & Douglass, H. R. (1947). *The modern junior high school.* New York: Ronald Press.

Hafner, A., Ingels, S., Schneider, B., Stevenson, D., & Owings, J. (1990). *National educational longitudinal study of 1988: A profile of the American eighth grader.* Washington, D. C.: U. S. Department of Education, Office of Educational Research and Implementation.

Hodgkinson, H. (1985). *All one system: Demographics of education, Kindergarten through graduate school.* Washington, D.C.: The Institute for Educational Leadership, Inc.

Hodgkinson, H. (1991). Reform versus reality. *Phi Delta Kappan, 73*(1), 9-16.

Jackson, A. (1990). From knowledge to practice: Implementing the recommendations of Turning Points. *Middle School Journal, 21*(3), 1-3.

Johnston, J. H. (1985, January). Four climates of effective middle level schools. *NASSP schools in the middle: A report on trends and practices.* Reston, VA: National Association of Secondary School Principals.

Lipsitz, J. (1984). *Successful schools for young adolescents.* New Brunswick, NJ: Transaction Books.

Lounsbury, J. H., & Clark, D. C. (1990). *Inside grade eight: From apathy to excitement.* Reston, VA: National Association of Secondary School Principals.

Mac Iver, D. J. (1990). Meeting the needs of young adolescents: Advisory groups, interdisciplinary teaching teams, and school transition programs. *Phi Delta Kappan, 71*(6), 458-464.

NASSP Council on Middle Level Education. (1985). *An agenda for excellence at the middle level.* Reston, VA: National Association of Secondary School Principals.

National Middle School Association. (1982). *This we believe.* Columbus, OH: National Middle School Association.

National Middle School Association. (1992). *This we believe.* Columbus, OH: National Middle School Association.

Oakes, J. (1985). *Keeping track: How schools structure inequality.* New Haven, CT: Yale University Press.

Regents Policy Statement on Middle Level Education and Schools with Middle Grades. (1989). *Regents policy on middle level organization and structure.* Albany, NY: New York State Department of Education.

Robinson, G. E. (1975). *Summary of research on middle schools.* Arlington, VA: Educational Research Service, Inc.

Sale, L. L. (1979). *Introduction to middle school teaching.* Columbus, OH: Charles E. Merrill Publishing Co.

Superintendent's Middle Grade Task Force. (1987). *Caught in the middle: Educational reform for young adolescents in California public schools.* Sacramento, CA: California State Department of Education.

Wiles, J. W., & Bondi, J. H., Jr. (1986). *Making middle schools work.* Alexandria, VA: Association for Supervision and Curriculum Development.

# SECTION II

Restructuring the Middle Level School:
Building a Knowledge Base

# 3

# Early Adolescent Developmental Needs and Characteristics

> "In no other stage of the life cycle, are the promises of finding oneself and the threat of losing oneself so closely allied."
>
> Erik Erikson

Early adolescence is a unique period of life when children begin the complex process of making the transition to adulthood. It is a process that not only encompasses physical development, but also influences social, emotional, and intellectual development. Early adolescence, which includes youth from 10 to 14 years of age, can best be described as a time of change and diversity. This change and diversity, which often is not well understood by parents and educators, frequently leads to anxiety and misunderstandings among young adolescents, their peers, and the significant adults who work with them daily.

Understanding young adolescents, their developmental needs and characteristics, is of prime importance for middle level educators engaging in the restructuring process. Without a comprehensive knowledge base regarding the developmental needs of the students they serve, middle level educators will continue to make well-intentioned, but uninformed organizational and programmatic decisions. Developmentally responsive middle level schools are and must be structured around a comprehensive knowledge base of the intellectual, physical, social, and emotional characteristics of the young adolescent learner. Failure to

consider carefully the implications of developmental characteristics will lead to the continuation of the inappropriate practices
shown to be so prevalent in the National Association of
Secondary School Principals' Grade Level Studies in the late
1980s (Lounsbury and Johnston, 1985; Lounsbury and
Johnston, 1988; Lounsbury and Clark, 1990).

## EARLY ADOLESCENT NEEDS AND
## CHARACTERISTICS: A BROAD PERSPECTIVE

The diversity of early adolescence is easily observed by walking
through the halls of any middle level school during a passing
period. One is overwhelmed by the differences in shapes and
sizes of young adolescents as well as the variation of behavior.
Not only is the early adolescent world one of diversity, it is one of
opposites. James (1980) suggests that young adolescents are at
one moment coordinated and awkward, shy and aggressive,
attentive and distracted, astute and absentminded. These students can also, at the same time, love and dislike their teachers
and peers and be "angelic" or "devilish."

Providing appropriate educational experiences for young adolescents demands that middle level educators have a comprehensive knowledge of the changes being encountered by the students they serve. John Hill's *Understanding Early Adolescence: A
Framework* (1980) provides a comprehensive structure for the
examination of the complexity of the change process in the lives of
young adolescents (see Figure 3-1). In his framework three sets of
interacting factors are identified, factors that profoundly influence the developmental process. These factors include (Hill, 1980):

**Primary Changes of Early Adolescence**
    Biological Change
    Psychological Change
    Changes in Social Definition

**Secondary Changes of Early Adolescence -
Psychosocial Issues in Adolescent Development**
    Attachment
    Autonomy
    Sexuality
    Intimacy
    Achievement
    Identity

**Figure 3-1**
Hill's Framework for Understanding Early Adolescence*

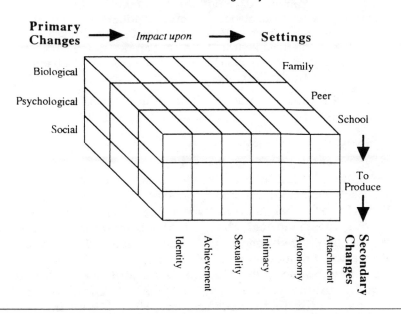

* Hill, J. (1980). Understanding Early Adolescence: A Framework. Carrboro, NC: Center for Early Adolescence. University of North Carolina at Chapel Hill. Reprinted by Permission.

### Settings
Family
Peer
School

In describing the framework Hill states (1980, p. 26):

> [I]n early adolescence the primary changes play the major role in bringing about the secondary changes. Biological changes raise new issues for autonomy, achievement, identity and the like. And so do changes in thinking ability. However, the impact of the primary changes on these psycho-social issues does not occur in a vacuum. It occurs in family, peer, school, community, media, church. . . . The variations in how the issues are resolved stem not only from individuals' past histories but also from their current social relationships. The others who are important in adolescents' lives—whom they encounter in family, peer, school, and community settings—react to primary changes with modified expectations and norms.

Hill goes on to say:

> Puberty, for example, does not directly dictate the initiation of sexual activity. How others respond to puberty is critical in determining who becomes sexually active. Changes in self-concept do not emerge only from looking at one's changing body in the mirror; they emerge also because of the reactions of parents and peers to the bodily changes (Hill, 1980; 26).

Understanding the nature of early adolescence is not only an awareness of the specific primary changes in biological, psychological, and sociological development, but an understanding of how these changes interact with secondary changes and the settings in which young adolescents live.

Steinberg (1989), in order to view adolescence from a variety of perspectives, also developed a framework. Largely based on the work of Hill, Steinberg's framework included similar components including **fundamental changes of adolescence** (biological changes, cognitive changes, and social changes), the **contexts of adolescence** (families, peer groups, schools, and the workplace), and the **psychosocial developments of adolescence** (identity, autonomy, intimacy, sexuality, achievement, and psychosocial problems). In the rest of this chapter, Hill's (1980) framework will serve as the structure for reporting the developmental characteristics of young adolescents.

## EARLY ADOLESCENT DEVELOPMENT: SPECIFIC COMPONENTS

### Component 1—Fundamental (Primary) Changes of Adolescence

Hill (1980) and Steinberg (1989) both suggest that there are three fundamental changes that take place in young adolescents: biological/physical, cognitive/psychological, and social. These changes are characterized by (1) the dramatic physical changes brought on by onset of puberty, (2) the emergence of more sophisticated thinking ability, and (3) the transitions into new and different roles with peers, parents, and other adults. These fundamental or primary changes are universal in all adolescents regardless of the society in which they live.

The following listing of biological/physical, cognitive/psychological, and social developmental characteristics drawn from the literature of research and practice provide an overview of early adolescent development.

## Biological/Physical Changes

1. The onset of puberty results in rapid acceleration of growth with dramatic increases in height and weight, further development in sex glands (testes and ovaries), development of secondary sex characteristics (breasts, pubic hair, continued development of sex glands), changes in the composition of the body—quantity and distribution of fat and muscle, changes in the circulatory and respiratory systems—increased strength and tolerance for exercise (Steinberg, 1989).

2. The most dramatic and visible changes in young adolescents are the biological changes that occur at puberty. Today young adolescents are experiencing biological changes five years earlier than a century ago (Superintendent's Task Force, 1987).

3. The process of physical growth varies with some parts of the body growing faster than other parts. Until all parts catch up, young adolescents may appear to be an assortment of mismatched parts.

   Bone growth is faster than muscle growth, a factor which may result in awkwardness, lack of coordination, and ungainly movements.

   Arms and legs grow faster than the trunk.

   Hands and feet mature before arms and legs.

   Uneven growth causes wide variation in energy with frequent fluctuations from high vigor to listlessness (Georgiady and Romano, 1977; Milgram, 1992; Superintendent's Task Force, 1987).

4. The biological change that takes place during adolescence is universal in all societies. There is considerable variation in time of onset and duration of the process.

   **Girls** begin the process of maturation some 18 to 24 months ahead of boys. The variation of onset of puberty for girls is from age 8 to age 13; the length of puberty in girls may vary from 1 1/2 to 6 years. (Hill, 1980; Steinberg, 1989).

   For **boys** the onset of puberty may begin as early as age 9 1/2 or as late as age 13 1/2. The length of puberty for boys varies from 2 to 5 years.

   It is entirely possible that in most middle level

schools there will be some girls and some boys who will have completed the physical maturation process. At the same time there will be other girls and other boys who have not yet started the process of puberty (Hill, 1980; Steinberg, 1989).

5.  The universality of puberty does not bring universal consequences. Perceptions of self are particularly influenced in young adolescents who are either early or late maturers (Adams and Gullotta, 1983; Hill, 1980; Steinberg, 1989).

> **Girls** are worried about physical changes that are brought about by sexual maturation. They are more concerned about physical appearance than boys. Physical contours, breast size, and any deviations in the perception of what is normal is particularly worrisome for girls (Milgram, 1992; Superintendent's Task Force, 1987).
>
> **Boys**, while less concerned about physical appearance than girls, are still concerned, particularly about height. They worry about receding chins, cowlicks, dimples, changes in their voices, and penis size (Milgram, 1992; Superintendent's Task Force, 1987).

6.  The physical maturation process, particularly in early maturers, may force some young adolescents to face responsibility for sexual behavior well before they achieve emotional and social maturity (Adams and Gullotta, 1983; Superintendent's Task Force, 1987).
7.  Young adolescents are physically at risk with the major causes of death homicides, suicides, and accidents (Superintendent's Task Force, 1987).
8.  Young adolescents are given little preparation for dealing with the impending physical changes they face (Adams and Gullotta, 1983; Clark, 1991).

## Cognitive/Psychological Changes

1.  Early adolescence is a time when many children make the transition from concrete to formal operations. It is generally believed that formal operational thinking begins at ages 11 or 12; however, there is considerable research that reports that a percentage of adolescents never reach this stage of thinking

(Milgram, 1992). Thinking in the formal operations stage enables young adolescents to generalize and discover relationships, deal with abstract ideas, make judgments, to see another's point of view, empathize, and put one's self in another person's shoes (Hill, 1980; Steinberg, 1989).

2. Although young adolescents display a wide range of intellectual development, they prefer active over passive learning, and they display a strong willingness to learn things they consider useful. Most young adolescents consider academic goals to be secondary in priority to the personal and social concerns that dominate their thoughts and activities (Clark, 1991; Superintendent's Task Force, 1987).

3. Young adolescents who have made the transition into formal operations differ in thinking from that of children in that:
   - they are better about thinking about what is possible instead of what is real
   - they are better at thinking through hypotheses
   - they are better at thinking about abstract concepts (Georgiady and Romano, 1977; Hill, 1980).

4. The young adolescent's transition to formal thinking is not limited to scientific thinking or performance on academic activities such as tests. It is a time of important changes in the way young adolescents think about other people, the way they communicate with others, and in the way they make decisions about right and wrong (values) (Milgram, 1992; Steinberg, 1989; Thornburg, 1980).

5. Young adolescents are able to go beyond the information given to consider possibilities, to reason on the basis of possibilities (not restricted to experience), and to think about one's own thoughts (reflective thinking). Thinking about possibilities enables young adolescents to envision and therefore anticipate possible responses of another person and have a series of counter-arguments. Many parents believe their children become very argumentative while in fact they become better arguers (Hill, 1980; Steinberg, 1989).

6.  Hypothetical thinking enables young adolescents to use the scientific method, to deal with hypothetical situations, and to reason through a series of "if then" propositions (Georgiady and Romano, 1977; Hill, 1980).

7.  The use of abstract thinking enables young adolescents to think about their own thoughts, resulting in introspection, self-consciousness, and intellectualization (Adams and Gullotta, 1983; Hill, 1980; Milgram, 1992; Steinberg, 1989).

8.  Formal operational thought is often related to social competence in that changes in relationships, in self-concept, and in values and plans can be partially traced to the new ways in which young adolescents think (Hill, 1980; Steinberg, 1989; Thornburg, 1980).

9.  Being able to introspect and reflect may lead many young adolescents to a form of extreme self-absorption with self called "adolescent egocentrism." This egocentrism is characterized in three ways: *imaginary audience*—when young adolescents imagine that their behavior is the focus of everyone else's attention and that everybody is noticing everything they do; *personal fable*—when each young adolescent believes that his or her own experiences are uniquely different, unlike those of anyone else; and *pseudostupidity*—when young adolescents with newly developed intellectual abilities combine these abilities with adolescent egocentrism, the result often is a tendency to look for and verbalize complicated solutions to problems when simple solutions would be sufficient. (Elkind, 1978).

10. Increased thinking capacity during early adolescence leads to social cognition. Young adolescents begin to reason about social phenomena by thinking about people, social relationships, and social institutions. Their level of interpersonal understanding expands to thinking about relationships with friends. Friendships become valued and they are reciprocal; friends negotiate, take turns, and depend on a sense of fair play (Hill, 1980; Milgram, 1992; Selman, 1980; Steinberg, 1989).

## Social Changes

1. Early adolescence is a time of change in social roles and status. Young adolescents cease to be children and begin the process of acquiring the rights, privileges, and responsibilities of adults (Steinberg, 1989; Thornburg, 1980).
2. The social changes in young adolescents are characterized by three areas of social redefinition:
   - The real or symbolic separation from parents
   - The increased emphasis on the differences between females and males
   - The passing on of cultural historical or practical information deemed important for adulthood (Georgiady and Romano, 1977; Steinberg, 1989)
3. Young adolescents begin to act and view themselves differently and they are treated differently by others (Hill, 1980; Steinberg, 1989).
4. Feelings toward parents change as young adolescents view their parents more realistically. Many look toward other adults to supplement guidance given by parents (Georgiady and Romano, 1977; Hill 1980; *Search Institute Source*, 1990).
5. Young adolescents often experience traumatic conflicts due to conflicting loyalties to peer groups and families. Some young adolescents may be rebellious toward parents but they are still strongly dependent on parental values. In most cases relationships between young adolescents and their parents are loving and supportive (Hill, 1980; Steinberg, 1989; Superintendent's Task Force, 1987; Thornburg, 1980).
6. Peer groups are important and friends are selected on the basis of similarity to one's self (Milgram, 1992).
   - Peer influence is strongest between ages 11 to 17.
   - Young adolescents are fiercely loyal to their peer group sometimes leading to cruel or insensitive behavior to those outside their group (Superintendent's Task Force, 1987).
   - Peers are standards and models for behavior.

- Peer group associations move from same sex friendships to both sex friendships. Both sex friendships do not supplant same sex friendships but supplement them (Georgiady and Romano, 1977; Steinberg, 1989).

7. Peer association is part of the normal development of the young adolescent, and participation in activities is a vehicle to social acceptance. Social isolates need careful watching, and conscious effort should be made to include them in social activities. They appear to benefit from well-functioning schools that regard socialization as part of their purpose (Milgram, 1992).

8. Young adolescents want to know that significant adults (parents and teachers) love and accept them. They need frequent but subtle affirmation of adult affection and support. Feelings of adult rejection drive young adolescents into the relatively secure, but sometimes inappropriate, social environment of the peer group (Georgiady and Romano, 1977; *Search Institute Source*, 1990; Superintendent's Task Force, 1987).

9. The continuity of social relationships is interrupted by the transition to new school settings. This interruption of relationships, in addition to the large and impersonal nature of the new school, often results in fear and feelings of anonymity (Clark, 1991; Simmons and Blyth, 1987; Superintendent's Task Force, 1987).

10. The process of social redefinition has important consequences for the early adolescent's psychosocial development in bringing about important changes in the areas of identity, autonomy, intimacy, sexuality, and achievement (Hill, 1980; Steinberg, 1989).

## Component 2—Psychosocial (Secondary) Changes in Early Adolescence

Hill (1980) believed that to understand the significance of the biological/physical, cognitive/psychological, and social changes in young adolescents one must be familiar with the secondary issues or changes that arise from these three fundamental changes. These issues which are identified as **psychosocial issues** describe the aspects of development that are both psychological and social in nature. Hill lists six issues and defines them as follows:

*Attachment.* Transforming childhood social bonds to parents to bonds acceptable between parents and their adult children.

*Autonomy.* Extending self-initiated activity and confidence in it to wider behavioral realms.

*Sexuality.* Transforming social roles and gender identity to incorporate sexual activity with others.

*Intimacy.* Transforming acquaintanceships into friendships; deepening and broadening capacities for self-disclosure, affective perspective-taking, altruism.

*Achievement.* Focusing industry and ambition into channels that are future-oriented and realistic.

*Identity.* Transforming images of self to accommodate primary and secondary change; coordinating images to attain a self-theory that incorporates uniqueness and continuity through time (p. 5).

These psychosocial issues identified by Hill (1980) and reinforced by Steinberg (1989) have major implications for middle level educators. Understanding the interactions of these issues with biological, cognitive, and social changes is crucial in the restructuring of middle level schools to be more developmentally responsive.

**Attachment/Autonomy.** Attachment, according to Hill (1980), is the process by which children change their perceptions and the nature of their relationships with parents. Basically it is a process of disengagement from parents, a process viewed by many researchers as a precondition to the development of autonomy.

Steinberg (1989) believes that autonomy can be organized into three basic types: (1) emotional—changes in close relationships, (2) behavioral—capacity to make independent decisions and capitalize on them, and (3) values—having a set of principles about right and wrong and about what is important and not important. The first two types of autonomy (emotional and behavioral) surface much earlier and become major issues in autonomy development in young adolescents.

The search for autonomy is not normally one of conflicts, and it has become evident that, in spite of the influence of peer groups, young adolescents still value and require guidance from significant adults (parents and teachers). Steinberg (1989) states:

In contrast to popular stereotypes, the development of autonomy during adolescence does not typically involve rebellion,
nor is it usually accompanied by strained or tense family relationships. Especially in households characterized by authori-
tative patterns of decision making, warmth, and flexibility, family relationships move toward increasing maturity gradually
and smoothly (p. 299).

The Search Institute reinforces Steinberg's statement. In their
study of early adolescent youth (Benson, Williams, and Johnson,
1987), they found that a majority of youth in grades 5 through 9
reported that they would turn to parents and other adults as
their *preferred* sources of help in problems dealing with school,
feelings, friends using drugs and alcohol, sexuality, feelings of
guilt, and life decisions. In addition, researchers found that the
nature of the problem or question determined who might be consulted. Parents were most likely to be consulted on questions
or issues that dealt with long-term consequences; when the
question was more short term, they tended to seek advice from
peers or other adults (*Search Institute Source*, 1987). It is apparent that young adolescents are willing to seek out parents and
other adults for advice in dealing with questions and issues in
their lives. It is also apparent as reported by the Search Institute
(*Search Institute Source*, 1987) that while some young adolescents have a rich variety of adults accessible to them, there are a
large number of them without such a support network. Of these
young people many

> . . . attend large, impersonal schools and have no connection
> with any youth serving organization. Though they may not
> themselves recognize it, this lack of adult support is a genuine
> deprivation and one that society should seek to remedy (*Search
> Institute Source*, 1987; 2).

Middle level educators should carefully consider the following
issues:

1. Puberty is strongly implicated in the early adolescents'
   disengagement process from parents. As children
   mature and take on the more visible physical changes
   of puberty (male and female body contours), the types
   of affection between parents and their children and
   the way in which it is demonstrated often changes.
2. Early maturers are more likely to be perceived as
   having more initiative; and as a consequence, they

are likely to be given more responsibility and treated differently by peers, parents, and other adults.

3. Formal operations skills permit young adolescents to "read" other people (particularly parents and teachers) in more complex ways. As a result, they are more persuasive in arguments, and they are more effective in managing the impressions they create in others.

**Sexuality.** Although sex drive is not necessarily related to the onset of puberty, the maturing young adolescent will experience a change in the nature of relationships with family and peers. Physical changes cause many adults to react differently to young adolescents than they did when they were children. Changes in the show of affection, touching, and expectancies often accompany the sexual maturing of young adolescents.

The following issues should be considered:

1. The onset of puberty does not necessarily lead to increased sex drive.
2. Sex is part of the average teenager's social life, particularly during middle and late adolescence.
3. Early sexual experiences have very different meanings for young males and young females.

**Intimacy.** Intimacy is the capacity to form close relationships with others, and its development is a fundamental feature of adolescence (Steinberg, 1989). While intimacy is more highly valued by girls than by boys, young adolescents of both sexes need close relationships with peers. These relationships, however, supplement but do not replace close family relationships. Same sex relationships remain important throughout the transition through adolescence and are supplemented but not supplanted by opposite sex relationships.

The issues that follow should be carefully considered:

1. Formal operational interpersonal skills and their integration with sexuality are required for more mature forms of intimacy.
2. Principles and concepts such as honesty, fidelity, openness require sophisticated thinking skills and require the simultaneous consideration of multiple perspectives on a given issue.
3. Intimacy first emerges in friendships with the same sex peers during early adolescence. Not until late

adolescence do opposite sex relationships become intimate (not to be confused with sex).

4. Girls have a greater capacity for intimacy than do boys. They develop closer relationships earlier, they are more interpersonally sensitive, and they place greater emphasis on intimacy in their early sexual relationships.

5. Dating during early and middle adolescence does not appear to contribute much to the development of intimacy. In fact, many psychologists believe that early dating may encourage shallow and superficial relationships.

**Achievement.** Adolescence is a period when major decisions are made about one's education and one's occupational future. Having early successful experiences in school leads to continuing success, and doing well in school usually leads to better jobs and higher occupational attainment (Steinberg, 1989).

Socioeconomic status has been found to be a powerful force in educational achievement. Young adolescents living in low socioeconomic families have fewer opportunities to succeed than their peers from more affluent families. The Search Institute (1990) in a study of "at risk" factors was able to "trace a pattern of factors that promote positive development of youth" (*Search Institute Source*, 1990; 1). They found that with the exception of one factor most of the factors could be altered in a young person's surroundings if the adults in that young person's family and community considered it important enough to do so. The one factor they found most difficult to alter was economic security or socioeconomic status. They state, "The single factor most difficult to alter is the provision of economic security. Poverty among families with children inhibits the kinds of nutrition, housing, and life experience crucial for healthy adolescent development" (*Search Institute Source*, 1990; 2).

Early adolescent success and/or achievement is affected, then, by many factors that can be altered by families, schools, and community. Middle level educators should carefully consider the following issues:

1. Differences appear in achievement scores of girls and boys during early adolescence. Psychologists are uncertain why these differences occur.

2. The ability to think about what is possible gives young adolescents a personal future.

3. The consequences of present achievement for future accomplishments are better understood and appreciated by young adolescents.
4. Differences in achievement come about not only as a result of differences in ability but also as a result of differences in opportunities.
5. Early successful experiences promote later successful experiences.

**Identity.** Identity, suggests Steinberg (1989), involves the way people think about themselves and it involves three viewpoints: (1) the conception of self, (2) changes in the way one feels about himself or herself, and (3) the degree to which one feels secure about who he or she is and where he or she is headed. Erikson (1968) defined the identity crisis as a struggle to establish a coherent sense of self-definition. This coherent sense of self-definition, believed Erikson, was a continuing process throughout adolescence in which young people experimented with different roles and personalities.

Part of the identity crisis of early adolescence is the development of positive self-concept, a process that becomes increasingly complex as the child matures into adulthood. Young adolescents with good self-esteem see themselves as persons of worth; those who lack self-esteem consider themselves to be inadequate or deficient. Low self-esteem has also been found to be related to many undesirable social consequences while moderate to high self-esteem appears to be necessary for effective functioning (Adams and Gullotta, 1983; Clark, 1991).

Perhaps one of the most important aspects of the identity crisis is the struggle for sexual definition (Thornburg, 1980). Young adolescents begin to confront what it is to be a female or a male and conform to what they understand to be the socially accepted stereotypes of feminism and masculinity. It is during this time that differences in females and males widen.

The Search Institute (*Search Institute Source*, 1988a, 1988b) reports many of the differences that affect the identities of females and males. Females regard themselves as less competent than males even though their grade point averages contradict their self perceptions of "smartness." They do better than boys in middle level schools, spend more time on homework, and have higher educational aspirations (1988a). Early adolescent girls are more socially competent and find it easier to make friends and share their feelings than do boys. Girls are also more concerned about physical attraction and popularity than are boys. Many girls also "fear success," believing that being too smart may be detrimental to being popular and accepted by boys.

Early adolescent males in working through their identity crisis—seeking what it is to be a male—exhibit a variety of fears and negative behaviors. The *Search Institute Source* (1988b) makes several observations regarding the adolescent male and the search for identity. The things that males fear most center on physical force or some kind of self-destructive or destructive behavior. Items such as getting beat up at school, fear of nuclear bombing of the U.S., and fear that their friends may get them into trouble top the list of male concerns. Females' greatest fears centered on the loss or disturbance of friend relationships.

Fewer boys than girls feel that it is wrong to disturb classrooms, steal something, lie to parents, use alcohol, or practice racial discrimination. The seemingly high approval by boys of these highly unsocial behaviors suggests "a disturbing disregard for honesty coupled with a belief that one's own welfare and interests should always come first" (*Search Institute Source*, 1988b; 1).

Boys appear less likely to help others than girls. Their level of generosity lags well behind that of girls, and it is exemplified by their unwillingness to initiate or carry out any activity to assist others. Boys also outnumbered girls in virtually every kind of negative behavior measured on the Search Institute study. Boys markedly exceeded girls in the frequency of participation in vandalism, beating someone up, gang fighting, and theft. Only in the area of "cheating" did girls come close to matching the frequency of boys. When substance abuse frequency was determined, with the exception of girls using tobacco to a greater degree, boys had a higher frequency of drinking, getting drunk, and using marijuana.

Both early adolescent females and males are indeed in "identity crises." The data from the Search Institute is disturbing and clearly points out the need for schools, parents, and community groups to develop appropriate supportive measures to assist young adolescents in making this important but difficult transition. The following issues need to be considered carefully:

1.  Puberty is a dominant factor in the early adolescent identity crisis. Self-concept changes to incorporate

new physical characteristics and perceived male and female roles.

2. Concepts of self and putting these concepts together into a stable picture of self requires formal operations thinking. Adolescent descriptions of self use qualifying terms and distinctions between real and apparent qualities.

3. Self-concept becomes increasingly complex as young adolescents make the transition to adulthood.

4. Individuals with good self-esteem see themselves as persons of worth; they respect themselves but do not necessarily feel superior to others. Individuals who lack self-esteem consider themselves unworthy, inadequate, or deficient.

5. Low self-esteem is related to many undesirable social consequences. Moderate to high self-esteem appears necessary for effective functioning.

6. Formal operations thinking contributes to identity crises in young adolescents because there is now a future into which they can extend themselves. The self is now much more differentiated, providing adolescents with a much wider range of options as they look to their futures.

## Component 3—The Contexts (Settings) of Early Adolescence

The third major component of Hill's framework addresses the settings or contexts in which young adolescents experience the developmental process, contexts that are different for each young adolescent. Hill (1980) and Steinberg (1989) both believe that the nature and structure of these contexts profoundly influence the way in which the primary changes of adolescence are experienced. Hill (1980) identifies these important settings for young adolescents as family, peer groups, and school. Steinberg (1989) adds the workplace to the list of settings or contexts, but the workplace is of lesser significance to young adolescents because most of them are still too young to work. To this list of settings, the community, with its vast array of social organizations, youth groups, and churches, must be added.

**Families** play an important role in the lives of young adolescents. Despite the many changes that have taken place in families over the past half century, the family still exerts significant influence on the psychosocial development of adolescents. Contrary to what is accepted by many adults, the early adolescent years are not generally a time of rebellion and conflict with parents. Hill (1980) and Steinberg (1989) both contend that for the most part a generation gap does not exist and that for most families early adolescence is not a period of great upheaval.

Positive family relationships before and during early adolescence are factors that lead to social competence and confidence in young adolescents (Hill, 1980). A key influential factor in the development of social competence are parents who are warm but firm, exercise moderate control, and encourage reasoned decision making. Steinberg (1989) states:

> . . . an adolescent who has warm, concerned, and involved parents—whether they are married, divorced, or separated, and whether they are full-time workers or not—has one of the most important elements of a strong foundation that he or she will need to develop into a happy, capable, and caring adult (1989; 148).

A Search Institute study of 46,000 adolescents in grades 6-12 also supported the importance of the family (*Search Institute Source*, 1990). Sixteen external assets were found that had a positive effect in "protecting" adolescents from risk factors such as substance abuse, poor mental health, accidents, and suicidal activity. Of these sixteen assets, eight were found to exist within the structure of the family. These assets included *family support* (high levels of love and support), *parent(s) as social resource, parent communication, parent involvement in schooling, parental standards, parental discipline, parental monitoring,* and *time at home.*

**Peer Groups** also influence the development of psychosocial skills. While not replacing the influence of the parents, they are a powerful force in the socialization process. Peer reaction to biological changes has been found to be important in molding early adolescent self-concept, especially in young adolescents who are early or late maturers (Adams and Gullotta, 1983; Clark, 1991; Hill, 1980). Peer groups are also the primary source of information about sex.

The basic unit of the peer group is the clique, and cliques tend to be groupings of young adolescents with similar interests and from similar backgrounds. Status in the peer group comes not from the commonly accepted traits of popularity (friendly, outgoing, socially adept), but from doing the things that promotes the clique's goals (Steinberg, 1989).

An excellent example of the conflicts created by peer pressure can be drawn from the research of Fordham and Ogbu (1986) and Ogbu (1985, 1992). In examining achievement in minority youth they found that peer pressure often discourages minority students from making good grades. Case studies suggest that in some African-American peer groups students who adopt attitudes and behaviors that lead to school success or who achieve good grades may be subjected to negative peer pressures that include criticism and isolation from the group. These good students, reports Ogbu (1985), are put down by their fellow students as "acting White." This, of course, can be a powerful factor in discouraging further efforts at schoolwork.

While there is some debate about the positive influence of peer groups, particularly cliques, there is general consensus that good peer relationships are an important part of the normal social development of young adolescents (Milgram, 1992).

**Schools** are another important context or setting that influence psychosocial skills. Hill (1980) suggests that schools influence the socialization process in two ways. First, schools impact on early adolescent social development because of organizational factors. Grade level organization, for instance, may generate relationships with younger or older students depending upon the grade levels included in the school structure. Grouping practices such as tracking may create a variety of expectancies among students from the same neighborhood or attendance area. Tracking may also disrupt cliques and force the formation of new student groups.

Second, Hill (1980) contends that what happens in the school may influence young adolescents. Processes and procedures such as time on task, teaching styles, and disciplinary practices influence the socialization process. There is evidence that middle level schools can and do provide positive experiences for many young adolescents. The effective implementation of programs such as interdisciplinary teaming and teacher advisories have been shown to provide supportive academic and social environments where young adolescents can achieve and be successful (George and Oldaker, 1985; Lipsitz, 1984; Mac Iver, 1990).

## EARLY ADOLESCENT DEVELOPMENT: IMPLICATIONS

In examining the developmental characteristics of young adolescents, it is clear that there are many factors that interact to influence the developing middle level student. Among these factors are the settings or contexts in which young adolescents live and learn, contexts in many cases that are not functioning in ways to promote positive climates for growth. Many middle level schools, a major context for young adolescents in their developmental process, in spite of their rhetoric, may not be functioning in ways that assist in the transition process from children to adults.

Middle level schools and middle level educators must be strong positive forces in the lives of their students, taking the lead in helping young adolescents develop healthy and successful lifestyles. How is this done? The Search Institute suggests two things: models and opportunities. "Having adults around them who are attentive, concerned about others, interested in education, and socially skilled provide the models" (*Search Institute Source*, 1991; 3). The importance of supportive teacher or other adult models is reinforced by Goodenow (1993) who reported that relationships with supportive teachers were found to have a positive effect on the motivation of middle level students. This was particularly true for girls where Goodenow found that their expectancies and values were maintained partially by their perceptions of good relationships with teachers.

In addition to supportive relationships with teachers, providing students with school and community service projects offers them opportunities for developing a sense of "being needed" and to enhance social and planning skills. (This concept of school and community service is further developed in Chapter 6). Finally, schools must provide the organizational structures and curricular programs that are developmentally responsive.

## SUMMARY

Early adolescence is a time of tremendous change. While understanding the reasons for and the ways that young adolescents change is an important first step for middle level leaders, acting upon that knowledge is even more important. Middle level programs must reflect what is known about young adolescents, their physical growth patterns, their emerging intellect, their new social sophistication, and their emotional vulnerability. Middle level leaders must ask themselves the following questions:

1. To what extent does our school provide the support necessary for every child to be successful (positive climate; opportunity to participate in activities)?

2. In what ways does our school provide young adolescents with opportunities to build a strong educational commitment (school performance; achievement motivation; educational aspiration)?

3. In what ways does our school help young adolescents build positive values (sexual restraint; helping others; concern about those in need; caring about the feelings of others)?

4. In what ways does our school help young adolescents develop skills in social competence (self-esteem; assertiveness; decision making; making friends; planning skills)?

5. In what ways does our school take the needs and characteristics of young adolescents under consideration when planning schedules and other school organizational structures?

6. In what ways does our school take the needs and characteristics of young adolescents under consideration when planning the core curriculum, the exploratory curriculum, and the elective curriculum?

7. In what ways does our school take the needs and characteristics of young adolescents under consideration when planning the cocurricular program?

8. In what ways does our school take the needs and characteristics of young adolescents under consideration when planning the counseling and guidance program?

Found in the answers to these questions are the building blocks on which the responsive middle level school is built. The next three chapters, which will focus on these questions, will examine middle level curriculum and programs that are developed with an understanding of the developmental characteristics of young adolescents.

# REFERENCES

Adams, G., & Gullotta, T. (1983). *Adolescent life experiences.* Monterey, CA: Brooks/Cole.

Benson, P. B., Williams, D. L., & Johnson, A. (1987). *The quicksilver years: The hopes and fears of early adolescence.* San Francisco, CA: Harper and Row.

Clark, D. C. (1991). Developmental traits. In J. W. Keefe, & J. M. Jenkins (Eds.), *Instructional leadership handbook* (pp. 153-154). Reston, VA: National Association of Secondary School Principals.

Elkind, D. (1978). Understanding the young adolescent. *Adolescence, 13*(49), 127-134.

Erikson, E. H. (1968). *Identity: Youth and crisis.* New York: Norton.

Fordham, S., & Ogbu, J. U. (1986). Black students' school success: Coping with the burden of "acting White." *Urban Review, 18,* 176-206.

George, P. S., & Oldaker, L. L. (1985). *Evidence for the middle school.* Columbus, OH: National Middle School Association.

Georgiady, N. P., & Romano, L. G. (1977). *Middle School Journal, 8*(2), 12-15; 22-23.

Goodenow, C. (1993). Classroom belonging among early adolescent students: Relationships to motivation and achievement. *The Journal of Early Adolescence, 13*(1), 21-43.

Hill, J. P. (1980). *Understanding early adolescence: A framework.* Carrboro, NC: Center for Early Adolescence.

James, M. A. (1980). Early adolescent ego development. *The High School Journal, 63*(6), 244-249.

Lipsitz, J. (1984). *Successful schools for young adolescents.* New Brunswick, NJ: Transaction Books.

Lounsbury, J. H., & Clark, D. C. (1990). *Inside grade eight: From apathy to excitement.* Reston, VA: National Association of Secondary School Principals.

Lounsbury, J. H., & Johnston, J. H. (1985). *How fares the ninth grade?* Reston, VA: National Association of Secondary School Principals.

Lounsbury, J. H., & Johnston, J. H. (1988). *Life in the three 6th grades.* Reston, VA: National Association of Secondary School Principals.

Mac Iver, D. (1990). Meeting the needs of young adolescents: Advisory groups, interdisciplinary teaching teams, and school transition programs. *Phi Delta Kappan, 71*(6), 458-464.

Milgram, J. (1992). A portrait of diversity: The middle level student. In J. L. Irvin (Ed.), *Transforming middle level education: Perspectives and possibilities* (pp. 16-27). Boston, MA: Allyn and Bacon.

Ogbu, J. U. (1985). Research currents: Cultural-ecological influences on minority school learning. *Language Arts, 62*(8), 60-69.

Ogbu, J. U. (1992). Understanding cultural diversity and learning. *Educational Researcher, 21*(8), 5-14.

Search Institute. (1987). Adolescent's search for trusted friends. *Source*, *3*(2), 1-4.

Search Institute. (1988a). The risky business of growing up female. *Source*, *4*(1), 1-4.

Search Institute. (1988b). The dangerous business of growing up male. *Source*, *4*(4), 1-4.

Search Institute. (1990). The troubled journey: New light on growing up healthy. *Source*, *6*(3), 1-4.

Search Institute. (1991). Backbone: Essential for survival on the troubled journey. *Source*, *7*(1), 1-4.

Selman, R. L. (1980). *The growth of interpersonal understanding: Developmental and clinical analyses*. New York: Academic Press.

Simmons, R., & Blyth, D. (1987). *Moving into adolescence*. New York: Aldine De Gruyter.

Steinberg, L. (1989). *Adolescence*. New York: Alfred A. Knopf.

Superintendent's Middle Grade Task Force. (1987). *Caught in the middle: Educational reform for young adolescents in California public schools*. Sacramento, CA: California Department of Education.

Thornburg, H. D. (1980). Early adolescents: Their developmental characteristics. *The High School Journal*, *63*(6), 215-221.

# 4

# Curriculum and Assessment in Responsive Middle Level Schools

> "If the middle school is to be based upon the developmental character-istics of early adolescents, then the curriculum ought to be redesigned along developmentally appropriate lines rather than just a slightly revised version of the traditional high school curriculum."
>
> James Beane

Middle level education has no really unique curricular struc-ture. At best the current structure is a patchwork of courses, activities, and experiences that may or may not have any relation to each other (Beane, 1990). Based largely on high school content organizational patterns, middle level curriculum has been described as being developmentally unresponsive, passive and undemanding, and unconnected to the daily lives of young ado-lescents (Lounsbury and Clark, 1990).

Many middle level educators believe that middle level schools must refocus their attention on the developmental needs of young adolescents as the central focus of content organization and instructional planning. To do so, middle level leaders must have a clear understanding of developmental appropriateness and a "vision" of what developmentally responsive curriculum and instruction would look like in their schools.

David Elkind (1989), in writing for early childhood educators, describes the differences between two major philosophies of education, developmentally appropriate curriculum and psychometric curriculum. His comparisons and descriptions are equally appropriate for middle level educators. Elkind contends that any philosophy of education must include some "conception of the learner, of the learning process, of the information to be acquired, and of the goals or aims of education" (1989; 113). Developmentally appropriate practice and psychometric practice deal very differently with these four areas, and understanding these differences provides important insights for curriculum development (see Figure 4-1). In developmentally appropriate practice the learner is viewed as a person with developing mental abilities, abilities that all students are capable of developing but at different rates and at different ages. This is compared to psychometric practice where the learner is viewed as having measurable abilities, abilities that must exist in some amount and therefore are quantifiable.

The learning process in developmentally appropriate practice is considered to be a creative and constructive process; in psychometric practice it consists of the acquisition of a set of skills that are dependent on the content to be learned. Developmentally appropriate practice views knowledge as a construction of the mind's interaction with the world while psychometric practice believes knowledge is something a student acquires that can be measured independent of the process of acquisition. The aim of developmental education is to produce thinkers who are creative and analytical. This is contrasted with the aim of psychometric education which is to maximize the acquisition of quantifiable knowledge and skill.

The focus of this chapter will be on middle level curriculum and student assessment. First, curriculum organization will be explored with emphasis placed on definitions, trends and issues, and current middle level content structures. Emphasis will also be placed on classroom instruction, with discussions of purposes, trends, promising programs, and current practice. Student assessment, which is a powerful, driving force in determining curriculum content and instructional procedures, will be the focus of the last section of this chapter.

## CURRICULUM IN THE MIDDLE LEVEL SCHOOL

### Curriculum—Some Definitions

The curriculum can be defined simply as the sum total of the experiences of the school. Broadly, this includes the content,

**Figure 4-1**
A Comparison of Developmentally Appropriate Practice and Psychometric Practice*

| Conceptions | Developmentally Appropriate Practice | Psychometric Practice |
|---|---|---|
| Conception of the Learner | Learner is viewed as having developing mental abilities<br>All students are assumed to develop these abilities although not at the same age<br>Matching curricula to the developing abilities of students is viewed as the most important task of education | Learner is viewed as having measurable abilities and any ability that exists in some amount is therefore quantifiable<br>Matching students with others of similar abilities is the most important task of education |
| Conception of the Learning Process | Learning is viewed as a creative and constructive process<br>Material learned interacts with the learning process<br>Little or no automatic transfer of learning from one subject to another subject | Learning is viewed as a set of governed principles and consists of the acquisition of a set of skills that are independent of the content<br>Learning reflects the concept that thought processes and content can be treated separately<br>Transfer between subject areas occurs automatically |
| Conception of Knowledge | Knowledge is always a construction of the mind's interaction with the world. The mind provides the categories of learning while the real world provides the content<br>A student creates and recreates reality out of his or her experiences with the environment<br>There can be differences in knowledge without reference to right or wrong. Differences rather than correctness is important not only with respect to knowledge, but also with respect to creative thinking | Knowledge is something a student acquires and can be measured independently of the process of acquisition<br>Knowledge is measured against an external standard that is independent of the learning. Such comparisons classify students as either right or wrong |
| Conception of the Aims of Education | The aim of education is to:<br>Facilitate developing abilities, learning as a creative activity, and knowledge construction<br>Produce thinkers who are creative and critical<br>Create environments where students are actively engaged in constructing and reconstructing their physical, social and moral world<br>Create students who want to know | The aim of education is to:<br>Maximize the acquisition of quantifiable knowledge and skills<br>Produce students who score high on achievement tests<br>Produce students who know what we want them to know |

* Adapted from Elkind, D. (1989). Developmentally Appropriate Practice: Philosophical and Practical Implications, *Phi Delta Kappan*, 71(2), 113-117.

the instruction, the activities, the school climate, and the social interaction that an early adolescent experiences during his or her sojourn at the middle level school. These experiences include the planned experiences of the school, commonly called the planned or intended curriculum, and the unplanned experiences commonly referred to as the hidden curriculum.

Curriculum may be classified in a variety of ways. These may include the recommended curriculum, the written curriculum, the supported curriculum, the taught curriculum, the tested curriculum, and the learned curriculum as suggested by Glatthorn (1987), or curriculum can include other classifications such as the formal, the informal; the perceived, the actual; and the operational and the experiential.

Most middle level educators are well aware of the written curriculum as it is represented by state guidelines and school district curriculum documents. For most middle level schools the written curriculum is illustrative of the "psychometric" philosophy of education with emphasis on the acquisition of a body of knowledge most commonly represented by state and district requirements built around the traditional subject areas. Testing is done for the purpose of determining scores that are perceived, perhaps erroneously, to represent the degree to which students have acquired the recommended knowledge and skills (tested curriculum).

The supported curriculum is a representation of the resources available to teachers (materials, textbooks, technology, class size, etc.). The taught curriculum, what the teacher teaches, is a product of teacher motivation, self-perceptions, social conditions, and experience. The tested curriculum is the measurement of student learning as determined by teacher-made tests, district curriculum tests, and standardized achievement tests. For most educators these four different types of curricula form the heart of the district and school curriculum and are classified as the intended curriculum.

The learned curriculum represents the sum total of what students have learned from the planned and unplanned experiences in school, the social as well as the academic, and includes changes in values, perceptions, and behavior. Much of value is learned by young adolescents from their interactions with peers and adults, and they are greatly influenced by positive school environments where teachers and other adults care for and nurture them (George and Oldaker, 1985). In spite of the importance of this "hidden curriculum" as an influence on student learning, it is infrequently assessed. As a result, what students learn is what is tested, usually consisting of discrete answers to specific questions, giving them a knowledge base that is unorganized, unconnected from other subject areas and the reality of their own lives, and quickly forgotten.

The recommended curriculum is the curriculum recommended by scholars, professional associations, and commissions. Often a reflection of policy groups and federal and state governments, it is usually general in scope and often insensitive to the realities of schools and classrooms. In many cases these recommendations are not known by teachers, and, if known, they have very little impact on curriculum and instruction.

It is, however, the written curriculum with its basis in psychometric education, combined with the traditional high school approach to organizing and teaching content, that has mitigated against middle level schools clearly defining a "theme" that unifies and guides the content and instruction of the school. Middle level educators, in their attempts to accommodate competing curricular philosophies and interests, have, for the most part, created fragmented programs "without any coherent or unifying theme" (Beane, 1990). Without a consistent focus, Beane suggests that middle level schools really have no uniquely, identifiable curriculum.

Creating a uniquely identifiable, focused, developmentally responsive middle level curriculum that strives to serve the needs of young adolescents is a complex and challenging task. It is an ongoing process that must address the many, and sometimes conflicting, beliefs and demands of the profession, the parents, the community, and the nation.

## Constraints to Implementing Developmentally Appropriate Middle Level Curriculum

The road to curricular change at the middle level is filled with roadblocks. Originating from a variety of sources at the national, state, and local levels, these roadblocks or constraints must be recognized and carefully considered in the process of curriculum development (Figure 4-2).

At the national level commission reports, such as *A Nation at Risk* (National Commission on Excellence in Education, 1983) and *Action for Excellence* (Task Force on Education for Economic

**Figure 4-2**
Constraints to Implementing Developmentally Appropriate Curriculum

1. National Commission Reports and Policy
   - Reports in the 1980s focusing exclusively on "academics" and excluding other aspects of the curriculum

2. Rigid State Regulations and Policies
   - Subject area competencies which reinforce the subject disciplines and specialization
   - Time requirements including number of minutes spent on various subjects and length of day
   - Standardized testing requirements which drive curriculum and instruction

3. Teacher Motivation
   - Concerns about affiliation, autonomy, feelings of usefulness, and achievement
   - Concerns about classroom management and control which lead to practices that make classroom life more predictable and thus more controllable

4. Assumptions about Parental and Community Expectations
   - Unsubstantiated and vague notions of expectations which often serve as an excuse to maintain the status quo

---

Growth, 1983), with their emphasis almost totally on "academics," have posed a major threat to the concept of developmental responsiveness. School boards throughout the nation have embraced the recommendations of these reports and have taken action that has often led to more rigid academic requirements in their high schools. These requirements frequently "filter down" to middle level schools with the result being reduction of and, in some cases, the elimination of exploratory, elective, and student activity programs. What many national policymakers fail to understand is that school improvement recommendations which focus solely on academics and obtaining higher achievement scores deny the importance of educational programs that respond to the developmental needs of adolescent learners (Clark and Clark, 1986).

While many states, through the work of task forces, policy statements, and networks, are significantly involved in the improvement of middle level education, many constraints still exist at the state level which create roadblocks to more developmentally responsive curricular structures. Included are rigid adherence to state subject area competencies, policies requiring a specific number of minutes of daily instructional time, minimal requirements for school day length, and standardized testing requirements, which for the most part are not aligned with state or district curricular goals or what is taught in the classroom (Freeman, Kuhs, Porter, Knappen, Floden, Schmidt, and Schwille, 1980; Natriello and Dornbusch, 1984).

The failure of most states to recognize middle level education as a separate administrative area also poses additional constraints on curriculum development. It is difficult to build a case for a uniquely different curriculum when states consider middle level schools as part of the elementary or secondary administrative units. In addition, this lack of recognition presents problems in the areas of financial allocations and certification requirements.

For many middle level educators, district level requirements are perceived as the primary forces in determining curriculum in their schools. Researchers have found that school district curriculum objectives and test results are strong influences on what teachers teach (Floden, Porter, Schmidt, Freeman, and Schwille, 1980; Leithwood, Ross, and Montgomery, 1982). If these requirements are in conflict with the developmental characteristics of young adolescents, major roadblocks to the development of appropriate curricular structures occur.

More subtle are the constraints that occur at the school site. Many middle level leaders, lacking a comprehensive knowledge of curriculum and young adolescent characteristics, find it difficult to conceptualize what a responsive curriculum should be. This factor, combined with a school culture that values control and orderliness, motivates many administrators to concentrate on "running a tight ship" and maintaining the status quo.

Teacher motivations also play an important role in curriculum development. Teachers are heavily influenced by their own needs for affiliation, autonomy, feelings of usefulness, and achievement (MacDonald and Leithwood, 1982). Teachers are also greatly concerned with classroom management, a concern that leads them to practices that make classroom life predictable and thus more controllable. Doyle (1986) reports that curriculum decisions are designed to achieve this goal, the result being standardization of curriculum by reducing or eliminating elements of novelty, simplifying the curriculum so it becomes easily managed, and making instruction routine in order to reduce the time needed for planning.

Also providing constraints to curriculum development at the middle level school are the teacher and administrator perceptions of parental expectations. These perceptions, which are often based on unsubstantiated, vague notions, frequently serve as a ready excuse for maintaining "academically" oriented programs. In many cases, these perceptions or misconceptions tend to reinforce the culture of the school which already supports traditional approaches to curriculum.

## Middle Level School Curricular Practices

Most middle level schools organize curriculum around three basic components, the core or basic curriculum, the exploratory curriculum, and the elective curriculum. In many middle level schools, exploratory and elective curriculum is used to describe all learning experiences not part of the basic curriculum. This three component structure is reinforced by Glatthorn (1987) who calls for the division of curriculum into basic/essential highly structured learnings that must be mastered by all students, basic/essential but less structured learnings for all students, and learnings that extend the curriculum but are not essential (Figure 4-3). Intertwined with these three components are also found curriculum structures designed to promote appropriate opportunities for social development.

**Core Curriculum.** The core curriculum of a middle level school is the content and skills that are considered to be basic for all students. This content, a core of common learnings, is for the most

**Figure 4-3**
Middle Level School Curriculum - Components and Elements

---

1. Core or Basic Curriculum
   - Scope and Sequence
   - Alternative Organizational Structures
   - Making Connections
   - Appropriate Instructional Strategies

2. Exploratory Curriculum (exploratory = essential; electives = enrichment)
   - Focus of Experiences
   - Appropriateness of Experiences
   - Organizational Structures

3. Social Curriculum
   - Planned Experiences (teacher advisories, social events, community service, etc.)
   - Unplanned Experiences (hidden curriculum - beliefs, values, interactions, climate, etc.)

---

part determined by the state and by the school district who also determine the procedures for assessing mastery. In most cases, the core of common learnings required by middle level schools consists of courses in reading/language arts, social studies, mathematics, and science. Students are usually enrolled in these classes the entire time they are in the middle level school. While the content and skills are largely determined by forces outside the schools, teachers and administrators have a variety of ways in which they can organize curriculum to be more developmentally responsive. These include reorganizing scope and sequence, implementing alternative organizational structures, making connections, and incorporating appropriate instructional strategies.

*Scope and Sequence.* The scope and sequence can be adjusted in many ways to be more developmentally responsive. Initially, teachers and administrators need to carefully examine the current requirements in each of the core subject areas. Content must be analyzed systematically to determine the breadth and depth of the requirements of the written curriculum. If any of the requirements appear to be inappropriate in terms of early adolescent developmental characteristics (intellectual, physical, social, or emotional maturation), teachers, administrators, and curriculum designers should reassess the requirements and modify or replace them with more suitable standards. Second, content area skills that are seen as being particularly relevant to young adolescents should be identified and emphasized. While the rest of the skills should receive attention, they should receive less emphasis. Setting instructional priorities is an important first step in addressing breadth and depth issues in the curriculum.

The sequence of content in each core course should be scrutinized to see if it can be organized in ways that would be more appropriate for adolescent learners. Many middle level schools have been successful in resequencing their course content to facilitate more individualized/personalized approaches to learning. This focus on individual needs is a feature of many mastery learning/continuous progress curricular structures. Although heavily subject-centered, these approaches, when designed with the characteristics of young adolescents in mind, can be responsive to student needs. With a basic belief that all students can learn, mastery learning and continuous progress programs focus on the diagnosis of student skills and student learning styles. This diagnostic information provides the basis for personalized curriculum sequencing and instruction, and offers students the opportunity to be more successful in completing the required curriculum of the school and district.

*Alternative Organizational Structures.* There are a variety of ways in which schools can use alternative organizational practices to make the curriculum more responsive within the constraints of the subject-centered curriculum. These include temporary grouping structures, flexible scheduling, alternative staffing, and community programs. Temporary grouping structures, which are replacing inappropriate tracking and ability grouping structures, offer numerous opportunities for students to receive special instruction or enrichment without danger of being labeled or stigmatized. Cooperative learning and team projects are excellent examples of flexible or temporary groupings. Programs for "at-risk" students, a form of temporary grouping, are also viewed as effective in meeting the special needs of students who, for whatever reasons, are having a difficult time experiencing success in school.

The use of alternative schedules also allows students to learn within more flexible time frames. The larger blocks of time that are usually available in team teaching arrangements allow teachers to adjust time and group size based upon the needs of students, the skill being learned, and the instructional strategy being used.

Many middle level schools are using a variety of alternative programs in their attempts to be more developmentally responsive. These include interdisciplinary teaming, teacher advisories, student activities, parent and community involvement, and youth service. These programs will be addressed in Chapters 5 and 6.

*Making Connections.* Connecting the various content areas around common themes is emerging as a viable way to help middle level students find more meaning in the curriculum of their schools. Numerous efforts are currently being made to facilitate these connections. Most notable among these efforts is the work being done to encourage reading and writing across the curriculum. This approach is successful in helping teachers see the relationships among the various subject areas and to begin to make connections that are meaningful for young adolescents.

The recent work of the National Council of Teachers of Mathematics is also encouraging. Their *Curriculum and Evaluation Standards for School Mathematics* (1989), which recognizes the need for all students to be literate in mathematics, calls for important changes in the mathematics curriculum and the way that it is taught. Special emphasis is placed on the teaching of mathematics as an integrated whole with a focus on learning that is active, constructive, and based on real problems (Frye, 1989).

Much of what occurs in middle level classrooms, particularly in the core areas, touches very little on the "real life" issues of young adolescents. In fact, most middle level students view school "as a thing apart—tolerated but not of immediate assistance to their lives" (Lounsbury and Clark, 1990). Connections can be made by actively involving young adolescents in the life of the school. By becoming major participants in school governance, in tutorial programs, and in youth service programs, both on and off campus, young adolescents can begin to see the important connections between the curriculum and their own needs.

In the various subject areas efforts need to be made to connect the skills and knowledge required to the needs and interests of students both in and out of school. While this requires some ingenuity, it brings increased relevance to the curriculum. Science educators are making significant efforts to connect with the lives of students. Especially important is the work of Paul DeHart Hurd (1989) at Stanford University who is leading the effort to develop a life science core for middle level students that is based on the developmental process of adolescence. At every phase of the Stanford Life Science Program the particular needs of young adolescents hold center stage. The two-year life science core program, while focusing on adolescent development as a basis of content, also seeks connections with other subject areas and features decision making, problem solving, logical thinking, making ethical judgments, and achieving consensus.

*Appropriate Instructional Strategies.* Classrooms are passive places (Gehrke, Knapp, and Sirotnik, 1992). Rather than being actively engaged in learning, middle level students are subjected to teacher talk, textbook reading, worksheets, and quizzes (Lounsbury and Clark, 1990). Such activities, which foster passive learning, limit student opportunity and contradicts what is known about how people learn. Berryman (1993) contends that passive learning has several unfortunate consequences including the (1) reduction of opportunities for exploration, discovery, and invention; (2) little opportunity for the learner to exercise control over learning; and (3) the creation of motivational and control problems.

While passive learning is still prevalent in a vast number of middle level schools, there are some schools that are making great strides in actively involving students in their own learning. Some of the more promising practices include cooperative learning and peer tutoring. Computer assisted instruction is also being used effectively to involve students in simulations and other activities which promote problem solving and critical thinking.

Cooperative learning, with its variety of approaches, is an excellent strategy for involving young adolescents in the learning process. Numerous studies (Aronson and Bridgeman, 1979; Braddock and McPartland, 1993; Slavin, 1983, 1985) attest to the value of cooperative learning in helping students to increase academic achievement and develop more positive attitudes to members of different racial groups. In addition, cooperative learning appears to be a viable alternative to school tracking procedures through the creation of roles of high status and responsibility for all students, which in turn facilitates positive peer climates for learning.

Peer tutoring, with its emphasis on helping relationships, has also been found to be very beneficial to young adolescents. In many cases both the tutors and those being tutored have improved in achievement, learned more effective social skills, and shown more positive attitudes (Conrad and Hedin, 1991).

Computer assisted learning continues to be an effective instructional strategy for young adolescents. Computer programs which focus on higher order thinking processes appear to be particularly effective in improving the achievement scores of minority youth (Pogrow, 1990). In addition, in finding that seventh and eighth grade girls had significantly more positive attitudes than boys toward the use of computers, Loyd, Loyd, and Gressard (1987) suggested that computers might be used to involve girls in subjects such as mathematics where they tended to have more negative attitudes.

Engaging students in learning, however, is more than just using a variety of instructional strategies. Elkind (1989) believes that students must see teachers as learners and teachers must see students as teachers. In this type of environment a community of learners is established. Elkind calls this authentic teaching, and he describes the authentic teacher as someone who asks "questions to gain information and understanding, not to test what students know or understand" (p. 117). This type of questioning places the teacher in a position of serving as an example of the enthusiastic learner.

The authentic classroom is in many ways like the world of work. Berryman (1993) suggests that structuring instruction to conform more to the ways students learn appears to improve the ability of that instruction to prepare students for the workplace. When the classroom takes on the characteristics of authentic work, Newmann (1989) found that students were much more engaged. The characteristics of classrooms emulating authentic work include extrinsic reward, intrinsic reward, sense of ownership, and realistic work conditions. In a classroom where authentic curriculum and instruction are being used, students see some payoff to what they are doing. Their work is valued and there is a purpose for what they are doing that goes beyond merely completing a task or receiving a grade (extrinsic reward). Work for many adults is enjoyable. Why should it not also be true for students? Curriculum and instruction that model the workplace allow students to be active learners, have an opportunity to become good at something, and experience a sense of accomplishment (intrinsic reward).

Students experiencing authentic curriculum and instruction are frequently given the opportunity to make choices and have some control over what they do and the way they do it. These choices give students a sense of efficacy which increases involvement (sense of ownership). Flexible use of time and natural working conditions foster engagement and productivity. Allowing students to follow a task through to completion increases the motivation to invest the time necessary to be successful (realistic work conditions). Authentic curriculum and instruction has shown gains in both academic and personal growth (Filby, 1992).

Teachers must believe that all students can learn and then provide them with the kind of learning opportunities "that make school important, challenging, joyful, motivating, and fair" (Epstein and Salinas, 1992). Active learning is a major step in achieving that goal.

**Exploratory Curriculum.** Young adolescents are going through major changes in their lives. Developmentally appropriate curricula should provide them the opportunity to explore the intellectual, emotional, social, and physical dimensions of those changes. This is commonly done in middle level schools through the exploratory curriculum.

An essential part of the middle level curriculum, the exploratory curriculum provides for essential, less structured learning experiences (exploratory courses) and student selected enrichment, participatory experiences (elective courses and activities). The exploratory curriculum, however, is more than just a sequence of courses. It is a process that provides opportunities for students to "explore their aptitudes, interests, and special talents and to develop an accurate and positive self-concept" across the entire range of the middle level school curriculum (Middle Level Council, 1985). The exploratory curriculum is a concept that permeates the entire school curriculum. Lounsbury (1990) confirms this when he suggests that the middle level school is an exploratory school "and everything done therein should be approached in an exploratory mode."

The major purpose of the exploratory curriculum in middle level schools is to allow young adolescents to achieve and demonstrate competence in a number of areas such as the arts, athletics, academics, and technology. In addition, the focus of the exploratory as well as the core curriculum is to provide opportunities for every student in the school to excel and be successful.

To accomplish these purposes, most middle level schools organize exploratory experiences around a sequence of required (essential) and elective (enrichment) courses that students take throughout their years in the middle level school. Included in the required sequence are courses in home economics, art and music, physical education, industrial arts, computers, and foreign language. In these essential, but less structured, courses young adolescents are given the opportunity to explore interests, talents, and skills. Frequently these courses allow them to make practical application of facts, skills and information being learned in other subject areas. Experiences in the exploratory areas tend to be active and provide numerous opportunities for hands-on activities and socialization.

Elective courses and activities programs are optional opportunities for enrichment which afford students choices, choices that frequently build on subject area and exploratory course experiences. Electives enable students to participate in high interest activities such as instrumental music, choral music, drama, and specialized art courses (ceramics, painting, sculpture); advanced courses in computers, technology, and foreign language; and special interest courses or topics in language arts, social studies, science, and mathematics.

Along with elective courses, activity programs allow students to pursue a variety of interests. Appropriate activities which support intellectual, emotional, social, and physical needs and can be developed from all areas of the curriculum will be discussed in Chapter 5.

Unlike the core or required curriculum, teachers and administrators play a major role in determining the nature of the exploratory experiences in the school. To develop successful, relevant experiences for students, middle level educators must determine the focus of their programs, identify suitable experiences and activities, and determine organizational structures that will support the "program focus" and make exploration a school-wide reality.

*Focus of the Exploratory Curriculum.* Determining a strong, mutually agreed upon focus or statement of purpose establishes the exploratory curriculum as a viable, ongoing part of the school, protecting it to some extent from those who advocate "academics" only for middle level schools. With a well-established sense of purpose, teachers and administrators can articulate their program to parents, community members, and school boards. In addition, a clearly defined purpose sets direction and makes it easier to integrate exploratory experiences across the curriculum away from the limitations of the concept of exploratory as a set of courses.

Several factors need to be examined in determining the focus of exploratory programs. First, should exploratory experiences assist students with current needs and interests? These might include experiences and mini-courses designed to assist middle level students to deal with their own problems and to explore personal interests. Second, should exploratory experiences be future-oriented and assist students in acquiring skills that will assist them when they become adults? Many of the current, but traditional, approaches to exploration have taken this focus by requiring all students to take courses in home economics and industrial arts. Third, should exploratory experiences focus on attitudes and values? Many middle level educators believe concern for others, honesty, responsibility for one's own actions, perseverance in task completion, and morality are values and attitudes which should be addressed as part of the exploratory curriculum. While there may be other important factors, these three must be addressed in the development of the focus or statement of purpose.

*Suitable Exploratory Experiences.* While the focus or purposes of the program lend guidance to the identification of suitable experiences, the criteria that must be continuously applied is one of developmental responsiveness. The fundamental question that must be asked is, "Is this course or experience developmentally appropriate for the young adolescents in our school?" This question applies to current experiences and activities as well as to those under consideration.

Other questions that need to be addressed in determining appropriate exploratory experiences are:

1.  What will be offered?
2.  Who determines what will be offered? How will teachers, administrators, parents, students, and school board members be involved in the selection process?
3.  What factors tend to influence the decision-making process? Community interests? Desires of school board members? Parental pressure? Teacher and administrator expertise? Tradition ("We've always done it this way")?
4.  What procedures are established to facilitate the decision-making process?
5.  How are the current experiences and/or planned experiences relevant to the needs and interests of the students in the school? Who determines relevancy?
6.  How does the exploratory program permeate the entire curriculum of the school? Who ensures that this occurs?

*Organizational Structures for Exploratories.* Operating, maintaining, and assessing successful exploratory programs is dependent on good organizational structures that facilitate collaborative decision making and communication. Decision-making structures must be established that allow teachers, administrators, parents, and students to participate in determining not only what the nature of exploratories will be but to also participate in determining how the program will operate in the school. Decisions to be made include:

1.  When should exploratory courses and experiences be scheduled? Morning? Afternoon? Before school/After school? As part of an extended lunch hour?

2. How frequently should they be offered? Every day? Twice a week? Once a week?
3. How long should they be? A standard period length? An extended period? Half a period?
4. What form should exploratories take? Standard 9-week courses? Mini-courses? Theme days? Incorporated into and organized by the team? Special projects?
5. How should they be staffed? By regular teachers? Staff members? Parents or community members?
6. What exploratory experiences should be required? Which ones should be elective?

Structures should also be developed that allow teachers, administrators, parents, and students to continuously assess the effectiveness of the program. If student needs are going to be met with relevant, interesting exploratory experiences, the program must be monitored and modified whenever necessary. This cooperative effort to implement, assess, and revise is crucial to a viable, successful exploratory program.

**The Social Curriculum.** The need to socialize is a central characteristic of all young adolescents, and middle level schools are the place where they do most of their socializing. Schools responsive to their students recognize this need and provide appropriate opportunities for them to socialize throughout the school day.

The importance of the social curriculum is underscored by the work of Wentzel (1993) who found that middle level students who reported frequent pursuit of multiple goals (social responsibility, academic-mastery, and positive evaluations) earned higher grades than those who did not. In addition, she reports that the results of her study confirm the belief that a primary goal of educational institutions is to socialize children into society by teaching work and responsibility oriented values. Middle level educators accomplish this goal through a number of planned and unplanned experiences.

There are two aspects of the social curriculum that should be emphasized: the planned social curriculum and the unplanned social curriculum (hidden curriculum). There are many planned activities which take place at school that facilitate socialization both in and out of the classroom. The centerpiece of the social curriculum is the teacher advisory program where the focus is on helping students develop effective socialization skills. The social curriculum, however, goes far beyond these experiences typically found in advisories. Some of these experiences include cooperative learning and task groups, student activities, participation in school governance, peer mediation, sports, and youth service. In addition, programs such as "adopt-a-student" or student mentoring, which provide students with a teacher or another student who serves as a special "friend," are effective in improving social skills. These special friends engage students, many of whom feel isolated and unsuccessful, in a variety of social and academic activities both in and out of school. These planned activities of the social curriculum not only provide students with the opportunity to socialize but offer chances to improve many important socialization skills such as communication with adults, acting responsibly, cooperative decision making, and conflict resolution.

For students from cultures other than the dominant culture, the social and academic cultures of the middle level school may require them to be productive in cultures that are very different from and in many cases in conflict to their own. In these instances, the planned social curriculum should provide activities that assist students in making the necessary adjustments to be successful. Ogbu (1992) suggests that this can be done by (1) helping teachers and administrators recognize that many students come to school with different and at times oppositional cultural frames, (2) providing teachers and administrators the opportunity to study minority cultures, and (3) establishing special counseling programs that help students learn to "accommodate" a different culture without "assimilation."

In many respects the social curriculum is much like the hidden curriculum. Values and attitudes are being projected by teachers, administrators, and other adults in ways that may positively or negatively affect young adolescents. The recent report of the American Association of University Women Educational Foundation (1992), for instance, documents ways in which the hidden curriculum in schools often creates environments which diminish girls' self-esteem and reduce expectancies and, at times, are even emotionally and physically threatening. A positive school social climate is possible when faculty and staff are cognizant of the special needs of *all* of their students and model positive, supportive behaviors. Being available to students between classes, before and after school, and at special events sends a strong message to young adolescents that teachers care about them. Equally important as being available is engaging in conversation with students about their lives and "things" of importance to them outside of school. This type of conversation with students helps them understand that adults in the school value them as persons, not just as students. Building strong positive relationships with teachers is a strong motivating factor for both boys and girls (Goodenow, 1993).

By participating with students in a variety of school activities such as field days, faculty/student athletic events, talent shows, and community projects, faculty and staff have a unique opportunity to form bonds with young people. This type of bonding between adults and students facilitates better communication, a feeling of cooperation and loyalty, and greater empathy for the other person's point of view. The availability of supportive teachers at events where both boys and girls are present is particularly important to young adolescent girls where the presence of a teacher or other adult is a key factor in protecting girls' physical and verbal space (Luria and Thorne, 1990; Maccoby, 1990).

Like the exploratory curriculum, the social curriculum should permeate every aspect of the school. It should become an integral part of every subject area, every teacher advisory group, and every school activity. By recognizing the importance of socialization to young adolescents, middle level educators can develop appropriate programs and activities that will capitalize on this significant force and use it to actively engage young adolescents in all aspects of the school life.

## The Integrated Curriculum

The works of Vars (1991, 1992) and Beane (1990, 1992) are typical of the attempts to use curriculum integration as a vehicle for developmentally appropriate middle level curriculum planning. As Vars (1992) points out, the attempts to move away from the subject-matter approach date back to the 1930s and 1940s. Curriculum integration and the "Core curriculum," not to be confused with today's usage meaning the "core of curriculum" (e.g., the required courses), with its strong emphasis on student concerns and social problems, has been well documented throughout the literature.

Beane (1990, 1991, 1992) takes an expansive view of integration in the middle level school, postulating that responsive schools should be organized around themes that deal specifically with early adolescent problems, needs, and concerns as they relate to the larger world in which they live. Believing that middle level schools should focus on general education specifically designed with early adolescent characteristics in mind, Beane suggests that teachers and administrators view students as young adolescents who are also participants in the larger world. Curriculum which integrates both personal and world questions and concerns forms the basis for the learning experiences of the middle level school (1991).

Middle level education should be general in nature with a focus on early adolescent characteristics. With this focus, the questions and concerns that young adolescents have about themselves and the world around them form the basis of Beane's approach to the development of integrated curriculum. In this organizational structure broad general themes built around issues and concerns become the core curriculum, replacing specific subject-matter courses. While Beane's ideas hold great promise, because of state and local curricular mandates and the generally high regard many teachers have for subject-centered curriculum structures, these ideas have not yet gained wide acceptance in practice.

Vars (1992) describes the integrated curriculum as a curriculum that seeks to assist students to see life as a whole, helping them "to put together in some meaningful way the many bits and pieces of experience both in school and out" (p. 67).

Typically, attempts to integrate curriculum occur in interdisciplinary teams where teachers from various subject areas are working with the same group of students. First efforts to integrate often take the form of correlation of content. Teachers from different courses modify the sequences of their courses so that related topics and issues are taught to students at the same time (Drake, 1991; Vars, 1992).

An example of this type of curriculum might be a unit on exploration of the new world. Featuring the circumnavigation of the globe by Magellan, the social studies teacher would study geography and map making; the science teacher would study early navigational tools and celestial navigation; the mathematics teacher would focus on rate of speed and other mathematical aspects of the trip including calculating the amount of provisions needed to feed the crew; and the language arts teacher would examine record keeping and provide experiences built around writing journals and diaries.

A truly integrated curriculum, however, is much more than just the correlation and resequencing of topics and themes. It is a restructuring of the curriculum so that the various subject areas are blended into a common theme that may form a new course or unit of study. In this type of "fused" curriculum teachers are more concerned with helping students deal with central concepts and values than being concerned about equal distribution of time among the subject areas (Vars, 1992). A typical integrated unit might have a theme such as the environment, with students engaged in studying and identifying local environmental issues and problems. They might conduct investigations that would yield data that would require analysis and graphing and the writing of a final report. Although a variety of skills are required to complete the project, they are subsumed under the theme and not separated out as specific subject area competencies.

Integrated curriculum is developed in most middle level schools through a process of evolution. Drake (1991) describes the process as one of dissolving subject area boundaries through a collaborative process that necessitates the changing of commonly held assumptions about curriculum and the adoption of new models. This process goes from correlation of content (as described earlier) where subject areas remain discrete, to interdisciplinary curriculum where the subject areas, while still existing, become more blurred, to integrated curriculum where subject areas are abandoned and replaced by common themes (Drake, 1991).

The process of integrating curriculum can be approached using a variety of strategies including the curriculum action plan (Jacobs, 1991) and curriculum planning wheels (Palmer, 1991). Jacobs' (1991) action plan makes provision for conducting external and internal action research, proposal writing, implementing and monitoring pilot units and program adoption, all accomplished over a three year period of time. Using planning wheels to plan for integrated curriculum allows teachers to keep their content area central and to examine the possibilities of integrating the logical, natural elements of other content areas (Palmer, 1991). Palmer (1991) found that planning wheels were an excellent vehicle for making cross-curricular connections with existing curriculums written in the single-subject mode.

The advantages of interdisciplinary curriculum are numerous. The opportunities for teachers to work together in developing learning experiences for their students creates a forum for action that focuses efforts on student needs, curriculum and instructional improvement, and reflective practice. Making connections among the various subject areas also helps teachers view their content area from a much broader perspective, thus reducing the fragmentation of learning that exists in most middle level schools. Generally speaking, teachers find greater satisfaction when working together on integrated curriculum and often have a renewal of energy and excitement. Planning and working together also makes teachers more appreciative of each other's skills and talents.

Teachers and researchers report that emphasis on interrelationships across the curriculum create powerful learning opportunities in the classroom, opportunities that help students find relevance in the content and become actively engaged in learning. Students remember more and become more proactive and creative thinkers because of the connections that integration makes with important issues in their lives (Berg, 1988; Jacobs, 1991). Also, as a result of integration, students see content areas as pieces of a whole rather than as separate entities. In the affective areas students become more involved and excited, demonstrate less competition and more cooperation, and learn to accept differences and appreciate the strengths and talents of their classmates.

Successful integration of curriculum is not without its pitfalls. The two biggest barriers to this approach are the current high degree of acceptance and support for single-subject curricula among teachers, administrators, parents, community members, and elected officials; and the amount of time needed to integrate curriculum and to identify or develop suitable resource materials and assessment procedures. Considerable anxiety is felt by many that essential subject matter will be shortchanged or compromised. Also of concern is the perceived lack of expertise on the part of many teachers as most of them were not exposed to planning for interdisciplinary curriculum in their initial teacher preparation programs. For many teachers the sheer effort and demands, both practically and intellectually, are daunting.

Probably the most critical area requiring administrative support is time. Time is needed to reach consensus on curriculum plans and criteria for testing and grading; for research, because new material is always being taught; for planning lessons that use untraditional approaches; for networking to make contact with those who can help expand the learning environment; and for public relations to maintain support for an innovative program. Overcoming these barriers and taking advantage of the opportunities offered by an integrated curriculum structure requires knowledgeable and visionary leadership. To facilitate the development of an integrated/interdisciplinary curriculum, administrators and leadership teams need to:

1.  Get comfortable with the concept of interdisciplinary curriculum and build a comprehensive information base. Believe in the value of interdisciplinary curriculum for helping students be more successful and make a commitment to implement it in their school.

2.  Develop a "vision" of how interdisciplinary curriculum would work in their school. Maintain that vision throughout the process of planning and implementation.

3.  Become "cheerleaders" and "coaches" for interdisciplinary curriculum during its planning and implementation stage. Maintain the effectiveness of interdisciplinary curriculum through vigilance, support, and encouragement.

4.  Help teachers validate a belief system that interdisciplinary curriculum is a worthwhile approach for young adolescents.

5.  Help change teacher attitudes about subject matter organization, autonomy, and learning.

6.  Assist teachers in building an information base about interdisciplinary curriculum. What is it? Why is it better than what they are doing?

7.  Promote cooperative decision making on the format of the interdisciplinary curriculum to be used at the school, content areas and teachers to be involved, the duration of units, and the nature of student assessment and evaluation.

8.  Help secure every extra moment of planning time for teachers to develop interdisciplinary curricula.

9.  Provide a support base for planning and implementation. Hustle resources, get extra pay, and provide extra "perks."

10. Communicate honestly with parents and community regarding the goals, values, benefits, advantages, and disadvantages of interdisciplinary curriculum.

11. Promote and secure widespread teacher, parent, and community involvement in the planning and implementation of interdisciplinary curriculum.

12. Assess the strengths and weaknesses of the faculty for the purpose of planning appropriate staff development experiences.

13. Assess and evaluate each stage of the planning and implementation and provide appropriate feedback that will facilitate improvement.

Enlightened leadership is crucial for success in developing appropriate curricular structures for young adolescents. Leaders who care about teachers and students, who have a vision of appropriate middle level curriculum, who have knowledge of parent and community expectations, and who are willing to be untiring advocates for young adolescents and their schools, can and do make a difference. Their efforts enable others to embrace their vision and create developmentally responsive curriculum.

## CURRICULUM AND STUDENT ASSESSMENT

Most assessment procedures found in middle level and other schools are inappropriate and fail to give an accurate picture of the range of student learning or an adequate measure of the accomplishment of school or district curricular goals. Current assessment procedures, for the most part, are not correlated with the school's curriculum, and assessment unduly influences the curriculum of the middle level school and the way in which it is taught. Fundamentally, what is assessed is what teachers teach, and often the limitations of the assessment procedures severely "cripple the instruction that goes on the classroom" (Glatthorn, 1987; Mitchell, 1990). Wiggins (1989) also comments on the strong influencing factors of assessment when he suggests that tests and examinations not only monitor standards, they also set them. Tests, says Wiggins (1989), should be central experiences of learning based on the performances or demonstrations of learning desired of all students. All too often this does not occur. For the most part tests continue to serve the primary function of reporting a "statistical" number, which is of little or no assistance to students and their teachers or to the politicians who use it to judge student progress and to rate schools.

## Current Assessment Practices

Standardized tests, contends Albert Shanker (Mitchell, 1990), are one of the five key reasons that American schools have fallen behind the schools of Europe. He suggests that standardized testing, which is required by most school districts throughout the nation, is one of the most characteristic and least productive features of American schooling. Resnick and Resnick (1985) support Shanker's belief when they suggest that American students are the most tested but least examined youngsters in the world.

Americans, however, take great stock in standardized test scores, believing that they are representative measures of student learning and school effectiveness. As a result, test scores, in spite of their severe limitations, have become a widely accepted means for judging school effectiveness (Fetler, 1986, 1991; Fetler and Carlson, 1985; Frechtling, 1989).

Standardized tests as the sole measure of student learning and school effectiveness are inappropriate for the following reasons (Freeman et. al., 1980; Glatthorn, 1987; Mitchell, 1990; Wiggins, 1989; Wolf, 1989):

1.  Standardized tests are not aligned with district or state curriculum guides. Lack of alignment is also evident when major standardized tests are compared to content of textbooks.
2.  Standardized tests, in the name of statistical accuracy and economy, deny the importance of context-sensitive human judgments of ability in the assessment process. These impersonal measures of a single performance are inadequate measures of student learning.
3.  Standardized tests do little to enhance or encourage higher order thinking skills. Much of current assessment practice, including standardized tests, mitigates against giving students the opportunity to become thoughtful respondents to and judges of their own work.

4. Standardized tests, when used for grade promotion or tracking assignments, reduce the curriculum to a disjointed series of exercises and discrete unconnected facts which tend to be representative of the tests.

Standardized tests, while providing scores for comparisons, leave much to be desired when it comes to enhancing student learning and ascertaining progress over a period of time. A one time only score generated from standardized tests is not a comprehensive representation of student learning. Separating assessment from instruction, an occurrence which commonly happens with standardized tests used in schools, often yields findings that may not tell a great deal about what students have learned from their classroom experiences (Maeroff, 1991).

What is needed, according to Wiggins (1989), is an opportunity to observe students' repertoires, not the pure rote recitation of answers to recall questions. To assess understanding, teachers must have the opportunity to explore a student's answer by conducting a dialogue. Only then can it be assumed that the student has been fully examined (Wiggins, 1989).

While standardized tests are severely limited in their ability to measure student learning, many educators concede that teacher-made exams are even more unsatisfactory (Brandt, 1992). Due to lack of training in test preparation, what classroom teachers measure on tests has very little correlation with what they have taught (Glatthorn, 1987). Teachers often opt for time-saving options such as short quizzes and true/false items rather than developing more comprehensive but time consuming assessment procedures which include problem solving, writing, performances, and exhibitions.

The tendency is to attempt to quantify student learning as commonly found on both standardized and teacher-made tests and exams. Wolf (1989) contends that these one-time assessments communicate to students that assessment comes from without and is not their personal responsibility; that what matters is not a thoughtful range of intuition or knowledge, but performance on a "slice" of skills that appear on the test; that first draft work is good enough; and that achievement matters to the exclusion of development.

It is obvious that options to current assessment practices need to be found if developmentally appropriate practices are to be generated and implemented. Emerging assessment approaches, such as performance assessment (student demonstration of the same behavior that the assessor desires), and its close relative, authentic assessment (student not only demonstrates desired behavior, but does so in a real-life context) (Meyer, 1992), are promising options for middle level educators.

## Goals of Student Assessment

What American education needs, according to Mitchell (1990), are testing procedures that will accomplish three important goals, goals that bring the assessment process back into the control of educators. She suggests that assessment should:

1.  Complement the curriculum and encourage expansion, not contraction.
2.  Encourage teachers to assume professional responsibility for, or ownership of, evaluation.
3.  Make schools accountable on their own terms, not those of politicians.

In describing the aims of the assessment procedures for Project Zero, Wolf (1989) presents two goals in designing assessment, goals that are equally appropriate for middle level programs. These include:

1.  Designing ways of providing information for teachers and school districts while at the same time modeling personal responsibility in questioning and reflecting on one's own work.
2.  Finding ways to capture growth over time so students can become informed and thoughtful assessors of their own learning histories (Wolf, 1989; 36).

Building upon the work of Mitchell (1990) and Wolf (1989), the goal of assessment in middle level schools should be to involve teachers and administrators in designing tasks and performances that are representative of the curriculum, that support instruction, and that involve students in questioning, in problem solving, in demonstrating, in performing, and in judging the quality of their own work.

## Important Concepts of Authentic Assessment

The main function of authentic assessment is to evaluate student work from a variety of viewpoints. Wiggins (1989) suggests that authentic assessments must replicate the challenges and standards that typically face people in the workplace. These challenges might include writing proposals, preparing reports, and conducting group research. Students must be heavily involved in the evaluation process through the monitoring of their own progress, judging the quality of their work, and taking the responsibility for seeking assistance. Authentic assessment is sensitive to individual student and school contexts and facilitates accurate and equitable evaluation by emphasizing the importance of human judgment and dialogue, refusing to accept as valid a score generated from a "one time performance."

The following listing of concepts of authentic assessment are drawn from research, literature, and practice. They include (Elkind, 1989; Farr, 1991; Glaser, 1988; Smith and Wigginton, 1991; Wiggins, 1989):

1. A real, authentic test replicates the authentic tasks that one might face in the workplace and/or real life.
2. An authentic test should be future oriented. Knowledge should be assessed in terms of its constructive use for learning in the future.
3. An authentic assessment should guide rather than judge. Authentic assessment allows educators to find out if students can create their own answers, chose their own learning activities, and determine the basis for their assessment.
4. An authentic assessment must serve the needs of students. Assessments which do not yield useful and valid information about how students perform tasks should not be administered.
5. An authentic assessment system should document what students have done and/or learned over a period of time.
6. An authentic assessment system asks students to prove that they have mastered the objectives. It prepares students to monitor their own progress and design their own remediation.
7. An authentic assessment system expects every student to understand that the progress of each student is the concern of every other student in the class.
8. An authentic assessment allows teachers to watch learners pose questions, tackle and solve slightly

ambiguous problems, build a body of evidence, plan
and arrange arguments, and take purposeful action
that confronts problems.

Assessing performance using authentic procedures also stim-
ulates higher level thinking processes. Some researchers suggest that educators begin to look at thinking as a performance
and draw comparisons between thinking and what performers
do. Like preparing for a performance, serious thinking requires
risk, working with ill-defined problems, data collecting, guessing
and observing. Thinking also requires work over a long period of
time, working through barriers, rehearsing, and internalizing
criticisms. And finally, thinking involves interpretation and making sense of information, ideas, and beliefs (Wolf et. al., 1991).
Assessing a student's ability to learn and to use these thinking
processes requires alternative forms of assessment, assessment
such as authentic or performance assessment.

## Authentic Assessment—Key Issues

The implementation of authentic assessment systems in middle
level schools is a complex process that intertwines with curriculum improvement and school restructuring. The adoption of
authentic assessment reflects a significant shift in what schools
value and carries with it far-reaching implications for content
organization and classroom instruction. When combined with
the restructuring of the curriculum to be more developmentally
responsive, authentic assessment can be a powerful force to
move the school away from a "factory-based-delivery of the facts
model to a new paradigm in which students are active learners
and questioning thinkers" (ASCD, 1991). Wiggins (ASCD, 1991)
contends that "assessment is the Trojan horse of school reform
because of its power to reshape what and how schools teach."

Another promising feature of authentic assessment is that it
involves teachers and administrators at virtually every stage of
the process. They are intensely involved in designing, adminis-
trating, scoring, and analyzing, a process that offers  educators
the benefits of feedback on student achievement and extensive
professional development (Mitchell, 1990).

Authentic assessment also legitimizes the wide-spread cus-
tom of teaching to the test. In the case of authentic assessment,
however, teaching to the test offers the advantage of actually
teaching to the curriculum of the school, not drilling discrete

facts for discrete answers (Mitchell, 1990). Wiggins (1989) also suggests that teachers teach to the test. Teachers, however, must be involved in designing the test and the test must offer students a genuine, authentic challenge. When using authentic assessments, the common practice of "springing" a surprise test on students is no longer a goal, because as Maeroff (1991) contends, students are taught by their teachers to provide evidence of their own learning.

Any discussion of the key issues of authentic student assessment must also address some of the complications that this form of assessment presents to educators. It is, for instance, much easier to propose an outcome than it is to determine the criteria and establish the performance levels that are represented by student achievement or exhibitions (Maeroff, 1991). Authentic assessment, still in its infancy, is time consuming, labor intensive, and tends to be imprecise, although appropriate procedures have been successfully developed to insure reliability and validity. Two of the more difficult areas in implementing authentic assessment are convincing teachers to participate and coming up with a "score" that will satisfy the needs of parents and politicians who are looking for criteria for making comparisons and judgments (Mitchell, 1990). Before authentic testing can become a reality in practice, Maeroff (1991) suggests that procedures must be developed so it can be done more quickly, more efficiently, less expensively, while making provision for an acceptable level of standardization that will satisfy politicians.

## Implementation of Authentic Assessment Systems

Implementation of authentic assessment programs requires that middle level educators carefully consider a number of factors (Figure 4-4). First, appropriate assessment must serve four important audiences (Farr, 1991):

1. *Students* must know what they are supposed to be learning and have the opportunity to reflect on their work.
2. *Parents* need to know what their children can do so they can provide assistance and encouragement.
3. *Teachers* need to know what students can do so that they can help them become more proficient.
4. *Decision makers* need reliable information about learning and achievement to make informed decisions.

**Figure 4-4**
Authentic Assessment - Some Considerations

The Implementation of Authentic Assessment Procedures at the Middle Level School
Requires that School Leaders Consider the:

1. Needs of the Various Constituents
   • Students
   • Parents
   • Teachers
   • Decision Makers

2. Challenges to Existing School Culture and Belief Systems

3. Criteria which Supports Authentic Assessment

4. Procedures to be Used in Accurately Assessing Student Learning

5. Relationship of Authentic Assessment Plans to Current Grading/Reporting
   Procedures

6. Procedures for Inquiry, Reflection, Staff Development, Collaborative Decision
   Making, and Implementation

The success of the authentic assessment program will be largely dependent upon how effectively it serves these four audiences.

Second, alternative assessment programs of any kind create challenges to the existing school culture and the values of those who function in that culture. New values should be nurtured and developed at the school level, and new conditions which support authentic assessment must be established within teams and individual classrooms. Zessoules and Gardner (1991) identify four critical conditions for establishing an authentic assessment culture in classrooms:

1.  The nurturing of complex understandings
2.  The development of reflective habits of the mind
3.  The documentation of students' evolving understanding
4.  The use of assessment as a moment of learning

Assessment must also be multidimensional, be complemented and supported by classroom practices, be responsive to students in terms of improvement of the quality of their work, and be able to engage teachers in reflection and debate about their visions of excellence and its implications for changing what is taught (Wolf et. al., 1991).

Third, middle level leaders must be familiar with the criteria that supports authentic assessment. This knowledge provides the basis for implementing comprehensive and effective programs. The most comprehensive listing of criteria for establishing authentic assessment programs comes from Wiggins (1989). He arranges his criteria around the categories of *structure and logistics, intellectual design features, standardized grading and scoring,* and *fairness and equity.* These criteria (see Figure 4-5) provide excellent guidelines for the organization of authentic assessment in middle level schools. In developing authentic testing, Wiggins (1991) is careful to point out that the process is reversed to facilitate a focus on accountability that serves student learning. Construction of authentic testing includes the specification and approval of a task, the devising of a fair and incentive-

**Figure 4-5**
Wiggins' Criteria for Authenticity*

*Structure and Logistics*
1. Authentic tests are public, involving an audience, client, and panel
2. Authentic tests do not rely on unrealistic, arbitrary time constraints, or secret questions or tasks
3. Authentic tests require collaboration with others

*Intellectual Design Features*
1. Authentic tests are not needlessly intrusive, arbitrary, or contrived for the sake of shaking out a single score or grade
2. Authentic tests are contextualized, complex, intellectual challenges, not fragmented and static bits or tasks
3. Authentic tests are representative challenges within a given discipline

*Standards of Grading and Scoring*
1. Authentic tests measure essentials, not easily counted errors
2. Authentic tests use multifaceted scoring systems instead of a single aggregate grade
3. Authentic tests exist in harmony with school-wide aims; they embody standards to which everyone in the school can aspire

*Fairness and Equity*
1. Authentic tests ferret out and identify strengths
2. Authentic tests minimize needless, unfair, and demoralizing comparisons and do away with fatalistic thinking about results
3. Authentic tests can be and should be attempted by all students—with tests "scaffolded up," not dumbed down as necessary to compensate for poor skill, inexperience, or weak training

* Adapted from Wiggins, G. (1989). A True Test: Toward More Authentic and Equitable Assessment. *Phi Delta Kappan, 70*(9), 703-713. Printed by permission of the Center on Learning, Assessment, and School Structure.

building plan for scoring, and the consideration of questions of reliability.

Fourth, consideration must be given to the procedures to be used to accurately assess student learning. Currently, because of its ability to involve students in self-assessment and to assess their growth over a long period of time, portfolio assessment is at the forefront in schools currently using authentic assessments. Also frequently used are student exhibitions, exit (end of year) interviews and performances, essays, and problem solving projects.

Fifth, the implementation of authentic assessment requires that careful consideration be given to current grading and/or reporting practices. Many educators are questioning the effectiveness and adequacy of letter grades in reporting the complexity of student learning. In addition, research is showing that particularly for "at risk" young adolescents, letter grades provide little or no motivation to achieve. Mac Iver (1990) has found handwritten comments and progress grades to be "significantly associated with principals' reports of lower retention rates, lower projected drop-out rates, and more successful programs for students in the middle grades." The comprehensiveness and magnitude of authentic assessment demands that educators look for better ways to accurately report student learning.

Sixth, crucial to the implementation of authentic assessment programs is a well-organized plan which provides for staff development, pilot studies, and collaborative decision making. School administrators and teacher leaders play a crucial role in the implementation process. Serving as advocates of authentic assessment they must:

1.  Encourage and allow teachers to incorporate authentic assessment in their classrooms
2.  Seek out ways to support teachers as reflective professionals working together to confront the issues central to authentic assessment
3.  Elicit support from the widest possible audience for authentic assessment
4.  Confront and deal effectively with the pressures for standardization and accountability (Zessoules and Gardner, 1991).

The process of organizing and building a developmentally appropriate authentic assessment program is a complex process, a process that needs careful planning and broad-based involvement. The concepts of authentic assessment are attractive to middle level educators because of their responsiveness to the characteristics of young adolescents, but unless authentic assessment comes to be seen as so essential that it justifies disrupting the habits and spending practices of conventional schooling, it will never be successfully implemented (Wiggins, 1989).

## SUMMARY

Developing a curriculum which is responsive to the needs of young adolescents is a challenging task. Struggling for an identity of their own, middle level schools have most often, and inappropriately, taken on the structures of high schools with their subject-centered organization, rigid schedules, and passive instruction. While some middle level schools have begun to break away from the high school influence, middle level education is still fragmented by differences of opinion and bound by cultures that support outdated and unresponsive views of education. Existing for the most part without any unifying theme or a consistent focus, middle level schools really have no uniquely, identifiable curriculum.

The middle level curriculum, usually structured around core courses, exploratory courses, and elective courses, must focus on the needs and characteristics of the early adolescent learners. The curriculum must be less passive and uninviting. Dull classrooms must be transformed into exciting places where learning demands involvement and participation. The content must move beyond topics of textbooks and the written curriculum to the issues of middle level students as they adjust to the daily pressures that confront them. The curriculum must also connect the great issues of America and the world, both past and present, to the lives of young adolescents.

Skill learning must also be a part of the curriculum and instruction of the responsive middle level school, but skills cannot be isolated from the lives of students. They must be connected to the needs and characteristics of the young adolescent. Communicative, investigative, and computational skills must be taught in ways that have application to each student's experience, thus allowing him or her to construct his or her own knowledge. Finding relevance in academic and social skills instruction is critical to the developing young adolescent.

Assessment is also a critical issue in curriculum development. The most innovative and developmentally responsive curriculum can quickly be made inoperable by the use of inappropriate assessment procedures. The process of evaluation must be closely linked with the goals of the curriculum and instruction. This linkage will align more participatory instructional approaches with assessment procedures that are also participatory in nature, thus assessing real learning with authentic procedures. Authentic instruction and authentic assessment are cornerstones of the developmentally responsive middle level school.

By building on the foundation of developmentally appropriate education, on a knowledge of early adolescent needs and characteristics, and on a comprehensive information base about curriculum and instruction, middle level leaders can structure the kinds of programs that will ensure success for all students.

## REFERENCES

American Association of University Women Educational Foundation. (1992). *The AAUW report: How schools shortchange girls (Executive summary)*. Washington, D.C.: American Association of University Women Educational Foundation.

Aronson, E., & Bridgeman, D. (1979). Jigsaw groups and the desegregated classroom: In pursuit of common goals. *Personality and Social Psychology Bulletin, 5*, 438-446.

Association for Supervision and Curriculum Development. (1991). Alternative assessment drive change. *ASCD Update, 33*(2), 5.

Beane, J. A. (1990). Rethinking the middle school curriculum. *Middle School Journal, 21*(5), 1-5.

Beane, J. A. (1991). Middle school: The natural home of integrated curriculum. *Educational Leadership, 49*(2), 9-13.

Beane, J. A. (1992). Turning the floor over: Reflections on a middle school curriculum. *Middle School Journal, 23*(3), 34-40.

Berg, M. (1988). The integrated curriculum. *Social Studies Review, 28*(1), 38-41.

Berryman, S. E. (1993). Learning for the workplace. In L. Darling-Hammond (Ed.), *Review of research in education* (Vol. 19, pp. 343-401). Washington, D.C.: American Educational Research Association.

Braddock, J. H., II, & McPartland, J. M. (1993). Education of early adolescents. In L. Darling-Hammond (Ed.), *Review of research in education* (Vol. 19, pp. 135-170). Washington, D.C.: American Educational Research Association.

Brandt, R. (1992). Overview: A fresh focus for curriculum. *Educational Leadership, 49*(8), 7.

Clark, S. N., & Clark, D. C. (1986, September). Middle level programs: More than academics. *Schools in the middle: A report on trends and practices.* Reston, VA: National Association of Secondary School Principals.

Conrad, D., & Hedin, D. (1991). School-based community service: What do we know from research and theory. *Phi Delta Kappan, 72*(10), 743-749.

Doyle, W. (1986). Classroom organization and management. In M. C. Wittrock (Ed.), *Handbook of research on teaching (3rd ed.)* (pp. 392-431). New York: Macmillan.

Drake, S. M. (1991). How our team dissolved the boundaries. *Educational Leadership, 49*(2), 20-22.

Elkind, D. (1989). Developmentally appropriate practice: Philosophical and practical implications. *Phi Delta Kappan, 71*(2), 113-117.

Epstein, J., & Salinas, K. (1992). *Promising programs in the middle grades.* Reston, VA: National Association of Secondary School Principals.

Farr, R. (1991). The assessment puzzle. *Educational Leadership, 49*(3), 95.

Fetler, M. (1986). Accountability in California public schools. *Educational Evaluation and Policy Analysis, 8*(1), 31-44.

Fetler, M. (1991). A method for the construction of differentiated school norms. *Applied Measurement in Education, 4*(1), 53-66.

Fetler, M., & Carlson, D. (1985). Identification of exemplary schools on a large scale. In G. Austin, & H. Garber (Eds.), *Research on exemplary schools* (pp. 83-86). New York: Academic Press.

Filby, N. (1992, Spring). *Toward a community of learners.* San Francisco, CA: Far West Laboratory for Educational Research and Development.

Floden, R. E., Porter, A. C., Schmidt, W. J., Freeman, D. J., & Schwille, J. R. (1980). *Responses to curriculum pressures: A policy capturing study of teacher decisions about content.* East Lansing, MI: Michigan State University, Institute for Research on Teaching.

Frechtling, J. (1989). Administrative uses of school testing programs. In R. Linn (Ed.), *Educational measurement* (pp. 475-484). New York: American Council of Education and Macmillan Publishing Company.

Freeman, D., Kuhs, T., Porter, A., Knappen, L., Floden, R., Schmidt, W., & Schwille, J. (1980). *The fourth grade mathematics curriculum as inferred from textbooks and tests.* East Lansing, MI: Michigan State University, Institute for Research on Teaching.

Frye, S. M. (1989). The NCTM standards—Challenges for all classrooms. *Arithmetic Teacher, 36*(9), 4-7.

Gehrke, N., Knapp, M., & Sirotnik, K. (1992). In search of the school curriculum. In G. Grant (Ed.), *Review of Research in Education* (Vol. 18, pp. 51-110). Washington, D.C.: American Educational Research Association.

George, P. S., & Oldaker, L. (1985). *Evidence for the middle school.* Columbus, OH: National Middle School Association.

Glaser, R. (1988). Cognitive and environmental perspectives on assessing achievement. In E. Freeman (Ed.), *Assessment in the service of learning: Proceedings of the 1987 ETS Invitational Conference* (pp. 40-42). Princeton, NJ: Educational Testing Service.

Glatthorn, A. A. (1987). *Curriculum leadership.* Glenview, IL: Scott, Foresman and Company.

Goodenow, C. (1993). Classroom belonging among early adolescent students: Relationships to motivation and achievement. *The Journal of Early Adolescence, 13*(1), 21-43.

Hurd, P. D. (1989). A life science core for early adolescents. *Middle School Journal, 20*(5), 20-23.

Jacobs, H. H. (1989). *Interdisciplinary curriculum: Design and implementation.* Alexandria, VA: Association for Curriculum and Supervision.

Jacobs, H. H. (1991). Planning for curriculum integration. *Educational Leadership, 49*(2), 27-28.

Leithwood, K. A., Ross, J. A., & Montgomery, D. J. (1982). An investigation of teachers' curriculum decision making. In K. A. Leithwood (Ed.), *Studies in curriculum decision-making* (pp. 14-46). Toronto, Ontario: Ontario Institute for Studies in Education.

Lounsbury, J. H. (1990, May). Middle level schools—Once around the elephant. *Schools in the middle: A report on trends and practices.* Reston, VA: National Association of Secondary School Principals.

Lounsbury, J. H., & Clark, D. C. (1990). *Inside grade eight: From apathy to excitement.* Reston, VA: National Association of Secondary School Principals.

Loyd, B. H., Loyd, D. E., & Gressard, C. P. (1987). Gender and computer experience as factors in the computer attitudes of middle school students. *Journal of Early Adolescence, 7*(1), 13-19.

Luria, Z., & Thorne, B. (1990, August). The construction of gender in psychology. Paper presented at the annual meeting of the American Psychological Association, Boston.

Maccoby, E. (1990). Gender and relationships: A developmental account. *American Psychologist, 45,* 513-520.

MacDonald, R. A., & Leithwood, K. A. (1982). Toward an explanation of the influences on teacher curriculum decisions. In K. A. Leithwood (Ed.), *Studies in curricular decision making* (pp. 35-51). Toronto, Ontario: Ontario Institute for Studies in Education.

Mac Iver, D. J. (1990). A national description of report card entries in the middle grades. Report No. 9. Baltimore, MD: The Johns Hopkins University, Center for Research on Effective Schooling for Disadvantaged Students.

Maeroff, G. I. (1991). Assessing alternative assessment. *Phi Delta Kappan, 73*(4), 272-281.

Meyer, C. A. (1992). What's the difference between authentic and performance assessment? *Educational Leadership, 49*(8), 39-40.

Mitchell, R. (1990). Authentic assessment. *Basic Education,* 33(10), 6-9.

NASSP Council on Middle Level Education. (1985). *An agenda for excellence at the middle level.* Reston, VA: National Association of Secondary School Principals.

National Commission on Excellence in Education. (1983). *A nation at risk: The imperative for educational reform.* Washington, D. C.: United States Government Printing Office.

National Council of Teachers of Mathematics. (1980). *An agenda for action: Recommendations for school mathematics of the 1980s.* Reston, VA: National Council of Teachers of Mathematics.

Natriello, G., & Dornbusch, S. (1984). *Teacher evaluation standards and student effort.* New York: Longman.

Newmann, F. (1991). Authentic work and student engagement. *Newsletter, 5*(3). Madison, WI: University of Wisconsin-Madison, National Center on Effective Secondary Schools.

Ogbu, J. U. (1992). Understanding cultural diversity and learning. *Educational Researcher, 21*(8), 5-14.

Palmer, J. M. (1991). Planning wheels turn curriculum around. *Educational Leadership, 49*(2), 57-60.

Pogrow, S. (1990). Challenging at-risk students: Findings from the HOTS program. *Phi Delta Kappan, 71*(5), 389-397.

Resnick, D. P., & Resnick, L. B. (1985). Standards, curriculum, and performance: A historical and comparative perspective. *Educational Researcher, 14*(4), 5-20.

Slavin, R. E. (1983). *Cooperative learning.* New York: Longman.

Slavin, R. E. (1985). Cooperative learning: Applying contact theory in desegregated schools. *Journal of Social Issues, 41,* 45-62.

Smith, H., & Wigginton, E. (1991). Foxfire teacher networks. In A. Lieberman, & L. Miller (Eds.), *Staff development for education in the '90s.* New York: Teachers College Press.

Task Force on Education for Economic Growth. (1983). *Action for excellence.* Denver, CO: Education Commission of the States.

Vars, G. F. (1991). Integrated curriculum in historical perspective. *Educational Leadership, 49*(2), 14-15.

Vars, G. F. (1992, Spring). Integrative curriculum: A deja vu. *Current Issues in Middle Level Education, 1*(1), 66-78.

Wentzel, K. R. (1993). Motivation and achievement in early adolescence: The role of multiple classroom goals. *The Journal of Early Adolescence, 13*(1), 4-20.

Wiggins, G. (1989). A true test: Toward more authentic and equitable assessment. *Phi Delta Kappan, 70*(9), 703-713.

Wolf, D. P. (1989). Portfolio assessment: Sampling student work. *Educational Leadership, 46*(7), 35-39.

Wolf, D., Bixby, J., Glenn, J. I., & Gardner, H. (1991). To use their minds well: Investigating new forms of student assessment. In G. Grant (Ed.), *Review of research in education* (Vol. 17, pp. 31-74). Washington, D.C.: American Educational Research Association.

Zessoules, R., & Gardner, H. (1991). Authentic assessment: Beyond the buzzword and into the classroom. In V. Perrone (Ed.), *Expanding student assessment* (pp. 47-71). Alexandria, VA: Association for Supervision and Curriculum Development.

# 5

## Responsive Middle Level Programs: Interdisciplinary Teaming, Teacher Advisories, and Student Activities

> "In the years ahead it must become more apparent to our youth than it is now that we genuinely value them and are conscientiously developing educational programs that match their nature and needs . . ."
> John Lounsbury and
> Donald Clark

Good middle level schools are developmentally responsive to the needs of the young adolescents they serve. Responsive middle level programs do not occur automatically. They come about as a result of the hard work of middle level educators who not only have a comprehensive knowledge base about early adolescent needs and characteristics but who are also aware of the wide variety of successful programs that are appropriate for their students.

Chapters 5 and 6 will give an overview of programs that have been recognized as being appropriate for young adolescents and how these programs meet the specific needs of middle level students. Programs to be described include: interdisciplinary teaming programs, teacher advisories, student activity programs, parental involvement programs, and youth service programs.

### INTERDISCIPLINARY TEAMING

Interdisciplinary teaming is considered by many middle level educators as one of the "cornerstones" of responsive middle level schools (Hafner, Ingels, Schneider, Stevenson, and Owings, 1990; Tye, 1985). When properly implemented, it facilitates teachers working together in smaller focus groups as recommended by Lipsitz (1984) and the Carnegie Task Force on Education of Young Adolescents (1989). Found in approximately 40 percent of America's middle level schools (Alexander and McEwin, 1989; Mac Iver, 1990), interdisciplinary teaming is defined as

> . . . two or more teachers from different subject areas working together to plan, instruct, and evaluate groups of students in two or more classrooms while making use of a wide variety of instructional strategies and learning resources in large group, small group, and directed study settings (Clark and Clark, 1987).

## Rationale for Interdisciplinary Teaming

The advantages of interdisciplinary teaming are numerous. The structuring of smaller focus groups through the teaming of teachers facilitates strong support systems for both middle level students and their teachers, increases the flexibility of learning time, provides a better vehicle for instruction, and creates opportunities to make connections across the various subject areas (Alexander and George, 1981; Clark and Clark, 1987, 1992; George and Oldaker, 1985; Mac Iver, 1990).

Interdisciplinary teaming environments have been shown to benefit middle level learners in a variety of positive ways. Positive climates and smaller focus groups, facilitated by interdisciplinary teams, have been shown to directly influence psychosocial development and indirectly influence achievement (Epstein, 1981). Other benefits drawn from research confirm the strong linkage of interdisciplinary teaming organizations to developmentally appropriate practices for young adolescents (Arhar, 1992; Clark and Clark, 1992; Epstein, 1981; Fenwick, 1992; George and Oldaker, 1985; Mac Iver, 1990; Mitman and Lambert, 1992; Rutter, Maughan, Mortimore, Houston, and Smith, 1979).

**Benefits to Students.** Interdisciplinary team organizations when properly implemented:

1.    Provide a more comfortable transition from elementary to middle school by creating environments that are conducive to learning and by reducing feelings of anonymity and isolation.

2.  Allow teachers to focus collectively on the individual needs of their students and provide greater opportunities for recognition and support.
3.  Enable the creation of positive, nurturing environments for learning.
4.  Enhance school environments that facilitate the development of positive student attitudes toward teachers, a greater interest in subject matter, a sense of personal freedom, and a sense of self-reliance.
5.  Promote a climate that fosters more positive relations among culturally diverse students.
6.  Provide an atmosphere of support that influences students to behave in more positive ways, resulting in less inappropriate behavior, truancy, and tardiness.
7.  Contribute to successful efforts to reduce dropouts.
8.  Promote student insight into the logical relationships between the branches of knowledge.
9.  Facilitate increased opportunities for communication between teachers and teachers, students and teachers, and students and students, often creating strong feelings of affiliation.
10. Provide better and more comprehensive communication between the home and school.

Numerous benefits for teachers also are found in interdisciplinary teaming organizations. Collaboration with other teachers facilitates communication, enhances satisfaction, and increases opportunities for professional development (Arhar, Johnston and Markle, 1989). Other benefits also include a support system among teachers that encourages innovation and the provision for professional autonomy and decision making about instructional and organizational issues (Clark and Clark, 1987). The following listing of additional benefits of interdisciplinary teaming for teachers reflects research and practice (Arhar, 1992; Clark and Clark, 1992; Fenwick, 1992; Mitman and Lambert, 1992).

**Benefits for Teachers.** Interdisciplinary teaming organizations:

1.  Reduce the sense of teacher isolation found in most schools. Team organizations establish the necessary frameworks that allow teachers to work together in

solving common instructional problems and to jointly focus on the needs of their students.

2.  Create a positive climate in the school by increasing teachers' sense of efficacy and renewing enthusiasm for teaching.
3.  Empower teachers to work collaboratively, giving them the autonomy to make instructional decisions based upon the individual needs of their students.
4.  Promote major changes in instructional practice. Collaborative planning of instruction which focuses on early adolescent needs and characteristics is likely to result in teachers seeking out and using more developmentally responsive teacher strategies such as cooperative learning and peer tutoring.
5.  Enhance positive communication with parents.

While there are many benefits that occur when interdisciplinary teaming organizations become a part of the school, middle level leaders also need to be cognizant of some of the potential problems. Although benefits far outweigh the problems, middle level leaders must actively address these problems if they are to be successful in creating effective teams.

1.  Teaming is a social enterprise. Successful teams are built around teachers who are skilled in human relations, planning, and decision making. When these skills are not present, the effectiveness of the team may be greatly limited.
2.  Effective interdisciplinary teams are built around teachers who like each other, work well together, and share like "beliefs" about the instruction of young adolescents. One of the major reasons teams fail is the lack of compatibility of team members.
3.  Interdisciplinary teaming programs involve change, and some teachers will resist change. Some teachers prize their individual classroom autonomy and will resist attempts to involve them in collaborative efforts with other teachers. Teachers who see themselves as rigorous content specialists may resist efforts to integrate their content area with other content areas. Resistance may also come from teachers who do not have good social, planning, or decision-making skills.

4.  Interdisciplinary teaming takes more teacher planning time. Team members who are still responsible for the instructional planning and management of their own classrooms must also allocate additional time for team planning. While some teachers will initially view this new time requirement as a burden, they soon come to value this shared time with their colleagues.

Interdisciplinary teaming organizations provide for better use of faculty, better strategies for dealing with diversified populations, better frameworks for the use of a variety of educational alternatives, and better opportunities for creating personalized instructional programs (Clark and Clark, 1987).

## Organization of Interdisciplinary Teaming

Although no two schools organize interdisciplinary teams in the same way, many schools organize their teams around the required core subjects of the middle level curriculum. The core subjects are grouped back-to-back so that team members have the flexibility to adjust time frames based upon instructional and student need. These interdisciplinary teams usually include two to four teachers from two to four subject areas who are responsible for approximately 60 to 120 students. A typical four subject "core team" would be organized as follows:

- Teachers—1 Language arts teacher, 1 social studies teacher, 1 mathematics teacher, and 1 science teacher
- Students—Approximately 120 heterogeneously grouped students (e.g., 30 students per teacher x 4 = 120 students)
- Periods—4 periods scheduled back to back and 1 common planning period for individual and/or team planning

While this is a common organizational pattern for teams, there are many other variations. For example, some sixth grade teams are scheduled with only two teachers who are given a four period block in which they are responsible for teaching the four core subject areas of language arts, social studies, mathematics, and science. This arrangement facilitates a smoother transition for sixth graders in that it provides encounters with fewer teachers during the day than in a typical six period schedule.

In many cases, a special education teacher becomes a fifth member of the team, bringing his or her students to the team.

This collaborative model, which facilitates cooperative efforts between regular and special education teachers, provides an excellent opportunity for special education students to be "mainstreamed" into the regular classroom settings and for students in the regular classrooms to benefit from the special skills and training of the special education teachers.

Various other options are available to teachers and administrators in organizing their teams. Some of these include the **F**ocus **O**n **C**oncentrated **U**nified **S**tudies schedule as seen in Figure 5-1 which limits the number of subjects taken by students each quarter and the Shelburne Plan which incorporates the whole faculty into interdisciplinary teams which are built around thematic units (Figure 5-2).

The **F**ocus **O**n **C**oncentrated **U**nified **S**tudies schedule, as used by Amphitheater Middle School in Tucson, is organized around teams of four teachers in the core subjects of language arts, social studies, mathematics and science. The students assigned to the team do not take all four subjects each day, rather half of them take two periods of language arts and two periods of social studies, while the other half takes two periods of math and two periods of science. At the end of each nine week quarter students are rotated (see Figure 5-1).

Using thematic units Shelburne Middle School (Figure 5-2) organizes their interdisciplinary teaming around exploratory experiences. Every teacher in the school is involved in one of three teams. One third of the students are assigned to each of the teams where they spend twelve weeks before being reassigned to another team.

The number of teachers on teams varies greatly, but teams of two to four teachers seem to be most commonly found (Clark and Clark, 1990a; Mac Iver, 1990). When too many persons become part of a team, it becomes more difficult to manage the logistics of planning, scheduling, and grouping; content integration; and facilities. Limiting the number of team members also reduces the potential for personality conflicts.

Teacher self-assignment to a team (voluntary) seems to have a slight advantage over being appointed to a team by an administrator, although both arrangements are found to be equally effective "in building team spirit among students, in recognizing and solving problems of individual students, and in using other team members as sources of social support" (Mac Iver, 1990; 462).

**Figure 5-1**
**Focus On Concentrated Unified Studies**
Amphitheater Middle School - Tucson, Arizona

| 6th GRADE SCHEDULE—MONDAY THROUGH THURSDAY | | | | | | |
|---|---|---|---|---|---|---|
| Trimester | Period 1<br>8:25-10:20 | Period 2<br>10:25-12:15 | Period 3<br>12:20-12:50 | Period 4<br>12:55-1:25 | Period 5<br>1:30-3:20 | Period 5<br>Music Students<br>1:30-3:20 |
| 1st 12 Weeks | Science/Math | English/Social Studies | Lunch | Home Base | Computers | Physical Education |
| 2nd 12 Weeks | Science/Math | English/Social Studies | Lunch | Home Base | Physical Education | Music |
| 3rd 12 Weeks | Science/Math | English/Social Studies | Lunch | Home Base | Musical Theater | Physical Education |

*(continued)*

**Figure 5-1** *(continued)*

| | 7th GRADE SCHEDULE—MONDAY THROUGH THURSDAY | | | | | |
| --- | --- | --- | --- | --- | --- | --- |
| *Quarter* | *Period 1*<br>*8:25-10:20* | *Period 2*<br>*10:25-12:15* | *Period 3*<br>*12:20-12:50* | *Period 4*<br>*12:55-1:25* | *Period 5*<br>*1:30-3:20* | *Period 5*<br>*Music Students*<br>*1:30-3:20* |
| 1st Nine Weeks | Science | Math | Lunch | Home Base | Physical Education | Physical Education |
| 2nd Nine Weeks | English | Social Studies | Lunch | Home Base | Lab 2000 | Music |
| 3rd Nine Weeks | Science | Math | Lunch | Home Base | Physical Education | Physical Education |
| 4th Nine Weeks | English | Social Studies | Lunch | Home Base | Conversational Spanish | Music |

*(continued)*

**Figure 5-1** *(continued)*

### 8th GRADE SCHEDULE—MONDAY THROUGH THURSDAY

| Quarter | Period 1<br>8:25-10:20 | Period 2<br>10:25-12:15 | Period 3<br>12:20-12:50 | Period 4<br>12:55-1:25 | Period 5<br>1:30-3:20 | Period 5<br>Music Students<br>1:30-3:20 |
|---|---|---|---|---|---|---|
| 1st Nine Weeks | Science | Math | Home Base | Lunch | Physical Education | Physical Education |
| 2nd Nine Weeks | English | Social Studies | Home Base | Lunch | Technology 2000 | Music |
| 3rd Nine Weeks | Science | Math | Home Base | Lunch | Physical Education | Physical Education |
| 4th Nine Weeks | English | Social Studies | Home Base | Lunch | Art | Music |

### SCHEDULE FOR FRIDAY (ALL STUDENTS)

| Period 1<br>8:25-9:50 | Period 2<br>9:55-11:20 | Period 5<br>11:25-12:45 | Lunch<br>12:45-1:15 | Special Activities<br>1:15-3:20* |
|---|---|---|---|---|

Special activities are offered in the afternoon.
*Buses leave at 1:15 and 3:25

**Figure 5-2**
Interdisciplinary Curriculum
Shelburne (Vermont) Middle School*

---

Year's Theme: A Limited Earth

*Interdisciplinary Teams/Units:*

> TECHNOLOGY TEAM
> > Theme: Energy Options for Shelburne - Year 2000
> > Team Members: (Teachers of mathematics, science, industrial arts, home economics, and a fifth grade teacher)

> HUMANITIES TEAM
> > Theme: Comparative Cultures - China/Vermont
> > Team Members: (Teachers of social studies, language arts, art, music, physical education, and a fifth grade teacher)

> COMMUNICATIONS TEAM
> > Theme: Languages are Codes - Communicating by Codes
> > Team Members: (Teachers of language arts, foreign language, typing, mathematics, physical education, and a fifth grade teacher)

*Duration of Units:*
> 12 weeks (each student spends 12 weeks in one interdisciplinary team, experiencing all three units in the span of the school year)

*Schedule:*
> Tuesdays and Thursdays 12:15-1:55 (Electives are scheduled on Mondays, Wednesdays, and Fridays)

---

* Adapted from Winton, J. (1988). Interdisciplinary Studies at the Shelburne Middle School. Schools in the Middle, Reston, VA: National Association of Secondary School Principals.

Once teams have been identified, it is crucial that team members establish procedures that will facilitate effective and efficient functioning. The first important step in organizing a team appears to be the establishment of leadership (Glatthorn and Spencer, 1986). These leaders need to be teachers who understand and know how to apply the skills of collaborative leadership. Glatthorn and Spencer (1986) suggest:

> Typically such leaders do not have access to three important sources of power: They cannot reward; they cannot punish; and they have little formal authority. In such a situation, the research suggests that they need to rely on other power sources: their expert knowledge; their control of information; and their attractiveness as individuals. They will need to be trained for this sensitive use of power (p. 156).

The importance of team leaders is confirmed by Mac Iver (1990) who reports that teams with leaders (whether elected, appointed, or rotated) appear to function better than those without leaders. He found that teams with leaders spent significantly more of their common planning time on team activities. In addition, principals reported more frequent benefits from interdisciplinary teams in schools where there were team leaders (Mac Iver, 1990).

Team planning is another important function of successful interdisciplinary teams. More team planning time appears to positively affect team effectiveness (Mac Iver, 1990). A certain degree of structure is also important to effectively functioning teams. Some middle level educators recommend that team meetings be guided by an agenda with time allocations for each agenda item so that planning meetings remain focused and productive. In addition, Merenbloom (1991) suggests that weekly, quarterly, and yearly goals help to direct the work of the team and provide structure for planning. He states: "Teams should be goal oriented; they should identify needs of students on that team and then work to meet those needs" (Merenbloom, 1991; 29). Keeping a weekly team log which addresses team goals is an excellent way to maintain goal orientation, while at the same time providing a record of team planning.

While establishing team goals and weekly agendas are important organizational functions, it is equally important that teams establish procedures and guidelines for team operation. These guidelines should address the following items (Clark and Clark, 1987):

1. Establish common and/or compatible classroom management and team management procedures. The expectancies for appropriate student behavior should be consistent among the team members.
2. Develop policies and practices for flexible student grouping within the team. Tracking should be avoided; flexible grouping for a variety of instructional experiences should be established.
3. Develop a variety of schedule alternatives (within the block of time scheduled for the team) and establish assignments that will provide equal opportunity for flexibility of time, group size, and teaching load for each teacher on the team.
4. Identify areas appropriate for large group instruction, places where the entire team can get together for films, guest speakers, and other all team activities.

5. Examine course content and establish systematic procedures to begin the integration of subject matter.
6. Establish compatible and appropriate procedures for evaluating student work and awarding grades.

Interdisciplinary teaming is a social as well as an educational enterprise. Teachers and administrators must be given the opportunity to develop the skills necessary to make teaming successful. This requires time for planning, reflection, and growth.

## TEACHER ADVISORY PROGRAMS

Middle level educators have long supported teacher advisory programs as a major component of developmentally responsive middle level schools. With the aid of a caring teacher advisor, it is believed that schooling during the middle years can become a more positive and less stressful experience. Alexander and George (1981) suggest that every middle level guidance program should include provision for students in the school to have at least one adult who will serve as an advocate. This would assure familiarity and continuity in providing advice on academic, personal, and social matters. Others also confirm the importance of every child having at least one adult advocate (Garvin, 1987; Lipsitz, 1984).

Teacher advisory programs which facilitate teachers serving as advocates for a group of young adolescents have also been strongly supported by the Carnegie Task Force on Education of Young Adolescents (1989) and the Center for Research in Elementary and Middle Schools, (CREMS) Johns Hopkins University (Mac Iver, 1990). In *Turning Points*, the Carnegie Task Force recommends that all middle level schools actively work toward "creating a climate of learning" (1989; 37). One of the strategies advocated for accomplishing this purpose is teacher advisory groups. Carnegie Task Force members believed that "every student should be well known by at least one adult" and that:

Small-group advisories, homerooms, or other arrangements enable teachers or other staff to provide guidance and actively monitor the academic and social development of students (Carnegie Task Force, 1989; 40).

The significance of teacher advisory programs in middle level schools is further enhanced by their inclusion in four major national studies of middle level schools. These include: the ASCD Study (Cawelti, 1988), the Alexander and McEwin Study (1989), the CREMS Study (Mac Iver, 1990), and the NASSP National Study of Eighth Grade (Lounsbury and Clark, 1990). The data from these studies indicate the following percentages of schools with teacher advisory programs: ASCD—29%; Alexander and McEwin—39%; CREMS—66%; NASSP—Eighth Grade Study—45%.

Even with the widespread acceptance of the importance of teacher advisory programs, it is interesting to note that with the exception of the CREMS study less than half of the middle level schools are reporting teacher advisory programs in their schools. Of those schools reporting teacher advisory programs there is strong reason to believe that many of the programs are not functioning as they were intended to function, thus limiting the effectiveness of these programs in meeting early adolescent needs (Lounsbury and Clark, 1990; Mac Iver, 1990).

## Rationale for Teacher Advisories

As a part of the school guidance program, teacher advisory programs focus specifically on the instructional and social aspects of guidance, areas that do not require specialized professional preparation. Teachers and administrators, for example, are well qualified to serve as advocates for young adolescents and to assist them in planning and achieving appropriate academic and personal/social goals. Keefe (1991) reports:

> Students are asked to make many important educational, career, and personal/social decisions, generally without much guidance. In advisement, a team of professionals and paraprofessionals works together to help students on an ongoing basis—the kind of assistance counselors do not have the time to provide (p. 161).

Some of the most frequently mentioned purposes of teacher advisories include:

1. Promote opportunities for social/emotional development in young adolescents
2. Assist students with academic and learning problems
3. Facilitate positive involvement between adults (teachers, administrators, staff) and students
4. Provide an adult advocate for every young adolescent in the school

5.  Encourage communication among students, parents, and teachers
6.  Promote positive, safe school environments

While there is still a need for considerably more research about the effectiveness of teacher advisories, there are some findings that support the importance of advisories in middle level schools. Mac Iver (1990) found that when teacher advisory groups focused on social and academic support activities a strong relationship existed to the reduction of dropouts. Connors (1986) found evidence that teacher advisory programs helped students grow socially, contributed to positive school climate, helped students learn about school and make friends, helped students get along with their classmates, and enhanced student and teacher relationships. George and Oldaker (1985) suggest that when teacher advisories are combined with other middle level programs such as interdisciplinary teaming and flexible scheduling, student self-concept improves, drop-out rates decrease, and school climate becomes more positive.

**Benefits to Students.** Teacher advisories:

1.  Promote improvement in teacher/student relationships
2.  Help students to make the transition to new school environments
3.  Give students feelings of more control over decisions
4.  Foster and promote an atmosphere of equality
5.  Help students develop a sense of positive self-worth
6.  Assist students in improving attitudes necessary for responsible citizenship
7.  Provide opportunities for students to be known by at least one adult in the school
8.  Assist students with social growth, including getting along with others and learning to make new friends
9.  Provide each student with an adult advocate
10. Provide greater opportunities for group work and participation in youth service activities

**Benefits to Teachers.** Teacher advisories:

1.  Improve teacher/student relationships on a personal level

2. Enhance opportunities to gain greater awareness and understanding of student behavior
3. Allow students to see teachers as people with likes and dislikes, hobbies, and interests
4. Contribute to a more positive school climate
5. Facilitate better home/school cooperation

Although the recent research regarding the effectiveness of teacher advisories is showing positive results (Connors, 1992; Mac Iver, 1990; Putbrese, 1989; Vars, 1989), it remains one of the most difficult of all of the middle level concepts to be implemented (Fenwick, 1992; Lounsbury and Clark, 1990).

Some of the obstacles to establishing viable teacher advisory programs include:

1. Teacher perceptions of lack of knowledge and skill to serve as advisors. Although no special skills in counseling are required to serve as a caring, nurturing advocate for young adolescents, many teachers feel that they do not have sufficient skills to function effectively in an advisory role.
2. Teacher beliefs that it is not the function of teachers to fulfill any other role than as a content specialist. Many teachers believe that asking teachers to take on additional roles detracts from their ability to be expert subject-matter teachers.
3. Being both an advisor and instructor to a group of students requires a change in roles that may be difficult for some teachers.
4. Insufficient time for planning of teacher advisory period activities. If teachers are not given time to plan for advisory activities, it does impinge on instructional planning time. In some cases the advisory period is considered as an additional subject, and as a result, contract negotiations have reduced or eliminated advisory programs (Clark and Clark, 1990b).
5. Renewed pressure for emphasis on academics. Many community members, parents, and a few educators believe that any program that takes time away from academic time should be eliminated.
6. Insufficient time and resources to plan advisory programs, develop or select materials, and prepare

teachers. Teachers need to have the opportunity to plan their advisory programs and to receive the necessary staff development to feel comfortable in their roles as advisors and advocates.

## Organization of Teacher Advisory Programs

Teacher advisory programs are organized in a variety of ways depending on the school, the faculty, and the needs of students. In most successful programs, the advisory period is scheduled regularly, varies in length from 25 to 40 minutes, frequently meets first thing in the morning, focuses on a variety of activities based on student needs, and includes virtually all certified staff as advisors.

Most frequently advisories are scheduled as a separate, designated, uniform period of time during the day and all students and certified staff participate. Advisories are often scheduled during the first period of the day, but they are also frequently scheduled during midmorning, either before or after lunch, or at the end of the day. In other cases, the additional time for the advisory period is allocated to interdisciplinary teams, and the teachers mutually decide when the advisory period will be scheduled.

The length of the advisory periods varies from 15 to 45 minutes, with most middle level educators preferring a period of 20 to 30 minutes in length (Clark and Clark, 1990a; Connors, 1992; Epstein and Mac Iver, 1990). Frequency of advisory periods also varies from daily meetings to as infrequent as once a month. Most middle level schools have a preference for daily meetings (Clark and Clark, 1990a; Epstein and Mac Iver, 1990).

Using a variety of criteria, groups of 15-30 students are assigned to each teacher advisor (Keefe, 1991). Most frequently advisory groups are comprised of students from a single grade level, a format preferred by many middle level educators (Clark and Clark, 1990a). Other middle level educators prefer teacher advisory groups that consist of equal numbers of students from each grade level. McEwin (1981) suggests that there are some advantages to this organization in that it provides for greater continuity of the advisory group and provides a good first step to multiage grouping in other areas of the curriculum.

Another organizational issue with teacher advisory programs is the question of teacher longevity with their advisory groups. Some programs provide for a new advisory teacher each year.

Other schools make provision for the teacher to remain with the same group of students for the entire time they are enrolled at the school. The latter format has certain advantages in that it allows teachers and students to get to know each other much better over a longer period of time (George, 1987).

Advisory programs differ widely in their approaches, but there is general agreement that the focus should be on young adolescents' intellectual, social, and emotional needs. Some schools organize their advisory groups around school-wide themes such as the environment, social issues, study skills, and relationships. Specific activities and lessons are developed by a school committee or purchased from a publisher and used daily or weekly by all advisory groups. The Grizzly Activity Period (GAP) at Granite Mountain Middle School in Prescott, Arizona is organized around monthly themes with a series of ongoing events integrated into the themes (see Figure 5-3).

Other schools rotate various types of focus activities around a repeating weekly schedule. Such a schedule might be as follows:

| | |
|---|---|
| Monday | Study Skills |
| Tuesday | Self-Concept/Values |
| Wednesday | Individual Academic Conferences |
| Thursday | Group Projects |
| Friday | Youth Service Activities |

The time required for preparation of materials presents a major constraint to the success of teacher advisory programs. In many cases these materials are developed by a group of teachers at each school and then given to the rest of the teachers to implement in their classrooms. In other cases, however, the teacher advisor is expected to develop materials and activities for use in his or her advisory group. As a result, even within a given school there is a great variation in the quality of the experiences being offered to young adolescents (Lounsbury and Clark, 1990; Mac Iver, 1990). It should be noted that in California more positive results were found when teachers created their own programs and materials. Canned programs developed by publishers, programs imposed by district edict or an enthusiastic administrator, or by any other means were failures without exception (Fenwick, 1992).

In the CREMS Study, Mac Iver (1990) reports that the most common activities in teacher advisories were taking attendance,

**Figure 5-3**
**Grizzly Activity Period (GAP) - An Advisor/Advisee Program***
**Granite Mountain Middle School - Prescott, Arizona**

| ONGOING GAP EVENTS | AUGUST/SEPTEMBER | OCTOBER | NOVEMBER | DECEMBER |
|---|---|---|---|---|
| Student Council reports, campaigns, elections; directed study period; sustained silent reading; Channel One News; Channel One News trivia question; review deficiencies and report cards; class assignment sheets; club days; sport days; GAP evaluation | *Here We Go Grizzlies*<br>Ice breakers and mixers<br>Student handbook trivia<br>Grizzly paws<br>Welcome dance posters<br>Note taking and study skills<br>Blue and White Day<br>Grizzly T-Shirt Day | *Octoberfest*<br>Friendship bracelets<br>Draw-a-pumpkin<br>Pumpkin carving contest<br>Halloween dress-up day<br>Magazine campaign competition | *Sharing and Caring*<br>Canned food drive<br>Gobbler Grams<br>Prejudice and dislike<br>Cards for the needy<br>Newspaper drive<br>Military pen pals<br>Holiday goodies exchange | *Holiday Traditions*<br>Holiday cards for cafeteria<br>Room/door decorating contest |
| | JANUARY | FEBRUARY | MARCH | APRIL | MAY |
| | *America Bowl*<br>America Bowl competition<br>Yellow ribbon day | *Heart and Soul*<br>Valentine cards for cafeteria<br>Friendship notes | *Name That Tune*<br>Name that tune game<br>Grizzly top five<br>Test taking skills | *Go Fly a Kite*<br>Kite building<br>Standardized testing<br>Earth Day<br>Campus clean-up<br>Recycling drive<br>Tree planting<br>Newspaper drive | *International Olympics*<br>Research of country<br>International food tasting<br>GAP evaluation<br>Olympic day |

* Adapted from Aycock, D.; Gygax-Kane, T.; Leeners, B.; Rose, D.; Sherrill, M.; and Summer, F. (1990). Grizzly Activity Period - An Advisor-Advisee Program. Prescott, AZ: Granite Mountain Middle School.

distributing notices, making announcements, and orienting students to rules and regulations. He did, however, find that 28 percent of the schools who had teacher advisory programs were focusing at least once a month on academic/social support activities. In these schools typical advisory group activities included: career and guidance, self-concept and leadership skills, academic issues, social relationships, peer group interaction, health issues, moral and ethical issues, multicultural and intergroup relationships, and in some cases, personal and family relationships.

Planning for advisories, including the determination of topics and activities, is just as important as planning for any other course in the curriculum. In addition, it is imperative that along with well-planned, purposeful activities teachers come to each advisory meeting with enthusiasm and a belief that the advisory period will be a valuable and profitable learning and developmental experience for each student.

Administrators, counselors, and teachers all play important roles in creating and maintaining successful teacher advisory programs. The building administrator is a key person in promoting the program and showing enthusiastic support for the concept in his or her school. In addition, the principal ensures that there is always a place for teacher advisories in the school schedule, exhibits a thorough understanding of teacher advisories and all of the components, arranges for continuing staff development, communicates with parents, school board members, and community members about the program, manages the continuous evaluation of the program, ensures that all faculty are effectively participating in the program, models good guidance practices in his or her own interaction with students, and when possible, participates as an advisory group leader (McEwin, 1981; Vars, 1989).

Teacher advisory programs expand the role of the guidance counselor. In addition to their continuing role of dealing with major social/emotional problems, arranging special services for needy students, and handling referrals, counselors are often called upon to serve as coordinators for the school's advisory groups. In many cases this requires the coordination of staff development, creation of learning activities that are appropriate, and ensuring that these learning activities are implemented throughout the school (Vars, 1989). In addition, counselors must provide enthusiastic support to administrators, teachers, and students; serve as a consultant to teacher advisors; and work with teachers and students, both in and out of the classroom, on problems and issues of importance to young adolescent learning and development.

The most important person in the success of advisory programs is the teacher advisor. Vars (1989) believes that, "In the hands of a skillful adviser, advisory groups reach a high level of trust and function as effective support groups" (p. 3). Skillful advisors are able to establish personal, caring relationships with their students, they are available to talk with students, they serve as listeners and "sounding boards" for student concerns, and they serve as academic advisors. Teacher advisors also make referrals, conduct and supervise appropriate activities, communicate with parents, and serve as an advocate for each child in the group by assuming the responsibility for the social and emotional education of their students (James, 1986; McEwin, 1981).

A successful teacher advisory program requires the efforts of a dedicated faculty and staff who are knowledgeable about the purposes of advisory programs and comfortable in their roles as administrators, counselors, and teacher/advisors. In implementing a program it is important that faculty and staff consider carefully the following tasks:

1. Identify and list goals and functions of the advisory program.
2. Describe the role of the principal in contributing to the success of the advisory program.
3. Describe the role of the counselor(s) in the advisory program.
4. Describe the role of the classroom teacher in the successful operation of advisory programs.
5. Determine the length, frequency of meetings per week, and time of day advisories will be scheduled.
6. Identify and list appropriate activities for the advisory meetings.
7. Determine procedures for assigning students to advisors (single grade, multigrade, number of students per advisor, degree of faculty and staff participation).
8. Determine procedures for developing or purchasing resources for use in the advisory meetings.
9. Determine staff development needs and schedule appropriate inservice sessions for advisors.

Successful teacher advisory programs are built around faculties and staffs who have a total commitment to common goals and a belief that the advisory program will be worth the time and effort. When this commitment is present, important strides can be made toward meeting the academic, social, and emotional needs of young adolescents.

## STUDENT ACTIVITY PROGRAMS

Student activity programs, sometimes called cocurricular or extra-curricular programs, are an important part of the middle level program. These programs, which usually include opportunities for school involvement, decision making, and socialization, are necessary because of the special contributions they make to the academic, social, and emotional development of young adolescents (Clark and Clark, 1990a; Glatthorn and Spencer, 1986).

One of the major purposes of any middle level activity program is to provide opportunities for all students to get meaningfully involved in some aspect of the school program, involvement that results in student engagement in a variety of learning and social experiences. It is essential, therefore, that participation be voluntary in nature and open to any student who desires to participate. State and school district regulations such as "no pass, no play," which have become a major feature in high schools, have "trickled" down to middle level schools, placing limitations on participation. Often times the very students eliminated from participation are the ones who could profit most from a continuing involvement in a school activity.

Appropriateness of the activity is also another important consideration. Many middle level schools tend to have "high school" type activity programs that feature sophisticated activities such as dances and high profile athletic programs where competition is intense and inappropriate for young adolescents. These types of activities need to be revised to be more in keeping with the developmental needs of middle level students.

Vars (1981) cautions that care must be taken in the type of activities provided for young adolescents. He suggests that activities like "informal social hours, camping and spontaneous parties, rather than evenings devoted entirely to social dancing" (p. 15) are best suited to the needs of young adolescents. Eichhorn (1966) stressed the importance of activities that include the participation of the entire student body in social events rather than the couple-like events found at the high school level. He recommended games (ping pong, shuffleboard, table games, circle games), square dances, vaudeville shows, and student performance activities.

Clubs built around academic learning interests such as math, science, environment, drama, journalism, and "reading for fun" are appropriate for middle level students. Also appropriate are special interest activities that meld the interest of students and teachers into both short-term and long-term involvements. Such activities as model airplane building, tie dyeing, barbecuing, handicrafts, rocketry, and stamp collecting have been used successfully by middle level schools.

Student government/council is one the most frequently found activities in middle level schools (Clark and Clark, 1990a; Valentine, Clark, Nickerson, and Keefe, 1981), and the way student councils function in their schools can make an important contribution to the lives of students and the climate of the school. Hovland (1990) believes that student government is the "linchpin" for a good student activities program. When student government is established in ways that ensure that each student has a voice in the school, feels empowered, and has the opportunity to participate either directly or indirectly in the governance of the school, students have a sense of ownership and pride. This empowerment sets a tone for all other activities in the school.

Johnston (1985) contends that student councils in effective middle level schools serve two, very important, distinct functions. First, the student council influences school policy and practice in an advisory fashion. The council advises the principal and faculty, discusses likely student reactions to suggested changes, and tries to affect the final outcome through persuasive arguments. Second, the council acts as service club for the school, undertaking projects that improve the quality of life at the school and securing a variety of opportunities for student participation in school events.

Athletic programs, particularly interscholastic sports, remain as one of the most popular type of activities at middle level schools. With significant modifications, such as "no cut policies," minimal playing times for all team members, and emphasis on participation rather than entirely on winning, interscholastic sports programs can make important contributions to student well-being and school climate. Despite more than 40 years of recommendations to the contrary (Clark and Thornburg, 1982), "high competition" interscholastic sports activities, which involve a very small percentage of students, are still found in many middle level schools throughout the nation. Clark and Thornburg reported that as early as 1952 a joint commission including teachers and physical educators recommended that sports activities not be offered prior to ninth grade. In the 1970s the Educational Policies Commission of the National Education Association and the American Association of School Administrators issued a strong statement recommending that varsity type sports not be permitted for junior high school boys and girls. Their recommendation was based on the opinions of 220 physicians who believed that because bone growth was still tender, muscle growth was uneven, and endurance was low due to rapid growth, intensive competition was potentially damaging to young adolescents between ages 12 and 15 (Kindred, Wololkiewicz, Michelson, Coplein, and Dyson, 1976).

The research on the effectiveness of middle level activities programs is incomplete. Educators, however, have noticed that students who participate in activities programs tend to have fewer discipline problems, better attendance, increased academic achievement (grades) while participating, and fewer out-of-school problems (Hovland, 1990). Two studies from the 1970s support the long-range benefits of participation in student activities. In a study conducted by the American College Testing Service, Munday and Davis (1974) found that out of four factors used in predicting future success (major achievement in school activities, high grades in high school, high grades in college, and high ACT scores) the only factor that could be used to predict success in later life was achievement in school activities.

Wallach (1972) also found, in examining factors that would predict how a successful person might be at a chosen career after college graduation, that there was no correlation between high scores on the SAT and success in life. His study did find that the best predictor of success in mature life was a person's performance in independent self-sustained ventures. He reported that youngsters who had hobbies, interests, and jobs, or who were active in school activities, were more likely to be successful in later life.

## Rationale for Student Activity Programs

Student activity programs provide opportunities for creative outlets that enhance character, promote personal growth, and augment classroom learning. According to Giroux and Hawley (1991) activities programs should foster continued educational development, student involvement in school, community service, and citizenship. Glatthorn and Spencer (1986) suggest that appropriate middle level activity programs include diverse activities that develop and reward multiple talents, encourage healthy boy/girl interaction without compulsory dating and dancing, and include activities that enable middle level students to develop social and interpersonal skills.

The purposes of student activity programs in the middle level school should be built around the needs of young adolescents that cannot be met solely in classrooms. These needs, as identified by Glatthorn and Spencer (1986), include a need for:

1.  Leadership and decision-making skills
2.  Healthy interactions with members of the same and the opposite sex
3.  Development of multiple talents
4.  Development of interpersonal skills
5.  Development of new relationships
6.  Development of new interests
7.  Change of pace
8.  Opportunities to celebrate and perform
9.  Opportunities to serve

**Benefits to Students.** The following list of benefits of activities programs to students has been drawn from the research and rhetoric of middle level education. Student activity programs:

1.  Get students involved in the life of the school
2.  Build self-esteem through participation in a variety of activities
3.  Develop and expand students' social and interpersonal skills
4.  Augment and expand students' classroom learning experiences and provide a "change of pace"
5.  Increase opportunity for individual achievement and recognition
6.  Decrease behavior problems and increase school attendance during times of participation
7.  Develop leadership skills and empower students to participate in the governance process of the school

8.  Develop important skills for living and working as adults
9.  Expand students' interests in lifetime leisure activities

**Benefits to Teachers.** While the advantages of an activities programs to teachers are not as apparent, it is clear that a well-organized program will foster a positive school climate. The obvious benefit to teachers, then, is happy students who day after day feel that their needs are being met. Some other benefits for teachers include:

1.  Opportunities to work with young adolescents in different settings
2.  Opportunities to share interests with students
3.  Opportunities to work closely and informally with students in the pursuit of a mutual goal
4.  Opportunities to coach or guide a group of young adolescents

While there is widespread support for student activity programs at the middle level school, there are also major concerns. First, the issue of when activities should be offered raises concerns about providing opportunities for everyone to participate, while at the same time not taking time away from classroom learning time. This is of particular concern in schools where a vast majority of the students are bussed to and from school, thus limiting their access to after school programs.

Second, the desire of a school to offer activities that are developmentally appropriate may be in conflict with parental and community demands for competitive sports programs that emphasize winning and more sophisticated "high school" activities such as night dances and proms. Third, schools wishing to develop a variety of activities for their students may find it difficult to find properly prepared volunteers (teachers and/or parents and community members) who will take the time and make the effort to sponsor activities, chaperone events, and coach interscholastic and intramural teams.

## Organizing Student Activity Programs

Successful student activity programs are organized in a variety of ways. At Orange Grove Middle School in Tucson the traditional student council approach to student participation in school governance has been expanded to include four student committees:

the principal's committee, recycling/environmental committee, activities committee, and Ambassadors—community service committee. Each committee is composed of an elected representative from each teacher advisory group whose length of term is determined by his or her advisory (one semester minimum). Over the period of a year a vast majority of the students at Orange Grove get an opportunity to participate directly in making decisions and establishing policy for the school.

In dealing with the ever present concerns regarding the scheduling of activities, Sierra Middle School, also in Tucson, added a half-an-hour period to the lunch hour. Called the x period, teachers and parents volunteered to sponsor a variety of high interest activities and clubs. These activities are offered twice weekly and students sign up to participate. On the other three days students are involved with teacher teams in study skills instruction.

The organization of developmentally responsive student activity programs requires that knowledgeable faculty and staff involve students, parents, and community members in a comprehensive planning process. As in any other planning or change process, the initial step must be a careful examination of the expectations of each of the groups. From that examination a mission statement and a listing of purposes should follow. In order to maintain congruence with the middle level school philosophy, a belief that every child should have the opportunity to participate should be a cornerstone of that philosophy. In developing the program the following questions should be asked:

1.  When will activities be scheduled to afford most students the opportunity to participate? If activities are scheduled during the regular school day (many middle level educators believe they should be), will they take time from other curricular activities?
2.  Will there be both long-term and short-term activities?
3.  How will the activities support classroom learning? How will they be integrated into the core, exploratory, and elective areas?
4.  What will be the nature of the social activities? How will teachers, administrators, students, parents and community members be involved in the decision? How often will they be scheduled?

5. How will the student government be organized in a manner that students will feel that they have a legitimate voice in school decision making? Where will the representatives come from? How will they be chosen? How will they interact with their peers?
6. What will be the nature of the athletic program? Will it include intramurals? Interscholastic competition? Where will the emphasis be placed? Will all students who try out get an opportunity to participate? Will there be eligibility requirements?
7. Who will sponsor these activities? What types of preparation will they receive? Will they receive compensation? How will parents and community members be involved?
8. How will the success of the program be determined? How will individual success be determined and recognized? Who will be involved in program evaluation?

A carefully planned and organized student activities program will have many positive benefits for students, teachers, administrators, parents, and community members. Positive benefits will be realized by assuring widespread involvement, variation of experiences and activities, and recognition of participation and success.

## SUMMARY

The three programs (interdisciplinary teaming, teacher advisories, and student activities) discussed in this chapter all play important roles in the developmentally responsive middle level school. Interdisciplinary teaming with its emphasis on collaboration has a positive influence on both teachers and students. Teachers are placed in situations where they have more autonomy over curriculum and instruction. They can plan integrated units, they can interact about problems experienced by specific students, and they can, and do, support each other professionally, socially, and emotionally. Interdisciplinary teams benefit students in a variety of ways including smaller focus groups, more teacher attention and support, integrated curriculum that makes connections to issues of importance, and more flexibility of learning time.

Teacher advisories provide an adult advocate for each student in the school. In addition, advisory periods focus on social skills, academic skills, and a variety of other issues critical to middle level students and their teachers. While admittedly a difficult program to initiate and maintain, teacher advisories have been found to support student needs and facilitate communication with parents.

Student activities provide numerous opportunities for young adolescents to become involved in the life of the school. Through participation in student government, clubs, and athletics, students expand their social skills through participation that is fun as well as instructional. Activities also facilitate cooperation and communication and afford students the opportunity of working closely with teachers and other students in the accomplishment of mutual goals or objectives.

While interdisciplinary teaming, teacher advisories, and student activities have all proven to be beneficial to both students and faculty, these benefits come about only after careful planning, implementation, and assessment. Teams must be functioning in the ways they were intended to function in order to be successful. Likewise, teacher advisories must keep the focus on social, emotional, and academic support. They must be facilitated by teachers who are enthusiastic about the program and who care about being advocates for young adolescents.

Student activities should be considered as an important part of the curriculum providing supporting experiences in academic and social learning. Activities, however, must be carefully monitored to ensure that they are developmentally responsive. Care also must be taken to plan and provide activities that are not only fun and enriching, but that are emotionally and physically safe.

Middle level leaders have the responsibility not only to assist in the planning and implementation of these three programs but to ensure that once implemented the programs are meeting the established objectives. When that happens, interdisciplinary teaming, teacher advisories, and student activities can make a major contribution to a positive school learning and emotional climate.

## REFERENCES

Alexander, W. M., & George, P. S. (1981). *The exemplary middle school.* New York: Holt, Rinehart and Winston.

Alexander, W. M., & McEwin, C. K. (1989, September). *Schools in the middle: Status and progress.* Columbus, OH: National Middle School Association.

Arhar, J. M. (1992). Interdisciplinary teaming and the social bonding of middle level students. In J. L. Irvin (Ed.), *Transforming middle level education: Perspectives and possibilities* (pp. 139-161). Needham Heights, MA: Allyn and Bacon.

Arhar, J. M., Johnston, J. H., & Markle, G. C. (1989). The effects of teaming on students. *Middle School Journal, 20*(3), 24-27.

Aycock, D.; Gygax-Kane, T.; Leeners, B.; Rose, D.; Sherrill, M.; and Summer, F. (1990). Grizzly activity period: An advisor-advisee program. Prescott, AZ: Granite Mountain Middle School.

Carnegie Task Force on Education of Young Adolescents. (1989). *Turning points: Preparing American youth for the 21st century.* Washington, D.C.: Carnegie Council on Adolescent Development.

Cawelti, G. (1988, November). Middle schools a better match with early adolescent needs, ASCD survey finds. *ASCD Curriculum Update.* Alexandria, VA: Association for Supervision and Curriculum Development.

Clark, S. N., & Clark, D. C. (1987, October). Interdisciplinary teaming programs: Organization, rationale, and implementation. *Schools in the middle: A report on trends and practices.* Reston, VA: National Association of Secondary School Principals.

Clark, S. N., & Clark, D. C. (1990a). *Arizona middle schools: A survey report.* Phoenix, AZ: Arizona Department of Education.

Clark, S. N., & Clark, D. C. (1990b). Teacher advisory programs in Arizona middle level schools. *Scope, 90*(3), 35-45.

Clark, S. N., & Clark, D. C. (1992). The pontoon transitional design: A missing link in research on interdisciplinary teaming. *Research in Middle Level Education, 15*(2), 57-81.

Clark, D. C., & Thornburg, H. (1982). Student activities: Report of a national survey. *Journal of North Carolina League of Middle/Junior High Schools, 31,* 21-22.

Connors, N. (1986). *A case study to determine the essential components and effects of an advisor/advisee program in an exemplary middle school.* Unpublished doctoral dissertation, Florida State University, Tallahassee, FL.

Connors, N. (1991). Teacher advisory: The fourth R. In J. L. Irvin (Ed.), *Transforming middle level education: Perspectives and possibilities* (pp. 162-178). Needham Heights, MA: Allyn and Bacon.

Eichhorn, D. H. (1966). *The middle school.* New York: The Center for Applied Research in Education, Inc.

Epstein, J. L. (1981). Secondary school environments and student outcomes: A review and annotated bibliography. Report No. 315. Baltimore, MD: Center for Social Organization of Schools, The Johns Hopkins University.

Epstein, J. L., & Mac Iver, D. (1990). *Education in the middle grades: National practices and trends.* Columbus, OH: National Middle School Association.

0

Fenwick, J. (1992). *Managing middle grade reform—an "American 2000" agenda.* San Diego, CA: Fenwick and Associates, Inc.

Garvin, J. (1987). What do parents expect from middle schools? *Middle School Journal, 19*(1), 3-4.

George, P. S. (1987). *Long-term teacher-student relationships: A middle school case study.* Columbus, OH: National Middle School Association.

George, P. S., & Oldaker, L. (1985). *Evidence for the middle school.* Columbus, OH: National Middle School Association.

Giroux, T., & Hawley, D. (1991). Cocurricular programs. In J. Keefe, & J. Jenkins (Eds.), *Instructional leadership handbook* (pp. 43-44). Reston, VA: National Association of Secondary School Principals.

Glatthorn, A. A., & Spencer, N. K. (1986). *Middle school/junior high principal's handbook: A practical guide for developing better schools.* Englewood Cliffs, NJ: Prentice-Hall, Inc.

Hafner, A., Ingels, S., Schneider, B., Stevenson, D., & Owings, J. (1990). *A profile of the American eighth grader: NELS '88 student description summary.* Washington, D.C.: U. S. Department of Education, Office of Educational Research.

Hovland, D. (1990). Middle level activities programs: Helping achieve academic success. *NASSP Bulletin, 74*(530), 15-18.

James, M. A. (1986). *Adviser-advisee programs: Why, what and how.* Columbus, OH: National Middle School Association.

Johnston, J. H. (1985, January). Four climates of effective middle level schools. *Schools in the middle: A report on trends and practices.* Reston, VA: National Association of Secondary School Principals.

Keefe, J. W. (1991). Advisement. In J. Keefe, & J. Jenkins (Eds.), *Instructional leadership handbook* (pp. 161-162). Reston, VA: National Association of Secondary School Principals.

Kindred, L., Wololkiewicz, R., Michelson, J., Coplein, L., & Dyson, E. (1976). *The middle school curriculum: A practitioner's handbook.* Boston, MA: Allyn and Bacon, Inc.

Lipsitz, J. S. (1984). *Successful schools for young adolescents.* New Brunswick, NJ: Transaction Books.

Lounsbury, J. H., & Clark, D. C. (1990). *Inside grade eight: From apathy to excitement.* Reston, VA: National Association of Secondary School Principals.

Mac Iver, D. (1990). Meeting the needs of young adolescents: Advisory groups, interdisciplinary teaching teams, and school transition programs. *Phi Delta Kappan, 71*(6), 458-464.

McEwin, C. K. (1981). Establishing teacher-advisory programs in middle level schools. *Journal of Early Adolescence, 1*(4), 337-348.

Merenbloom, E. Y. (1991). *The team process: Handbook for teachers.* Columbus, OH: National Middle School Association.

Mitman, A. L., & Lambert, V. L. (1992). *Instructional challenge: A casebook for middle grade educators.* San Francisco, CA: Far West Laboratory for Educational Research and Development.

Munday, L. A., & Davis, J. C. (1974). Varieties of accomplishment after college: Perspectives of meaning of academic talent. ACT Research Report No. 62. Iowa City, IA: American College Testing Service.

Putbrese, L. (1989). Advisory programs at the middle level—The students' response. *NASSP Bulletin, 73*(514), 111-115.

Rutter, M., Maughan, B., Mortimore, P., Houston, J., & Smith, A. (1979). *Fifteen thousand hours: Secondary schools and their effects on children.* Cambridge, MA: Harvard University Press.

Tye, K. A. (1985). *The junior high: School in search of a mission.* Lanham, MD: The University Press of America.

Valentine, J. W., Clark, D. C., Nickerson, N. C., & Keefe, J. W. (1981). *The middle level principalship—Volume I: A survey of middle level principals and programs.* Reston, VA: National Association of Secondary School Principals.

Vars, G. F. (1989, January). Getting closer to middle level students: Options for teacher-advisor programs. *Schools in the middle: A report on trends and practices.* Reston, VA: National Association of Secondary School Principals.

Vars, G. F. (1981). A new/old look at the needs of transescents. *Transescence, IX*(2), 15.

Wallach, M. (1972). Psychology of talent and graduate education. Paper presented at the International Conference on Cognitive Styles in Higher Education. Montreal, Canada.

Winton, J. J. (1988, October). Interdisciplinary studies at the Shelburne Middle School. *Schools in the middle: A report of trends and practices.* Reston, VA: National Association of Secondary School Principals.

# 6

# Programs which Involve Parents and Community: Parent Participation and Youth Service

> "By learning that they can make a difference in the lives of others, students discover the power to control their own lives."
>
> Sen. Edward M. Kennedy

Although the programs described in Chapter 5 (interdisciplinary teaming, teacher advisories, and student activities) provide supportive environments where students can learn and experience success, middle level leaders must look beyond the school and actively engage parents and the community in the education of young adolescents. Opportunities must be given to parents to become involved in the school and to contribute in meaningful ways to the education of their own children, and in fact, to all of the children in school. Learning in the community, particularly through providing service to others, provides unique experiences for middle level students to expand the learning that occurs in the school setting. In this chapter, the rationale for and the benefits and organization of parent participation and youth service programs will be presented.

## PARENT INVOLVEMENT PROGRAMS

Educators have always recognized the importance of parental involvement in the education of their children. Yet, in spite of the

154

clearly documented evidence of the benefits of parental involvement in students' achievement and attitudes toward school, parental participation drops off steadily during the upper elementary years and in some instances is almost nonexistent in middle level schools (Carnegie Task Force, 1989; Epstein, 1986).

Even though they say otherwise, middle level educators often do not encourage strong parent participation programs, and in some cases participation is actually discouraged (Carnegie Task Force, 1989). For many minority parents, schools are perceived as unfriendly places filled with bad memories of their own lack of success. These memories, coupled with their own lack of positive relationships with their children's teachers, tend to deepen the feelings of alienation that parents have toward the school (Comer, 1980).

Because of the many benefits to students, educators, and parents, effective parent involvement programs should be promoted, organized, and implemented. Schools need to reach out to parents, offer them meaningful roles in school governance, and involve them more in their children's education.

## Rationale for Parent Involvement Programs

The major purpose of parent involvement programs is to actively engage parents in the education of their children. Davies (1991), in examining parent participation programs across the nation, found three common themes of importance: a focus on providing success for all children, a commitment to programs designed to serve the whole child, and an emphasis on sharing the responsibility for the development of students.

Many of the parent involvement programs developed throughout the United States are developed around Epstein's (1987) five-element model of parent involvement:

1. Basic family obligations—health, safety, and positive home environment
2. Basic school obligations—communication with parents regarding their child's programs and progress
3. Parent involvement at school—volunteer activities, support of sports, performances, clubs, and other activities
4. Parent involvement in learning at home—supervising homework and helping children with skills that will be beneficial in the classroom

5.    Parent involvement in school—governance, decision
      making, advocacy, participation in parent/teacher
      groups, and advisory councils

Out of these five elements have emerged programs that emphasize parenting skills, communication, parental participation in
the classroom and school activities, parent involvement with student learning at home, and governance activities.

Helping parents meet basic family obligations, Epstein's element number one, is a concern of many middle level educators
and parents. As a result, middle level counselors and health
coordinators in numerous middle level schools have developed
programs that are designed to promote parent/child relationships, the development of healthy lifestyles, and a greater understanding of early adolescent development. These programs often
include parent workshops, video tapes, reading materials, and
special informational and recreational activities involving educators, students, and parents.

Middle level schools have an obligation to communicate effectively with parents (Epstein's second element). Successful parent
involvement programs deal with parents' needs for information
on school programs, procedures, and curricula. Communication
vehicles such as newsletters and parent networks are viable
techniques for informing parents.

Epstein and Herrick (1991) found that newsletters developed
by parent advisory groups were effective in communicating what
was going on in classrooms and the school. When asked what
information they would like to see in the newsletters, parents
requested information about how to help their children achieve in
school subjects, how to improve their writing and study skills,
and ways to deal with hygiene, sex, and drug issues (Epstein
and Herrick, 1991).

Parent communication networks are effective in getting parents involved in the life of the school. Lipsitz (1984) found that
parent advisory committees can function as "a successful communication link that scotches rumors, advocates for the school
at board meetings and for parents at school meetings, and
advises the administration about issues of current concern in the
school" (Lipsitz, 1984; 155).

Participation by parents in school activities, Epstein's third
element of parent involvement, also has positive results.
Dornbusch (1986) reported that parent participation that

amounted to no more than appearing at "back-to-school night" positively influenced his or her child's grade. Other parent participation such as conducting parent tours, chaperoning activities, going on field trips, assisting teachers, working in the office or library, tutoring students, and coaching intramural teams have all been found to have a positive influence on middle level students.

Successful parent involvement, which includes sharing in the education of their children at home, is the fourth element identified by Epstein. Johnston (1990) suggests that among the services that schools offer to families are those services that are designed to involve parents in helping to deliver the curriculum to their children. These services range from informal advice to parents on how to help their children complete projects, get ready for a test, or do homework to systematic parent workshops that help parents understand the nature of their children, school procedures and practices, and specific ways that they can tutor their children. In California, many middle level schools are providing special programs for parents of "at risk" students. These programs include opportunities to attend parenting seminars, to learn about early adolescent development, and to gain skills in helping students practice good study skills (Fenwick, 1992).

Lipsitz (1984) reports that the successful schools in her study all dealt with parental anxiety by offering classes or workshops that dealt with "adolescent development, aspects of peer relationships, and school life." She states:

> This service, about which many parents are openly appreciative, binds them with loyalty to the school while helping them to understand family interactions and school practices they may have otherwise questioned (p. 196).

There is a strong link to parental involvement in school governance (Epstein's fifth element) and successful school improvement (Chapman, 1991; D'Angelo and Adler, 1991; Davies, 1991; Warner, 1991). Ideally, parent advisory groups involved in school governance perform the following tasks: secure information through surveys, questions, telephone polls, and interviews; review school practices, policies, and procedures; inform administration and staff of issues and concerns; and make recommendations for improvement. Johnston (1990) found the power of a parent advisory panel in a big-city middle school to be multifaceted. They communicated effectively with their reference groups, they got involved in the school by conducting surveys to identify important issues and concerns, and they reviewed virtually every proposed policy change and many current school practices. This involvement, combined with a responsive administration and staff, led to student performance on conventional measures that exceeded virtually every other school in the region. The use of parent advisory boards is growing rapidly, and this expansion points to the impact that they are having on school performance and success (Johnston, 1990).

**Benefits to Students.** Some of the benefits of parent involvement in schools to the well-being of students are as follows (Chrispeels, 1991; Comer, 1980; Solomon, 1991):

1.  Students receive long-term support from parents and other adults at home in conjunction with support from teachers and staff at school.
2.  Students receive help in learning at home from parents who are more skilled and knowledgeable in assisting the learning process.
3.  Students' attitudes toward school and school work are influenced positively when their parents are involved in the school.
4.  Student achievement improves as a result of long-term parental involvement.
5.  Student achievement improves when their parents are trained to become tutors.
6.  Students receive a better education when schools, parents, and communities share the responsibility for education.

**Benefits for Teachers.** Comprehensive parent involvement also assists teachers in many ways. In addition to the benefits of better school climate and the focus on school improvement, teachers receive the following benefits (Davies, 1991; Epstein, 1981; Johnston, 1990):

1.  Teachers have a partner to support student learning at school.
2.  Teachers find they share common goals with parents regarding the education of their children.
3.  Teachers find that their job is easier and they are more successful.

4.  Teachers benefit greatly from parents' volunteer service as tutors, teaching assistants, campus supervisors, office aides, and library clerks.
5.  Teachers, by sharing the responsibility for early adolescents' learning and development with parents, can reduce the burden, the isolation, and the stress felt by many dedicated and hard-working professionals.

While all of the benefits that accrue to students, teachers, parents, and schools as a result of comprehensive parent involvement programs are not yet known, it is apparent that schools cannot be as effective if they operate in isolation from parents and the community. Effective middle level education is a collaborative process that includes the school, the family, and the community.

## Organization of Parent Involvement Programs

In organizing parent involvement programs it is helpful to identify the ways in which schools can enhance the way families can participate in the education process. Johnston (1990) identifies three areas: awareness of family variety, services to families, and provision for governance and other school participation activities.

There is incredible diversity in the make-up of families in any middle level school attendance area, and the initial stage in establishing a well-functioning parent involvement program is to raise the awareness of teachers and administrators about the richness of that diversity. Johnston (1990) describes this process of awareness as the first step in making a middle level school "family friendly."

The following procedures can be used to build awareness (Johnston, 1990):

1.  "Focus attention on school practices that affect family life, rather than upon making judgments about what is or should be normal family behavior" (p. 26).
2.  Conduct family impact assessment of programs and curriculum, rules, practices, and policies (impact of participation fees, child care and parent participation, appropriateness of projects to be completed at home, etc.).
3.  Focus attention for a portion of each faculty meeting on student and family needs that become apparent to faculty and staff members.

4.    Involve parent advisory groups in communicating
      family issues and needs to the faculty.

Middle level school educators who wish to actively involve
parents in their schools should be prepared to offer a variety of
services, services that will involve parents in the education of
their children both at home and at school. One of the most
important services that schools can provide is the effective communication of information. Many schools begin their parent
involvement programs by working to understand how and when
parents may be reached. These schools then "fine-tune their
communication to respond to the qualities, characteristics, and
needs of the parents" (D'Angelo and Adler, 1991; 350).

The following suggestions are made to guide the effective
communication of information (D'Angelo and Adler, 1991;
Johnston, 1990):

1.    Face-to-face communication is perhaps the most
      effective way of communicating with parents. This
      type of communication includes parent/teacher con-
      ferences, parent centers or parent rooms, parent
      workshops, etc.
2.    Technology, such as the telephone (teacher to parent;
      parent telephone network) and radio and TV stations
      (forums; community service announcements) can be
      used to inform parents. Video or audio tapes can be
      used to reach parents who cannot attend workshops.
3.    Newsletters and notices can also be effective in com-
      municating information to parents. Newsletters must
      be concise, readable, and address concerns of par-
      ents such as how to assist their child in completing
      homework assignments. Notices should be in the
      active voice, should ask for participation, and state
      how the activity will be helpful.

Communication, to be effective, must be adapted to the needs
of each school. Strategies used need to be determined based
upon the needs, characteristics, and expectancies of parents
and community members. Effective ways of distributing materials must also be developed. The best communication devices are
ineffective if they fail to reach the intended audiences. Strategies
must also be developed to make school meetings and workshops
appealing to parents. Topics which address family concerns,

activities which include student performance groups, meetings built around school/family potluck dinners are approaches that are successful in getting parent participation.

In addition to the communication of information to families, other services that schools provide which support active parent involvement include:

1. Home/school liaison workers who facilitate connections between the schools and parents.
2. School facilities made available for afternoon and evening social activities such as clubs, meetings, and recreational events.
3. Parents' room where parents can meet and discuss various issues of importance, coordinate parent activities, hold workshops, and organize school and community service projects.
4. Child care services for parents participating in school-related activities.
5. Scheduling of school events so that they coincide more closely with parent work schedules.
6. Regularly scheduled workshops which include information on parenting, early adolescent development, family life education, effective tutoring, and study skills.
7. Adult literacy classes which assist parents in becoming more competent readers and writers.

Two major ways in which parents have the opportunity to actively participate in schools are through involvement with parent advisory committees and volunteer service to the school. Participation on a parent advisory committee affords parents the opportunity to become involved in the decision-making process of the school. To function effectively middle level school parent/community advisory groups should be organized around the following guidelines:

1. Advisory groups should be composed of representatives from a broad section of the school community. Representation should include parents from all ethnic and socioeconomic groups.
2. Advisory group members should be selected based upon their dedication to the needs of early adolescent youth.

3.  Advisory groups should be involved in important tasks, tasks that are necessary for educational improvement, that are doable, and that give each member a sense of efficacy and accomplishment.
4.  Advisory groups need to be organized in ways that will facilitate goal achievement. This includes a clearly defined mission, appropriate and manageable tasks, and reasonable deadlines.
5.  Advisory groups need to develop a set of organizational procedures including leadership and member roles and responsibilities, procedural guidelines for the operation of meetings, frequency and location of meetings, identification of resources to support group activities and task assignments, and appropriate methods and procedures for reporting information.
6.  Advisory groups should be recognized frequently for the work that they do and their dedication to improving the educational experiences of young adolescents.

In addition to parent advisory groups, many middle level schools actively involve parents in school programs and classroom instruction. Parent volunteers make major contributions to schools by serving as teaching assistants, library and office aides, tutors, chaperones, and activity sponsors. To ensure that parent participation experiences are successful, middle level leaders need to:

1.  Identify tasks and activities that allow parents to participate in meaningful and important ways.
2.  Assign tasks and activities that fall within the skill level of the parent volunteer.
3.  Provide staff development opportunities to build skills that will assist parent volunteers in successfully carrying out their assignments.
4.  Assist teachers in identifying appropriate tasks and activities for parent volunteers.
5.  Organize a staff development program for teachers that will help them develop the skills they need for working with and supervising parent volunteers in a friendly and supportive manner.
6.  Recognize the special and unique talents of parents and place them in situations where they can use those talents.

7. Organize socials where teachers and parent volunteers can share ideas and concerns on an informal basis.
8. Recognize the work of parent volunteers often. Parent volunteers need to feel they are valued and the work that they do is having a significant impact on the school.

Effective parent involvement programs are a must for successful, developmentally responsive middle level schools. Middle level educators must understand, however, that effective parent involvement programs take time to develop and evolve. This developmental process most frequently requires the direction of a school/family coordinator who takes responsibility for the program.

Is the development of a comprehensive parent involvement program worth the time and effort? The evidence is conclusive that "any school can be successful when parents are productively involved in their children's education" and "any child can be more successful if schools link comprehensive parent involvement programs to curricula and to teaching and learning" (Solomon, 1991; 362).

## YOUTH SERVICE PROGRAMS

Youth service has become a curricular component of many middle level schools throughout the nation. The writers of *Turning Points* (Carnegie Task Force, 1989) suggest that "Every middle grade school should include youth service—supervised activity helping others in the community or in the school—in its core instructional program" (p. 45). Youth service has also been recommended by Boyer (1983), Wigginton (1985), Goodlad (1984), and the W. T. Grant Foundation (1988).

### Rationale for Youth Service Programs

While it is clear that there is a broad base of support for youth service programs in middle level and high schools, it is equally clear that there is concern among many middle level educators as to how these programs specifically benefit students. Many middle level leaders question if youth service programs are worth the time and effort required to make them successful.

The W. T. Grant Foundation Commission on Work, Family and Citizenship believes that giving all young people opportunities to serve enables them to "become contributors, problem-solvers, and partners with adults in improving their communities and the larger society." They state, "There is virtually no limit to what young people . . . can do, no social need they cannot meet." (Benson and Roehlkepartain, 1991; 1).

In a study of over 40,000 young people the Search Institute found that youth involved in youth service or helping relationships were less apt to be involved in at-risk behaviors (substance abuse, vandalism and theft, school absenteeism, depression, suicidal behaviors, and dropping out of school) than students who were not involved in service programs. They also described additional benefits of youth service programs for participants as: developing new social skills, building self-esteem, strengthening decision making and leadership skills, and nurturing an ethic of social welfare (Benson and Roehlkepartain, 1991).

Quantitative studies indicate strong support for peer tutoring with academic gains in reading and mathematics for both tutors and tutees (Hedin, 1987). In addition, other quantitative studies have also reported findings in support of youth service programs. Students who participated in youth service programs were more open minded, improved their problem-solving skills, and made gains in social and personal responsibility. Student participants also developed more favorable attitudes toward adults and became more socially competent in areas such as communicating effectively with groups, initiating conversations with strangers, and persuading adults to take their values seriously. Increases in self-esteem were found in students who tutored mentally disabled students and who engaged in helping roles. Students with behavioral problems who were assigned to service activities showed lower levels of alienation and isolation and had fewer discipline problems. It was also found that reflective sessions or discussion groups, when combined with youth service activities, assisted students to gain in both moral and ego development and made a clear difference with respect to intellectual and social dimensions of development (Calabrese and Schumer, 1986; Conrad and Hedin, 1982; Hedin, 1987; Newmann and Rutter, 1983; Rutter and Newmann, 1989).

An equally significant finding in support of youth service was the finding of Tobler (1986). In a meta-analysis of 143 drug prevention programs for adolescents, she found that of the five programs examined peer helping programs were the most effective in reducing drug usage.

The findings of qualitative research on youth service programs were equally convincing. Conrad and Hedin (1991), drawing from journal entries of over 4,000 students, concluded that "a helping relationship with another person is a much more compelling reason to act responsibly than are the demands and sanctions of school authorities" (p. 748). They also suggested that youth service programs give students a sense of connection with a wider range of people, places and problems.

After careful analysis of journal entries, Conrad and Hedin reported that youth service activities allowed adolescents the opportunity to explore some of the fundamental questions of life such as Who am I? Where am I going? Is there any point to all of it? Participants were "thinking and writing about the basic issues of adolescence and beyond: relationships, significance, connections, suffering, meaning, hope, love, and attachment" (1991; 749).

**Benefits to Students.** Researchers and practitioners report that students who participate in youth service programs:

1.  Show increases in self-esteem
2.  Feel that they are needed and that they are a valued member of the community
3.  Have increases in social and personal responsibility
4.  Feel less isolation and alienation
5.  Develop more favorable attitudes toward adults
6.  Have a better understanding of the connection between education and real life
7.  Have, in some cases, higher academic achievement

**Benefits to Teachers and Schools.** The following benefits have been found for teachers and for schools who participate in youth service programs. Youth service programs:

1.  Help build strong school/community relationships
2.  View young people as resources to the community
3.  Provide unique opportunities to work with values and attitudes
4.  Stimulate learning and social development
5.  Place information and learning in the context of real life situations
6.  Provide the impetus for the development of interdisciplinary curriculum
7.  Facilitate a more personalized process of student assessment

8. Involve the home and the community more actively in the education and development of youth by expanding formal learning beyond the walls of the school

9. Facilitate teacher/student planning and working together which results in closer relationships between students and teachers

10. Provide a vehicle for more dynamic approaches to teaching and learning

The findings of research give a strong base for youth service programs in middle level schools. The experiences of youth service programs are well tailored to meet the developmental needs of young adolescents. Educators at the middle level can take the necessary steps to develop comprehensive, viable programs, programs that will establish youth service as a continuing and important part of the curriculum.

## Organization of Youth Service Programs

In many cases youth service programs have come about as part of the school reform movement. Frequently they have provided the stimulus for more comprehensive school restructuring. Middle level teachers and administrators, in working to improve the educational experiences of their students, have looked to youth service as a way to get middle level students more involved in their schools and communities. Often youth service programs are initially centered within the school itself with students taking on duties as teacher, library, and office aides; peer tutors and cross-age tutors; and peer mediators. Youth service in middle level schools is regularly incorporated into the teacher advisory program, with the various teacher advisory groups expanding their service efforts into the community by participating in special community projects such as food drives, community beautification, and recycling.

Middle level educators must plan all service projects carefully so that they will have maximum benefits for students, the school, and those served. The following criteria, drawn from research and practice, provide guidance for the development of a school-wide comprehensive youth service program (Anderson, Kinsley, Negroni, and Price, 1991; Benson and Roehlkepartain, 1991; McPherson, 1991; Nathan and Kielsmeier, 1991; Schine, Bianco, and Seltz, 1991):

1.  Policies and procedures that will lead to an ongoing active, genuine commitment to youth service programs should be established by both schools and service receiving groups. A strong commitment from both school and community leadership to include participation by and with diverse populations is also necessary.

2.  Responsibilities of each participating group and individual should be clarified. Both students and adults need to understand their roles and responsibilities.

3.  Procedures for preparation of faculty and students, supervision and monitoring of activities, and systematic evaluation must be established.

4.  Opportunities for students to reflect regularly about their service experiences is essential in making connections between service and school learning and in the development of personal and social responsibility.

5.  Students should be involved in making the decisions about the type of service to be performed and the organization of the service activity.

6.  Service to be accomplished should be worthwhile, provide valuable learning experiences for students, and provide necessary service for the community or special group being assisted. These experiences should be ongoing and provide opportunities for students to build continuing relationships with members of the service group.

7.  Services to be provided should be valued by those receiving the service.

8.  Service projects should hold a reasonable promise for success and be manageable within the resources of the school and the community. This includes the logistics of time, transportation, and supervisory personnel.

9.  Service projects should integrate with the existing curriculum; and program goals and learning objectives, as well as activities, should be clearly articulated.

10. Regular and significant recognition should be given to the students and adults who participate in the program.

Youth service activities provide a unique opportunity for middle level educators to involve young adolescents in active learning environments. They provide an excellent vehicle for assisting students in making connections between school and "real life" and allow students to assume responsible roles within their schools and communities.

## SUMMARY

An old African saying states, "The whole village educates the child" (Davies, 1991), a message that should be embraced by all middle level educators. Schools, families, and communities must become more collaborative in sharing the role of educating young adolescents.

By actively encouraging parents to become involved, by giving them meaningful roles in decision making, and by assisting them in becoming more skilled in helping their children learn, middle level educators can establish powerful allies in the education of their children. These alliances, which typically place emphasis on improving home environments, establishing better parent/school communication, increasing parent involvement in school programs, encouraging parent involvement in home learning, and affording parent participation in school governance, not only benefit students but offer opportunities for teachers, administrators, and parents to share their concerns about the education of young adolescents. This sharing process often reduces feelings of isolation and stress for both educators and parents and unites them in school restructuring efforts.

Youth service programs, which offer students the opportunity to assist others, must be expanded. While these programs support many of the learnings that take place in the classroom, they also allow students to contribute positively to their schools and their communities. Becoming an asset to one's community and feeling needed by someone else are strong contributors to positive self-concept. Likewise, when the community is served well by young adolescents, it begins to view students as contributors, thus opening up new opportunities for service and new sources of support. Youth service programs provide an opportunity for the school and community to join together in enhancing the educational and developmental opportunities of American youth.

Parent and community involvement and youth service programs are not just another addition to the middle level program.

They are an integral part of the responsive middle level school and its efforts to create successful learning experiences for all of its students. It is, however, only through the vision and hard work of middle level leaders that these programs can become, and continue to be, viable contributors to the well-being of the students, the school, the family, and the community.

## REFERENCES

Anderson, V., Kinsley, C., Negroni, P., & Price, C. (1991). Community service learning and school improvement in Springfield, Massachusetts. *Phi Delta Kappan, 72*(10), 761-764.

Benson, P., & Roehlkepartain, E. (1991). Kids who care: Meeting the challenge of youth service involvement. *Search Institute Source, VII*(3), 1-4.

Boyer, E. (1983). *High school: A report on secondary education in America.* New York: Harper and Row.

Calabrese, R. L., & Schumer, H. (1986). The effects of service activities on adolescent alienation. *Adolescence, 21*(83), 675-687.

Carnegie Task Force on Education of Young Adolescents. (1989). *Turning points: Preparing American youth for the 21st century.* Washington, D.C.: Carnegie Council on Adolescent Development.

Chapman, W. (1991). The Illinois experience: State grants to improve schools through parent involvement. *Phi Delta Kappan, 72*(5), 359-362.

Chrispeels, J. H. (1991). District leadership in parent involvement: Policies and actions in San Diego. *Phi Delta Kappan, 72*(5), 367-371.

Comer, J. (1980). *School power: Implications of an intervention project.* New York: The Free Press.

Commission on Work, Family and Citizenship. (1988). *The forgotten half: Pathways to success for American youth and young families.* Washington, D.C.: William T. Grant Foundation.

Conrad, D., & Hedin, D. (1982). The impact of experiential education on adolescent development. *Child and Youth Services, 4*(3-4), 57-76.

Conrad, D., & Hedin, D. (1991). School-based community service: What do we know from research and theory. *Phi Delta Kappan, 72*(10), 743-749.

D'Angelo, D. A., & Adler, C. R. (1991). Chapter 1: A catalyst for improving parent involvement. *Phi Delta Kappan, 72*(5), 350-358.

Davies, D. (1991). Schools reaching out: Family, school and community partnerships for student success. *Phi Delta Kappan, 72*(5), 376-382.

Dornbusch, S. (1986). *Helping your kids make the grade.* Reston, VA: National Association of Secondary School Principals.

Epstein, J. L. (1981). Secondary school environments and student outcomes: A review and annotated bibliography. Report No. 315.

Baltimore, MD: Center for Social Organization of Schools, The Johns Hopkins University.

Epstein, J. L. (1986). Parents' reactions to teacher practices of parent involvement. *Elementary School Journal, 86*(3), 277-294.

Epstein, J. L. (1987). What principals should know about parent involvement. *Principal, 66*(3), 6-9.

Epstein, J. L., & Herrick, S. C. (1991). Improving school and family partnerships in urban middle grade schools: Orientation days and school newsletters. Report No. 10. Baltimore, MD: Center for Research on Effective Schooling for Disadvantaged Students, The Johns Hopkins University.

Fenwick, J. (1992). *Managing middle grade reform—an "American 2000" agenda.* San Diego, CA: Fenwick and Associates, Inc.

Goodlad, J. I. (1984). *A place called school.* New York: McGraw-Hill.

Hedin, D. (1987). Students as teachers: A tool for improving school climate and productivity. *Social Policy, 17*(3), 42-47.

Johnston, J. H. (1990). *The new American family and the school.* Columbus, OH: National Middle School Association.

Kennedy, E. M. (1991). National service and education for citizenship. *Phi Delta Kappan, 72*(10), 771-773.

Lipsitz, J. (1984). *Successful schools for young adolescents.* New Brunswick, NJ: Transaction Books.

McPherson, K. (1991). Project service leadership: School service projects in Washington state. *Phi Delta Kappan, 72*(10), 750-753.

Nathan, J., & Kielsmeier, J. (1991). The sleeping giant of school reform. *Phi Delta Kappan, 72*(10), 739-742.

Newmann, F. M., & Rutter, R. A. (1983). *The effects of high school community service programs on students' social development.* Madison: WI: University of Wisconsin, Center for Educational Research.

Rutter, R. A., & Newmann, F. M. (1989, October). The potential of community service to enhance civic responsibility. *Social Education, 53*(6), 371-374.

Schine, J. G., Bianco, D., & Seltz, J. (1992). Service learning for urban youth: Joining classroom and community. *Middle School Journal, 23*(5), 40-43.

Solomon, Z. P. (1991). California's policy on parent involvement: State leadership for local initiatives. *Phi Delta Kappan, 72*(5), 359-363.

Tobler, N. S. (1986). Meta-analysis of 143 adolescent drug prevention programs: Quantitative outcome results of program participants compared to a control or comparison group. *Journal of Drug Issues, 16*(4), 537-567.

Warner, I. (1991). Parents in touch: District leadership for parent involvement. *Phi Delta Kappan, 72*(5), 372-375.

Wigginton, E. (1985). *Sometimes a shining moment: Twenty years at Foxfire.* Garden City, NY: Anchor Press/Doubleday.

# SECTION III

Restructuring the Middle Level School:
Restructuring, Leadership, and Collaboration

# 7

# Restructuring and Middle Level Schools

> "Restructuring is the process of institutionalizing essential new beliefs and values in the school mission, structure and process."
>
> Richard McDonald
> Charles Mojokowski

School restructuring is built around the effective use of appropriate knowledge bases. In the case of middle level education, those knowledge bases, including the characteristics of young adolescents, middle level curriculum and instruction, and appropriate programs and practices as described in Chapters 3, 4, 5, and 6, are the foundation on which successful middle level schools are built. While the acquisition of this specific knowledge of middle level education is crucial to restructuring, using it to bring about school change is a process that does not occur automatically. It occurs only when educational leaders understand restructuring, its tasks, and the critical factors which support it in middle level schools (new leadership roles and collegial and participatory school cultures). These topics will be the focus of this chapter.

## WHAT IS SCHOOL RESTRUCTURING?

During much of the eighties, American schools were deeply involved in school improvement. These efforts largely focused on "improvement plans" that set out to increase accountability and raise student achievement scores. For the most part the reform efforts were narrowly focused on intellectual development, neglecting the other important areas of social, emotional, and physical development. Many middle level educators viewed these narrowly focused efforts as a major threat to the middle level concept of developmental responsiveness (Clark and Clark, 1986). Other educators, scholars, and policymakers were also concerned about the narrow focus of the reform movement and began to call for broader reforms. Cohen (1988) faulted school improvement efforts because they rarely got into curriculum, instruction, or other structural issues. As a leading advocate of restructuring, he suggested that school restructuring should be the "creating of multiple blueprints" for schools.

Restructuring can be classified in the categories of **technical**—changes in the curriculum and instruction of the schools, **political/social**—changes in student and parent relationships with schools, and **occupational**—changes which create more collegial workplaces and/or changes which involve teachers more in the governance process (Elmore, 1990). Ken Michaels (1988) characterized restructuring as the second wave of reform with an exciting and markedly different agenda. Among the components he identified as crucial to the restructuring process were: the school as the decision-making unit; a collegial, participatory climate among faculty, staff, and students; the flexible use of time; an environment which places emphasis on trust, high expectations, and fairness; and a curricular focus on students' understanding what they learn—knowing "why" as well as "how."

The report of the Michigan Association of Secondary School Principals, *Michigan Schools of the Future Task Force Report: Focus on Restructuring* (1990), defined restructuring as the "reforming of the interrelationships of an organization; a strategy used to analyze and redesign the organization or structure of education in order to improve student outcomes" (p. ii). They identified two key elements necessary for districts and schools promoting restructuring. These include:

- **Leadership** committed to initiating, encouraging, and sustaining the change process necessary for restructuring.
- **Belief** by the leadership that the people in the organization who actually engage children in learning are pivotal to the restructuring process (1990).

Throughout the restructuring literature great emphasis is placed upon "process." The LEAD Study Group (McDonald and Mojokowski, 1990) states: "Restructuring is a process, not a product. An organization never reaches the final state of being restructured." The Michigan Task Force (1990) also suggests that a school never becomes restructured—it is always in the process of restructuring. Lieberman and Miller (1990) expand upon the process by characterizing restructuring as steady work grounded in the day-to-day life of the school, a significant shift from the concept of innovation as an intermittent event.

In addition to the process orientation of restructuring, it is also unique from most previous reform efforts in its comprehensiveness or "wholeness." David (1991) states:

> In the past, reforms have tried to change one piece at a time, in a system of interlocking pieces. Restructuring, however, tackles all of the pieces (p. 11).

Lieberman and Miller (1990) echo David in their belief that for restructuring to occur a combination of factors must be present at the same time and over time. These factors include leadership, shared mission, school goals, promotion of collegiality, and provision for professional growth opportunities for teachers. They suggest that a comprehensive or "holistic" approach to restructuring might include significant values, standards, or beliefs; procedural means for accomplishing them; and organizational structures that provide continuous support and learning.

What drives restructuring efforts? David (1991) believes two major factors come into play. First, restructuring is driven by an emphasis on student performance based on the premise that all students can and must learn. The importance of student outcomes is also supported by Lieberman and Miller (1990) and the Michigan Task Force (1990). The second factor driving restructuring (David, 1991) is a strong, long-term commitment to fundamental and systemic change. The process of restructuring requires a long-term commitment from all involved to bring about the organizational and structural changes necessary for more developmentally appropriate middle level school programs and practices.

## WHAT ARE THE TASKS OF RESTRUCTURING?

Many listings of specific tasks of restructuring can be found in the literature. David (1991) sees restructuring tasks focusing on the identification of what students need to know and be able to do, the determination of learning experiences that will produce desired outcomes, the determination of what it takes to transfer schools into places where students will achieve the desired outcomes, and the identification of who will be responsible for ensuring that the desired results are obtained.

The tasks of restructuring suggested by Lieberman and Miller (1990) constitute what they call "the building blocks of restructuring." They include:

1.  A rethinking of curricular and instructional efforts in order to promote quality and equality for all students.
2.  A rethinking of the culture of the school.
3.  A two-pronged focus on a rich learning environment for students and professionally supportive work environment for adults.
4.  A recognition of building partnerships and networks.
5.  A recognition of the increased and changing participation of parents and the community.

While knowing the tasks of restructuring is an important first step in school restructuring, initiating a restructuring program in a middle level school is a very complex and time-consuming task. In citing management consultant Joel Barker, the Michigan Task Force (1990) suggests that two circumstances need to occur before restructuring can begin: (1) There must be an awareness that what is currently being done is not working, and (2) there needs to be a shift in existing "paradigms" so that the old truths are not maintained and new ways of doing things can be considered. Middle level restructuring, then, has a major task of confronting values and belief systems commonly held and reflected in practice by middle level teachers and administrators. New visions are needed of what middle level schooling might be like.

Elaborating on Barker's two circumstances, David (1990) believes that initiating restructuring in a school requires an **invitation to change**—reasons for and opportunities to change; **authority and flexibility**—autonomy to make decisions, freedom from constraining regulations; **access to knowledge**—the "biggest barrier to change" is the absence of knowledge and skills to do one's job differently; and **time**—time to learn, to plan, to test ideas, to maintain lines of communication.

## CRUCIAL FACTORS SUPPORTING SUCCESSFUL MIDDLE LEVEL RESTRUCTURING

While the studies done on successful school restructuring identify elements, factors, and components of successful restructuring efforts, two factors appear to be of particular importance to middle level educators. These crucial factors include:

1.  New leadership roles for administrators and teachers which require special characteristics and skills
2.  A school culture that promotes collegiality and participatory governance

These crucial factors will be addressed in the remaining part of this chapter.

### Middle Level School Leadership: Characteristics

Middle level school restructuring makes new demands on leadership. Middle level teachers and administrators must be visionary, they must change their current mind set, and they must be willing to let go of old ways of doing things. Administrators must not only be able to provide visionary leadership, but they must encourage and allow leadership to emerge from other members of the faculty. Schools need more leadership, not just stronger leaders (Schlechty, 1988). It must be acknowledged that instructional leadership inherently resides in the role of the teacher and the administrator role is to expect that s/he will be a leader of leaders.

The leadership challenge in school restructuring is how to get extraordinary things done by ordinary people. Effective leaders possess the hard-won ability to get the right things done at the right time (Drucker, 1985). Leaders build on strengths (theirs and others they work with), focus on positive opportunities, and view problems as challenges.

Seven leadership characteristics important to middle level restructuring have been identified by the authors. These include:

1.  A passion for middle level education—a vision of what a good middle level school might look like
2.  A good self-concept and a willingness to share decision making with others
3.  A concern for the well-being of all persons in the school
4.  A leadership style that is opportunity oriented

5. A model of school norms
6. A thirst for knowledge and information
7. A desire to become comfortable with and knowledgeable about change process

The effective middle level leader has a **passion for middle level schools and a vision of what those schools might be like**. S/he is motivated and excited about the possibilities of creating more responsive learning environments. Bennis (1987) believes that "every leader has a passion for the promises of life" and "if the basic ingredient for leadership is the passion for the promises of life, the key to realizing those promises is the deployment of self."

For the successful middle level leader, that "passion for the promises of life" includes a burning desire to do everything humanly possible to make his or her school developmentally responsive. Fulfilling this desire means developing one's skills and knowledge in every way possible.

Leaders must have a vision of what they believe good middle level schools should be like, a vision that is built around an informed belief system about the nature of early adolescent learners and a comprehensive knowledge base about successful middle level schools. Visionary middle level school leaders must have the ability to communicate their vision so that over time the vision becomes the shared vision of the entire faculty and staff.

**A good self-concept** is an important basis for developing a **willingness to share decision making**. Good self-concept is a crucial characteristic for successful leadership. Johnston, Markle, and Forrer (1984) suggest that in effective leaders there is a high congruence between the leader's perception of himself or herself and the view of the school and the community. Leaders who are knowledgeable and confident about their ability are likely to consult with others and share decision making with teachers, parents, and community members.

Shared decision making is a major component of middle level school restructuring. Leaders must be willing to involve other teachers and administrators in making major decisions about the direction(s) the restructuring will take. An able leader actively involves others in the leadership process. Peters and Austin (1985b) state: "Leadership is the liberation of talent. What people need from work is to be liberated, to be involved, to be accountable, and to reach their potential."

The concept of teacher empowerment, which is inherent in shared decision making, should not be viewed as the relinquishing of administrator authority. Robert St. Clair (1988), former president of the National Association of Secondary School Principals, feels that enhancing the professional status of teachers enhances the professional status of principals as well.

Shared decision making is a powerful technique for securing teacher involvement and commitment to the restructuring process. A crucial factor in the empowerment that comes from involvement in shared decision making is the importance of making informed choices based upon knowledge and information. Clark and Clark (1989) believe that teachers and administrators who are uninformed about the important issues in middle level education and about early adolescent development are least likely to make the kind of changes in their schools that will have a major impact on improving school culture or restructuring the organization of the school.

Effective middle level leaders **care about everyone in their schools**. The physical, intellectual, social, and emotional well-being of administrators, teachers, staff members, and students is crucial to the success of the restructuring efforts. Effective leaders care about teachers, support staff, students, and parents. A climate of caring, support, and nurturing is created, and as a result, everyone feels important and involved. This is a climate in which restructuring can take place.

Perhaps the following quote best illustrates the importance of caring:

> There are a lot of brilliant people in the world who are, and will remain, ineffective leaders. Why? Because they are so interested in themselves and their own accomplishments that they never get around to appreciating and understanding the feelings of other people who are sharing the world with them (Bits and Pieces, 1987).

**Looking for opportunities** is another important leadership characteristic. There is a willingness to accept challenges and to try new approaches. Peters and Austin (1985a) suggest that many organizations make it the norm **not** to be trying new things. They believe, however, that this is an error and that leaders must "reverse the normal"—making the workplace a full-fledged laboratory for learning and perpetual improvement.

Leaders must not only learn to live with change, they must insist that something productive comes from it. Middle level leaders who consider their schools to be "laboratories for learning and perpetual improvement" are well on their way to successfully restructuring their schools. Their leadership is not risk-focused but opportunity oriented.

Middle level leaders must **model the expected norms** of the restructuring school. Bennis states (1987): "As many leaders have learned, mere position and authority are not enough . . . a leader doesn't just get the message across. A leader is the message."

Leaders must be leaders in establishing appropriate "norms" for their middle level schools. To do this they must have a clear sense of school mission and a clear picture of school goals. The effective school leader must constantly be in the forefront of modeling cooperative working relationships and encouraging participation from a wide variety of persons in the decision-making process.

A **thirst for knowledge and information** is another important characteristic of successful middle level leaders. The "thirst for knowledge" is an attitude, an attitude that constantly pushes leaders beyond the "status quo." Leaders with a thirst for knowledge are not willing to settle into comfortable patterns. They are learners constantly asking questions, seeking new information, and constructing new visions.

Good leaders share this attitude with others in their school, and like a "virus" it is contagious and spreads throughout the school, fostering a climate of learning and inquiry. This climate of learning, called a community of learners (Barth, 1990), puts a premium on learning and the integration of new information into school "revisioning" and the decision-making process.

Being **comfortable with and knowledgeable about the change process** is another important characteristic of effective middle level leaders. Change is a complex process and leaders must be aware of its dynamics if their efforts to restructure their schools are to be successful. Ronald Havelock defines change as "any significant alteration to the status quo intended to benefit the people involved" (Wells, 1987). Middle level restructuring is based on the notion of change that intends to benefit the people involved: students, parents, teachers, administrators, and community members.

In bringing about change it is important to know what motivates people to change. The degree to which teachers and administrators are motivated to participate in the change process is influenced by the degree that they perceive change as:

1. Being more effective than what they are currently doing
2. Compatible with their own value system
3. Not too complex to implement, but intellectually challenging
4. Triable on a small scale with low visibility
5. Offering high visibility and recognition when successful

Change is almost always a painful process, for it requires the restructuring of one's personal and professional belief systems as well as those of the school culture. Leaders who understand the change process are patient, create nurturing, inquiring environments, establish mechanisms for networking and collaboration, and provide the time and resources necessary for the change process to be successful.

While comfort with and extensive knowledge of the change process is important, it must be recognized that restructuring middle level schools is hard work. Drucker (1986) believes that innovation makes great demands on "diligence, persistence, and commitment; and if these are lacking, no amount of talent, ingenuity, or knowledge will avail."

## Middle School Leadership: Skills

Drawing from the work of Thomas Sergiovanni (1984), the authors have identified five categories of leadership skills important in middle level school restructuring. The categories include (Sergiovanni's terms are shown in parentheses):

1. School management (technical)
2. Human relations and communication (human)
3. Curriculum and instructional management and improvement (educational)
4. Modeling and "purposing" (symbolic)
5. Creating school cultures (cultural)

The leader skilled in **school management** assumes the role of a management engineer. S/he emphasizes such concepts as planning, time management, contingency leadership, and organizational structure. Leadership in this category requires skill in planning, organizing, and coordinating the activities of the school. A competent school leader/manager is skilled at using various strategies and situations to ensure optimum success in the restructuring effort.

Leaders skilled in **human relations and communication** provide support, encouragement, and growth opportunities for teachers, administrators, and staff members by emphasizing such concepts as human relations, interpersonal competence, and motivation. These skilled leaders are able to build and maintain morale by using processes such as collaboration and decision making.

In the category of **curriculum and instructional management and improvement** leaders assume the role of clinical practitioners. At the middle level these leaders bring expert professional knowledge to the process of effective teaching, educational program development, and supervision.

Middle level curriculum and instruction leaders who are particularly strong in their knowledge of early adolescence and appropriate educational programming are able to use this knowledge for the purposes of diagnosing educational problems and for providing the supervision, evaluation, and staff development necessary to build successful programs. Many scholars and practitioners, including John Goodlad (1984), feel that this area of educational leadership is neglected or largely ignored. Part of this problem may be the traditional view of the principal as the only leader in the school and the fact that many principals feel ill at ease with curriculum and instructional issues. Perhaps this deficiency of leadership will become less apparent in restructuring schools where teachers take on more of the leadership tasks.

Sergiovanni (1984) believes that when leaders are effectively using the first three forces or skills (school management, human relations and communication, and curriculum and instructional management and improvement) they are providing the leadership necessary for competent schooling. When there is a deficit in any one of these three areas, it upsets the school's operation and less effective schools occur. These three factors are not enough, however, to provide for excellent schools. "Excellent organizations, schools among them, are characterized by other leadership qualities, forces described here as symbolic and cultural" (Sergiovanni, 1984; 7).

The leader who demonstrates **modeling and purposing** skills sends a strong message to others. By modeling important roles and behaviors, a signal is sent as to what is of value and of importance to the school. Symbolic leaders spend large amounts of time in classrooms, seek out and visibly spend time with students, downplay management concerns in favor of educational issues, and provide a unified vision of the school through proper use of words and examples. This is why symbolic middle level leaders share decision making, are active participants in school activities, and are involved in all staff development activities.

Warren Bennis (1987) argues that a compelling vision is the key ingredient of leadership in the excellent organizations he studied. Vision, according to Bennis, refers to the capacity to create and communicate a view of the desired state of affairs that induces commitment from those working in the organization.

Vision, then, becomes the substance of what is communicated as the symbolic aspects of leadership are emphasized. Middle level leaders must have a vision of the responsive middle level school and be able to communicate that vision to teachers, administrators, students, parents, and community members.

**Helping create positive school cultures** is another important leadership skill. Cultural leadership requires that the leader seek "to define, strengthen, and articulate those enduring values, beliefs, and cultural strands that give the school its unique identity" (Sergiovanni, 1984). Cultural leadership leads to the bonding of students, teachers, and administrators into a group who share the same beliefs about the mission and work of the school.

## School Cultures that Promote Collegiality and Participatory Governance

School cultures which facilitate restructuring usually include participatory decision making, site-based management or authority, and enhanced roles for teachers and parents. The LEAD Task Force (McDonald and Mojokowski, 1990) suggests that schools in the process of restructuring create cultures where teachers are given additional authority, responsibility is shared, innovation and experimentation is encouraged, a caring nurturing environment of trust and communication exists, and the focus of the school is on programs and services for its students. These schools also break down the isolation of teachers through their participation in planning and development. Increased communication with families and community members is facilitated by offering opportunities for significant involvement in the school. These changes are a result of school cultures whose norms support collegiality and participatory governance.

School cultures have the potential to either energize or undermine restructuring efforts. For that reason Saphier and King (1985) believe that "schools need to nurture and build on the cultural norms that contribute to growth." They have identified twelve cultural norms that affect school improvement, norms that can be "built where they do not exist." These norms include: (1) collegiality, (2) experimentation, (3) high expectations, (4) trust and confidence, (5) tangible support, (6) reaching out to knowledge bases, (7) appreciation and recognition, (8) caring, celebration, and humor, (9) involvement in decision making, (10) protection of what's important, (11) traditions, and (12) honest, open communication (Saphier and King, 1985; 142).

Schools with strong cultures celebrate collegiality, collaboration, risk taking, and experimentation. They also value both individuality and community. The crucial element, at least in terms of school restructuring, is that schools with strong cultures engage in continuous and increasing concrete/precise talk about teaching. Teachers and administrators frequently observe each other and provide each other with suggestions for improvement. They plan, design programs, conduct research, evaluate and prepare materials together, and they teach each other the practice of teaching (Lieberman and Miller, 1990). In effect, they have a culture that eliminates the professional and social isolation that exists in most schools. Teachers and administrators in these schools with strong cultures have structured a system of new norms that support collegial and collaborative climates.

Teacher empowerment is a term that is commonly associated with a positive change supporting school culture. The term empowerment is limiting in that it suggests that someone, usually the principal, is giving power to teachers. Empowerment in restructuring schools, viewed from a much broader perspective, suggests that the entire school is empowered. The teachers, administrators, students, and parents at the school are given the authority to make major decisions regarding school program, school structure, and organizational factors. This is the kind of empowerment that the Carnegie Task Force on Education of Young Adolescents (1989) envisioned when they recommended that "Decisions concerning the experiences of middle grade students should be made by the adults who know them best" (p. 54).

The Carnegie Task Force makes three suggestions for establishing greater school autonomy and site-based decision making.

These include giving teachers greater control and influence in the classroom—done largely through the organization of teaching teams; establishing school governance committees consisting of teachers, administrators, support staff, parents, and representatives of community agencies whose major responsibility would be shared decision making; and providing teachers with opportunities for leadership.

Enhancing the role of teachers by giving them more opportunities for leadership presents some interesting dilemmas. In most current school structures opportunities for teacher leadership are uncommon and not usually part of the accepted norms of the school culture. One exception to this is often found in successful middle level schools where teachers commonly hold leadership roles within interdisciplinary teaming structures. Another exception to this is in restructuring schools where teachers often play leadership roles in curriculum and instruction and in staff development programs.

One of the major roadblocks to teacher leadership is the sense of isolation that still exists in many schools. Teachers who do not have the opportunity to interact, plan, and problem solve together usually have few opportunities to engage in leadership functions. Lieberman and Miller (1990) suggest that "simultaneous leading and teaching" have never been formally acknowledged in conventional schools. As this new dual role becomes accepted in more and more schools, they advise that the following questions need to be asked:

- Who decides who will lead?
- What characteristics must teacher leaders have?
- What role are teacher leaders to play?
- Whom are teacher leaders to serve?
- How will these dual roles become legitimatized?

The whole concept of teacher leadership presents a challenge to the traditionally held beliefs of the administrator as **the school leader**. Sharing leadership, decision making, and authority go far beyond the accepted norms usually attributed to the role of the principal. Participatory or shared leadership is more than encouraging involvement and participation; it is more than building a good climate through effective human relations; it is more than listening, responding to, and acting on the ideas and suggestions of others; it is, in fact, a whole different philosophical approach to the management and structure of a school. As such, administrators of restructuring schools will be required to do more than just learn new skills. They will have to confront their own attitudes and belief systems about leadership.

Although site-autonomy, collegiality, trust, shared leadership, and collaborative decision making are key elements in school restructuring, different aspects of school culture may be emphasized. After extensive review of the literature and school improvement efforts, Joyce (1991) contends that the proponents of school improvement "emphasize different aspects of school culture at the outset—in other words, they choose to open different doors to school improvement. Each door opens a passageway into the culture of the school" (1991; 59). Five major emphases were identified by Joyce.

1. **Collegiality**—cohesive personal/professional relationships within the school and with parents and community groups.
2. **Research**—the study by the school faculties of the research on school effectiveness and/or successful school practices, strategies, etc.
3. **Site-specific information**—the collection and analysis of data by the faculty in regards to student success and school programs.
4. **Curriculum initiatives**—changes within content areas or across curriculum areas such as technology or interdisciplinary curriculum initiatives.
5. **Instructional initiatives**—the study of instructional alternatives and strategies.

While Joyce believes that any one of these emphases can change school cultures significantly, he is concerned about the dangers of advocating any one of the approaches as the "panacea" for school restructuring. Specifically he suggests that a synthesis of the ideas found in these approaches would be more appropriate and effective. He states:

> Major school improvement programs probably need to begin with agreement by all parties that all the doors will be open, with collegial faculties using research and site-specific information and studying and improving curriculum and instruction (Joyce, 1991; 61-62).

Levine (1991), in his studies of the creation of effective schools, identified nine important factors that emerged from research on multischool restructuring projects. These factors, which can serve as guidelines to middle level educators involved in school restructuring, are as follows:

1. Substantial staff development for all participants; at least part of it done during the regular teaching day
2. Issues of instructional improvement must be addressed fairly early in the school improvement project
3. Avoidance of getting "bogged down" in elaborate schemes of a particular practice in the early stages of the project
4. Sharply focused improvement goals which do not overload teachers
5. Significant technical assistance must be available
6. Programs are data-driven in the sense that appropriate information should be collected and used to guide participants in planning, decision making, and implementing
7. Avoidance of reliance on bureaucratic processes that stress forms and checklists as well as mandated components rigidly applied to schools and classrooms
8. Identification and use of materials, methods and approaches that have been successful in schools elsewhere
9. Judicious mixture of local school autonomy and control from the central office—a kind of "directed autonomy" (Levine, 1991; 390-393).

Levine's factors for effective school restructuring, along with a comprehensive knowledge of early adolescent development, middle level curriculum and instruction, and successful programs and practices, provide excellent guidelines for middle level restructuring.

## SUMMARY

Restructuring, with its emphasis on leadership, shared mission and goals, collegiality, and professional development, provides new challenges for middle level leadership. These challenges include rethinking the curriculum of the school, changing the culture of the school to be more supportive of change and new ideas, creating rich, safe learning environments for both students and adults, building partnerships and networks with other educational and social agencies, and increasing the participation of parents and community members in the operation of the school.

In meeting these challenges, both administrators and teacher leaders must recognize the importance of leadership by example. Their behaviors must be characterized by a passion and vision for middle level schools, a willingness to share decision making, and a concern for the well-being of all who attend or work in the school. Effective leaders of restructuring middle level schools are persons who are comfortable with change, who are engaged in continuous learning, and who are ready to seize available opportunities and act on them. These characteristics are symbolic of leaders engaged in school improvement.

Successful school restructuring is supported by cultures that energize the school improvement process. These cultures are typically built around a shared vision, collaborative decision making, high levels of participation, teacher leadership, and site-based management. Within these cultures are safe environments that allow all participants to inquire, to reflect, and to become actively involved in the school change process.

Organizing cultures which support middle level school restructuring will be the focus of the next chapter. Special emphasis will be placed on shared decision making and site-based management.

## REFERENCES

Barth, R. S. (1990). *Improving schools from within.* San Francisco, CA: Jossey-Bass Publishers.

Bennis, W. (1987). Leadership in the 21st century. In W. Butler, & W. Strode (Eds.), *The University of Southern California* (pp. 13-15). Louisville, KY: Harmony House Publishers.

*Bits and Pieces.* (1987). Fairfield, NJ: The Economic Press, Inc. F(7).

Carnegie Task Force on Education of Young Adolescents. (1989). *Turning points: Preparing American youth for the 21st century.* Washington, D.C.: Carnegie Council on Adolescent Development.

Clark, S. N., & Clark, D. C. (1986, September). Middle level programs: More than academics. *Schools in the middle: A report on trends and practices.* Reston, VA: National Association of Secondary School Principals.

Clark, S. N., & Clark, D. C. (1989, February). School restructuring: A leadership challenge for middle level administrators. *Schools in the middle: A report of trends and practices.* Reston, VA: National Association of Secondary School Principals.

Cohen, M. (1988). Restructuring schools: Frequently invoked, rarely defined. *ASCD Update*. 30(1), 1, 6-7.

David, J. L. (1991). What it takes to restructure education. *Educational Leadership, 48*(8), 11-15.

Drucker, P. F. (1985). *Innovation and Entrepreneurship*. New York: Harper & Row.

Drucker, P. F. (1986). Principles of innovation: The do's and don'ts. *Modern Office Technology, 31*(2), 12-16.

Elmore, R. (1990). On changing the structure of public schools. In R. Elmore (Ed.), *Restructuring schools*. Oakland, CA: Jossey-Bass.

Goodlad, J. . (1984). *A place called school: Prospects for the future*. New York: McGraw Hill.

Johnston, J. H., Markle, G. C., & Forrer, D. (1984). What the research says to the practitioner—About effective middle level principals. *Middle School Journal, 15*(3), 14-17.

Joyce, B. R. (1991). The door to school improvement. *Educational Leadership, 48*(8), 59-62.

Levine, D. U. (1991). Creating effective schools: Findings and implications from research and practice. *Phi Delta Kappan, 72*(5), 389-393.

Lieberman, A., & Miller, L. (1990). Restructuring schools: What matters and what works. *Phi Delta Kappan, 71*(10), 759-764.

McDonald, R., & Mojokowski, C. (Co-chairs). (1990). *Developing leaders for restructuring schools* (pp. 35-51). Washington, D.C.: Office of Educational Research and Improvement, U. S. Department of Education.

Michaels, K. (1988). Caution: Second-wave reform taking place. *Educational Leadership, 45*(5), 3.

Michigan Schools of the Future Task Force. (1990). *Michigan schools of the future task force report: Focus on restructuring*. Ann Arbor, MI: Michigan Association of Secondary School Principals.

National LEADership Network Study Group on Restructuring Schools. (1990). *Developing leaders for restructuring schools: New habits of mind and heart*. Reston, VA: National Association of Secondary School Principals.

Peters, T. J., & Austin, N. J. (1985). Bone-deep beliefs: Simple secrets of success. *Modern Office Technology, 30*(11), 16-20.

Saphier, J., & King, M. (1985). Good seeds grow in strong cultures. *Educational Leadership, 42*(6), 142-148.

Schlechty, P. (1988). Issue. *ASCD Update, 30*(1), 4-5.

Sergiovanni, T. (1984). Leadership and excellence in schooling. *Educational Leadership, 41*(5), 4-13.

St. Clair, R. (1988). Issue. *ASCD Update*, 30(1), 4-5.

Wells, R. L. (1987). Preparing students for career changes. In M. Gregory, & W. Daniel (Eds.), *Business education for a changing world: National Business Education Association Yearbook* (pp. 16-28). Reston, VA: National Business Education Association.

# 8

## Collaboration and Middle
## Level School Restructuring

> "No profession can survive, let alone
> flourish, when its members are cut
> off from others and from the rich
> knowledge base on which success
> and excellence depend."
>
> Roland Barth

Cultures which support change are built around collegial relationships which emphasize school improvement through collaboration. As discussed in Chapter 7, collaboration can take many
forms, including participatory decision making, site-based management, teacher empowerment, and teacher leadership.
Whatever the format of participation, research has shown that
collaboration enhances teachers' sense of efficacy, improves the
quality of decision making, creates positive school climate, and
supports school change (Lindelow, Coursen, Mazzarella,
Heynderickz, and Smith, 1989; Shedd and Bacharach, 1991;
Smith and Scott, 1990).

The focus of this chapter will be on collaboration and its
importance to the middle level restructuring process. School cultures of teacher and administrator isolation will be compared to
those that promote collaboration. In addition, strategies for
involvement will be discussed, and procedures for organizing
collaborative environments which focus on school change will
be presented.

## SCHOOL CULTURES OF ISOLATION
## AND OF COLLABORATION

### Cultures of Isolation

The rhetoric of middle level education is strongly supportive of collaborative environments, yet the research on practice suggests that in many middle level schools teacher and administrator isolation is a predominate factor (Clark and Clark, 1993; Lounsbury and Clark, 1990). The fact that less than half of the nation's middle level schools report the most common form of collaboration, interdisciplinary teaming organizations, lends additional support to the notion that most teachers perform their work in isolation. As a result, they receive no benefits from teaching with each other, from sharing expertise, or from support systems that are typically found in collaborative environments. These environments of isolation offer teachers and administrators few opportunities to engage in substantive dialogue or to exchange information (Shedd and Bacharach, 1991).

Teacher isolation in middle level schools is reinforced by many factors, including facilities which provide few suitable places for teachers to meet and confer and rigid schedules that provide little or no time for teachers to exchange ideas or plan together. It is, however, school cultural norms that provide the most significant barriers to collaboration. Commonly accepted norms of noninterference discourage the seeking of and the giving of advice. In fact, requests for peer assistance are often considered to be indicators of incompetence (Aston, Webb, and Doda, 1982; Rosenholtz, 1985a; Shedd and Bacharach, 1991). In addition to cultural norms that mitigate against collaboration, many teachers actively work to maintain isolation, an isolation they believe necessary to protect the time they need to meet all of the demands required of them (Flinders, 1988).

Teacher isolation has been found to work against school effectiveness and school improvement in a variety of ways. Drawing from research (Rosenholtz, 1985b; Sarason, 1982; Shedd, 1985; Shedd and Bacharach, 1991; Smith and Scott, 1990), teacher isolation has been found to:

1.    Impede teachers in the performance of their responsibilities

2.  Force teachers to learn by trial and error. When cut
    off from effective teacher role models, teachers tend
    to fall back on their own days as students
3.  Contribute to resistance to change
4.  Restrict the opportunities to engage in interaction
5.  Impede professional growth by making it difficult for
    teachers and administrators to exchange ideas
6.  Compound the problem of beginning teachers who
    find it difficult to build relationships where ques-
    tions can be asked and problems discussed without
    fear of evaluation

## Cultures of Collaboration

Collaboration, with its emphasis on collaborative planning, collegial relationships, and sense of community, provides middle
level teachers and administrators with a viable approach to
school restructuring. Involvement clearly enhances the ability
of the school to respond to problems and opportunities and
increases effectiveness, efficiency, and productivity (Shedd and
Bacharach, 1991). Involvement also leads to better decision making, enhanced relationships between teachers and administrators, and higher employee satisfaction (Smith and Scott, 1990).
In addition, collaboration facilitates better decisions by eliciting
more viewpoints and improves communication by opening more
channels. Human resources are also used more effectively in
collaborative environments, and the distance between decisions
and implementation is reduced (Lindelow et. al., 1989). It is evident from the research that collaborative environments increase
job satisfaction, help reduce conflict, reduce stress and burnout,
and raise morale and trust for school leaders (Shedd and
Bacharach, 1991).

Other benefits of teacher and administrator collaboration are
as follows (Little, 1982; Purkey and Smith, 1982; Rosenholtz,
1985b; Rosenholtz, 1989; Shedd and Bacharach, 1991; Smith
and Scott, 1990):

1.  Teachers in collaborative schools share ideas about
    instruction. They view teacher leaders as persons
    who show initiative, are willing to share with oth-
    ers, and are willing to assist others in solving
    instructional problems.
2.  Schools where teachers talk to each other, design
    their instruction together, and teach each other have

higher achievement scores than schools where teachers work in isolation. Collaboration is a strong predictor of student achievement.

3. Collegial relationships fostered by collaboration break down barriers between departments and among teachers and administrators. Collegiality also encourages intellectual discourse that leads to consensus and promotes feelings of unity and commonality among the staff.

4. Collaboration supports professional development and contributes to improved teaching and learning.

5. Collaborative environments are particularly helpful to beginning teachers.

6. Teacher participation is critical to the success of any change effort.

In spite of the many benefits of collaboration, especially participatory decision making, middle level teachers appear to be only minimally involved. Results reported in the National Association of Secondary School Principals' Study of Leadership in Middle Level Schools (Valentine, Clark, Irvin, Keefe, and Melton, 1993), indicated that leadership teams and staff committees had low levels of participation in decision making. Their involvement consisted most typically of making recommendations or participating in discussions.

## COLLABORATIVE APPROACHES—TEACHER LEADERSHIP, DECISION MAKING, AND INFLUENCE

School collaboration can and does take many forms including opportunities for teacher leadership, structures for participatory decision making, procedures for sharing influence, and participation in networks and partnerships (Figure 8-1). The many approaches available for the sharing of authority and influence may account for the differing perceptions of administrators and teachers about the decision-making processes in schools. Shedd and Bacharach (1991) reported that in an assessment of school decision making 93 percent of the principals reported "decision making in my school is a collaborative process." Only 32 percent of the teachers agreed with the same statement. Differences in perceptions were attributed to principals' belief that giving teachers opportunities to share opinions was collaboration. Teachers,

**Figure 8-1**
Approaches to Middle Level School Collaboration

1. Teacher Leadership
   • Team Leaders
   • Department Heads
   • Mentors/Coaches
   • Teacher Evaluators

2. Decision Making
   • Site-Based Management
   • Organizational Development
   • School Improvement Teams
   • Quality Circles

3. Influence and Communication
   • Standing Committees
   • Advisory Groups
   • Ad Hoc Committees/Task Forces

4. Partnership and Networks
   • Other Schools
   • Universities
   • Parents
   • Community Groups

however, "dismissed mere consultation, particularly if it involved a handpicked group of teachers . . ." (p. 141).

Building involvement in decision making presents some major challenges for middle level leaders. These challenges, which focus around issues of influence and authority, raise some interesting questions: How can authority be shared while still meeting the demands for administrator accountability expected by superintendents? How can schools be organized to facilitate broadly based participation in decision making? Who should be involved in decision making? Who should be involved in advisory (influencing) capacities? Answers to these questions lie in the various forms adopted for collaboration and the attitudes and willingness of middle level leaders to share decision making in ways that are meaningful and significant.

## Collaboration Which Facilitates Teacher Leadership

Traditionally high school and middle level teachers have been involved in school leadership. This leadership is most commonly organized around academic departments with teachers assuming the traditional roles of department heads. While important, this type of leadership has tended to be narrow in scope, focusing primarily on decisions regarding materials and curricular issues related to the department.

In collaborative schools teachers are assuming different kinds of leadership roles. Teachers are serving effectively as instructional leaders by assuming roles of **mentors** or **coaches**. Using their expertise, they work with other teachers in instructional improvement and curricular revision. Teachers are also playing key leadership roles in peer assessment programs. As **teacher evaluators** they direct assessment efforts and cooperatively develop individual teacher improvement plans.

Teachers also exercise leadership through memberships on decision-making councils, leadership of committees and task forces, and coordinators of career ladder programs. These roles all rely heavily on teacher expertise and their involvement in and influence on decision making.

## Collaboration Which Facilitates Decision Making

Collaborative decision making extends the authority to make significant decisions about the school and its programs to the various school stakeholder groups. This extension of decision making is most commonly organized around site-based management, organizational development, school improvement teams, and quality circles.

The most powerful forms of participatory decision making are found in **site-based management**. These large scale efforts aimed at consolidating the authority for school operation at the building level are largely dependent on the willingness of central office staff and the school board to enable teachers and administrators to make the decisions about what is best for the students at their schools. Within the parameters of the mission and goals of the school district, each school has the power to make decisions about curricula, programs, professional development, scheduling, personnel, assessment/evaluation, and budget.

In site-based management schools the decision-making process is almost always facilitated by school leadership councils composed of representatives from the various stakeholder groups in the school and community. The work of the school leadership council is usually augmented by specialized committees and task forces which involve faculty, staff, and parents as active participants in the management of the school. The success of site-based management depends upon the ability of the leadership to build trust, to provide for open channels of communication, to obtain widespread involvement, and to provide the necessary support systems for decision making.

**Organizational development**, with its emphasis on improving the ability of the various structures of a school to change or modify, provides an excellent vehicle for collaborative decision making. Based on the premise that schools can successfully change themselves, organizational development focuses on change and school improvement through clarifying goals, improving communication among various elements of the school community, and tapping the school's unused resources.

In organizational development, the development of a school improvement or restructuring plan is of critical importance. Of equal importance to success is the use of an outside facilitator to initiate the restructuring plan and to prepare teachers and administrators for the leadership tasks to continue the plan. With its emphasis on collaboration, organizational development facilitates decision making through the reexamination of goals, identification of group norms, and analysis of current practice. These collaborative efforts lead to a shared vision about the purposes of the school and a restructuring plan that is developed and implemented by those closest to the school: the teachers, administrators, students, and parents.

**School improvement teams** incorporate many of the elements of organizational development, although on a smaller scale. In most cases school improvement teams focus on specific elements of the school such as reducing the number of dropouts or improving the students' achievement in mathematics. School improvement teams may also be organized on a district-wide basis to study a particular problem and develop approaches for its solution. Collaboration facilitates the study of the issue and the decision-making process by involving those closest to the problem with the resources and authority to make the necessary changes.

**Quality circles** serve the purpose of providing structures for teachers to work collaboratively on school improvement, curricular programs, and instructional issues. Adapted from industry, quality circles consist of a small group of people (teachers) with common interests who meet regularly to define and solve problems. Trained in the use of techniques such as brainstorming, consensus, cause and effect analysis, data gathering and analysis, and effective communication, members of quality circles share power and influence decisions (Smith and Scott, 1990).

In middle level schools, the best example of the informal use of quality circles is found in interdisciplinary teaming structures. In these structures, teachers interact regularly, focusing on common issues and problems concerning curriculum and instruction, scheduling practices, and student achievement. This reflective practice gives teachers a sense of efficacy and empowers them to modify programs and practice to best suit the needs of their students.

## Collaboration Which Facilitates Opportunities to Influence and Communicate

Not all collaboration directly involves others in decision making, offering instead the opportunity to communicate ideas and to influence policy and decision making. Organizational arrangements such as standing committees, advisory groups, and ad hoc committees offer opportunities for teachers, parents, and community groups to advise and influence.

**Standing committees** are often organized around the various school structures of scheduling, content organization, student activities, instruction, instructional resources, and assessment. Although these committees may have some decision-making authority, their major function is to monitor programs and to make recommendation(s) for improvement. Standing committees are a continuing part of the collaborative governance of the school.

**Advisory groups**, which are found in many middle level schools, extend to the various constituencies of the school the opportunity to influence the decision-making process. These advisory groups perform a variety of functions including data gathering, making recommendations, sharing the opinions of various stakeholder groups, and communicating policies and decisions.

Parent/school/community advisory groups, the most common form of school advisory groups, are generally organized for the purposes of building closer bonds between the school, home, and community; to promote cooperation in the education of young adolescents; and to facilitate communication. Because of the continuing importance of these purposes, parent/school/community advisory groups play a significant part in the school governance process.

**Ad hoc committees** or **task forces** are committees organized to study a specific problem or issue and make recommendations for improvement. When their tasks are completed, ad hoc committees and task forces are usually disbanded.

## Collaboration Which Supports Partnerships and Networks

Involvement with others outside of the specific middle level school setting can enhance the restructuring process. **Networking** with other schools, for instance, provides opportunities for teachers and administrators to exchange ideas, tap into different perspectives, and build supportive networks. **Partnerships** with colleges and universities have the potential to involve practitioners and scholars in professional development activities, resource development, research, and initial teacher preparation. In addition, partnerships with community groups, social service agencies, service clubs, and local businesses offer numerous opportunities for educators and community members to collaborate on the education of young adolescents.

## STRUCTURING SUCCESSFUL MIDDLE LEVEL SCHOOL COLLABORATION

There are many ways in which teachers, administrators, parents, and community members can be involved in collaborative efforts. Whether the collaboration is direct involvement in decision making or participation as an influencer, leadership plays an important role in its success. Leaders, by valuing and recognizing the contributions of each teacher, staff member, student, and parent, give high visibility to the collaborative process.

Leaders also bolster collaboration by providing guidance in establishing procedures for the identification of tasks and the organization and operation of collaborative groups. Providing the necessary support systems for participatory decision making is also critical to success (Figure 8-2).

## The Tasks of the Collaborative Decision-Making Group

Determining the tasks of the decision-making group is the initial task in establishing successful collaboration. In making this determination, two factors must be considered: (1) who decides what the tasks will be and (2) what areas, topics, or tasks are "off limits"?

In many instances the work of decision-making committees is focused on particular tasks, topics, subjects, or issues assigned

**Figure 8-2**
Structuring Successful Collaboration

---

1. Determination of Tasks for Collaborative Groups
   - Who Decides?
   - What's "Off Limits?"

2. Organization of Collaborative Groups
   - Representation
   - Expertise
   - Appropriate Number of Members
   - Selection Process
   - Motivation of Group Members

3. Operation of Collaborative Groups
   - Role of Members
   - Procedures
   - Honesty and Trust

4. Support for Collaborative Groups
   - Meaningful Involvement
   - Time for Working Together
   - Recognition
   - Funding
   - Professional Development

---

to them by the school-site administration. Tasks assigned to a school collaborative decision-making group may also be related to the implementation of district goals or other agendas for improvement. In these cases, the tasks of decision making are carefully defined, and collaborative groups are empowered to act within the parameters of these definitions.

In some middle level schools, the tasks are largely determined by the participants, consisting of teachers, administrators, students, parents, and community members. The organizational development approach, for instance, which is presented in Chapter 9, involves representatives of stakeholder groups in the process of determining needs, clarifying purposes, establishing goals and objectives, developing a strategic plan, implementing the plan, and assessing the program. At every stage of the process collaborative groups determine the issues they will study and the scope of their decision-making authority.

In strategic planning (Chapter 9), individuals from the numerous school constituencies are usually organized into various groups that have specific responsibilities and tasks. The work of these groups is frequently coordinated by a school leadership council. This council, to the extent of its granted authority, is responsible for dealing with the major issues of school operation and improvement. It is frequently the function of the school leadership council to define the scope of decision-making responsibility and the procedures for operation of the standing committees, advisory groups, and ad hoc committees.

Within any school organizational structure there will be limitations placed on collaborative decision making. These limitations often include state and school district policies regarding personnel issues and curricular issues. In most schools, however, the authority to act on specific issues and make decisions comes as a result of a clear delegation of authority (empowerment) by the administration (Howard and Keefe, 1991). Determining factors as to the extent of the shared decision making are largely based on the school administrator's perceptions of authority, comfort level with collaborative decision making, confidence in the decision-making groups, and pressures for accountability from the district office.

## Organization and Operation of Collaborative Groups

Successful participatory decision making requires that special attention be given to the composition of the collaborative groups, including the requirements for expertise, the breadth of representation, and the processes for selection. Attention must also be given to the operational aspects of groups with emphasis placed on procedural guidelines, decision-making processes, and the building of trust.

**Organization.** In determining the composition of a collaborative decision-making group, the purpose of the group and its needs for specialized membership must be carefully considered. For example, the school leadership council and/or school improvement team has several important needs. These groups need expertise in the processes of collaboration and decision making, expertise in middle level school organization and program development, expertise in curriculum and instruction, expertise in early adolescent development and student services, expertise in professional development, expertise in communication with school constituencies, and expertise in program assessment. In addition to specific expertise, a school leadership council or school improvement team needs to be representative of the interests of the various stakeholder groups. Accommodating these two major needs are major factors in the selection of membership.

Harvey (1990) suggests that the composition of the leadership team should consist of five to ten members and be composed of decision makers (persons in authority), stakeholders, experts, supporters, resisters, and facilitators. More specifically, a school leadership council charged with the responsibility of developing and coordinating the strategic plan described in Chapter 9 might consist of teachers, parents, the principal, a counselor, a staff member, a school board member, community members, and a central office administrator.

In addition to expertise and representation, the selection of participants for involvement in collaborative decision making should include selection/identification procedures and motivation to participate. There are several ways of determining membership of collaborative groups, including appointment, self-selection, and election by fellow teachers. Marburger (1985) suggests that election by the faculty can ensure representative membership on committees as long as ability and not popularity is the criterion. He also suggests that self-selection can populate committees with persons with appropriate expertise and motivation.

People are motivated to become involved for a variety of reasons. Good collaborative group members are usually drawn from those persons who will be most affected by the decisions to be made and who have a high desire to be involved. Also of importance is the involvement of those who have the necessary expertise. Unfortunately, in some cases those with the expertise do not also have a high desire to participate. The offer of additional time for planning, special "perks" such as conference attendance and school visitations, and monetary grants may provide the incentives needed for participation.

For many persons, however, the prime reason for involvement is the sense of efficacy they realize from their participation. For that reason, leaders must structure collaborative decision-making groups so that participants have important work to do, have a clear sense of purpose, and are committed to achieving that purpose. Each member of a collaborative group must feel that his or her survival and success is in his or her own hands (Harvey, 1990).

Selection processes for each school will differ according to purposes of the groups and the belief systems of the administration. While each committee may be different, and selection criteria may differ, criterion must be developed and used to ensure the availability of expertise, the breadth of representation, and high levels of motivation.

**Operation.** Individuals and groups must thoroughly understand their role in the process of decision making. While this understanding can be facilitated by guidelines, the need for highly structured guidelines differs depending on factors such as the specificity or the openness of the task. Collaborative decision-making groups such as standing and ad hoc committees who are confronting specific tasks usually require less structure, while decisions made by the school leadership council, for instance, which are less defined and more open, have a greater need for a structured process.

In addition to processes for conducting deliberations, collaborative decision-making groups must also address the procedures for making decisions. With its ability to support serious consideration for each person's viewpoint and its emphasis on group process, many scholars and practitioners support the use of consensus. There are times, however, when voting or some other decision-making technique may be just as appropriate. Situations and issues must determine the appropriate strategies for making decisions (Shedd and Bacharach, 1991).

The ability of collaborative groups to work effectively is built on a climate of honesty and trust. "All forms of school-based management are based on a process of trust" (Lindelow and Heynderickz, 1989; 133), and building that trust must be one of the initial processes in establishing collaborative decision making. Harvey (1990) suggests that the first meeting of any collaborative group should be focused on team building, the discussion of hidden agendas, and the review of norms and beliefs. The importance of learning to listen and developing the necessary skills for using site-based management successfully are emphasized by Bergman (1992). He also stresses the importance of sharing information, understanding feelings, building trust, and promoting open communication.

Once the foundation of trust and honesty is in place, teachers, administrators, parents, and community members can use established procedures and processes to collaborate effectively in the restructuring of middle level schools.

## Supporting Collaborative Decision Making

Collaboration in decision making is supported by administrator commitment to involvement, provision of resources, and opportunities for professional development.

Building principals must exhibit a strong commitment to involvement in decision making, and this commitment must not only be verbalized but it must be backed by actions. Administrators exhibit support by becoming personally involved in collaboratives, by giving verbal support, and by monitoring progress. Administrators also have available to them numerous strategies they can use to encourage collaboration. These include advising teachers on instructional practice, running interference for teachers who wish to collaborate, incorporating collaborative practices into current school structures, and modeling effective procedures of classroom observation and teacher assessment (Smith and Scott, 1990). It is crucial that school administrators play an active role in influencing school norms, norms that support collaboration.

Numerous resources are necessary to support participatory decision making. Harvey (1990) suggests that the following factors support collaboration: time, effective leadership, funding, freedom to act, energy and excitement, recognition, opportunity to network, and empowerment. Of these factors the element of time is the most critical. Collaborators need time to study and analyze information; time for administrators and teachers to support improvement; time for faculties, parents, and community groups to examine and debate curriculum and instructional issues; and time to improve the norms of collegiality (Bird and Little, 1986).

Finding the time to collaborate, while difficult in most middle level schools, is absolutely essential. Although many schools use planning periods, lunch hours, before and after school as meeting times, it has been found that use of these time frames (discretionary time) have several disadvantages. First, the shortness of these time periods, which cannot be organized into larger blocks, limits exploration and reflection. Second, the belief of many teachers that discretionary time is their time for planning lessons and other instructional tasks also mitigates against the use of discretionary time for collaboration (Dawson, 1984). Providing time for teachers to collaborate by releasing students early from class or hiring substitutes makes available larger blocks of time for involvement and a more relaxing climate for interaction. In addition, the support of these types of arrangements gives teachers evidence of commitment by the administration to collaborative planning and decision making (Dawson, 1984).

Other resources important to involvement in decision making are recognition of participation and funding support. The recognition of good work does much to support positive climates of collegial collaboration. Verbal as well as written praise are essential in supporting participatory decision making. Decision making is time consuming and hard work; and teachers, parents, and community members need to feel that their efforts are appreciated.

Funding provides additional support of and incentives for involvement. Primarily used in the area of professional development, this funding provides the resources for participants to meet in larger blocks of time, attend conferences, visit schools, secure expertise, and purchase resource materials.

Professional development must also be a continuing part of the collaborative process. Preparing participants to be skillful in group process, team building, problem solving, change process, school improvement, and decision making is an important first step (Caldwell and Wood, 1992). For example, staff development, where emphasis was placed on organizational development issues such as problem solving, group process, and conflict resolution, was cited as the key element to success in site-based management in one school district (Bahrenfuss, 1992).

In addition to training on the processes of collaborative decision making, teachers, administrators, parents, and community members may require professional development that is focused on specific areas of curriculum, instruction, and program development. Specific expertise is essential to informed and effective decision making, and opportunities to develop expertise must be provided.

## ORGANIZING COLLABORATION FOR STRATEGIC PLANNING

The starting point of any school's move to collaborative decision making must be centered around a needs assessment that determines where the school is on a continuum between isolation and collaboration (Smith and Scott, 1990). Such an assessment can determine past and current experiences with collaborative structures, assist in making decisions about types of structures to adopt, and provide a basis for making professional development plans.

In addition to examining the current levels of collaboration, middle level leaders need to expand the knowledge base of faculty, staff, parents, and community members about the needs and characteristics of young adolescents, appropriate curricular structures, and successful middle level programs and practices. Techniques that can be used in building this awareness include (Clark and Clark, 1983):

1. **Seed planting**—giving ideas and suggestions to key teachers, parents, and community members.
2. **Articles**—duplication of articles that address important issues and/or report middle level research and successful practices.
3. **Books and resources**—purchase of middle level books, audio tapes, video tapes, and other appropriate materials.
4. **Workshops**—use of consultants and media presentations.
5. **Conferences**—sending teachers, administrators, parents, and community members to local, regional, and national conferences and conventions.
6. **Visitations**—visits or interchanges with other middle level schools.

With an understanding of the school's previous experience with participatory decision making and an awareness of early adolescent characteristics, appropriate curriculum, and successful programs and practices, the school faculty, staff and constituents have the foundation on which to construct successful collaborative decision-making structures.

Building on a foundation of knowledge and drawing from the research and practice described in this chapter, the following steps are recommended for organizing collaborative decision making for the strategic planning process presented in Chapter 9.

1. Organize the committee structure for the school. These committees should include the two school coordinating

committees (School Leadership Council, Staff Development Steering Committee); the school standing committees (Scheduling, Content, Advisories/Activities, Methods/Strategies, Resources, Evaluation, and Personnel); and advisory groups (parent/school/ community). Ad hoc/task force committees are established as needed.

2.  Determine membership of each committee using predetermined criteria (expertise, representation, selection procedures, and motivation). Each member of the committees must feel a sense of efficacy and empowerment. He or she must feel that there is a real need for his or her involvement and that by being involved he or she can make a real difference in the school.

3.  Define the purposes of each committee. For example, the purpose of the School Leadership Council might be to coordinate the development and implementation of the strategic plan by identifying tasks, determining responsibilities, providing resources, and establishing deadlines. The School Leadership Council should also clarify the purposes and goals of each of the Standing Committees as well its functions, the authority of the committee, the provisions for committee leadership, the resources available, and the deadlines for completion of the various tasks assigned to the committee.

4.  Provide information to all groups. This would include staff development on the processes of collaboration and decision making. Information, in a usable format, must be available to all committee members. All decisions and recommendations must be data driven, derived from research, literature, and successful practice.

5.  Provide adequate time for committees to meet. Meeting times convenient to all committee members must be established. Time allocation is particularly critical because it reflects the commitment of the district and the school leadership to the involvement of all constituency groups in the process of reflection so necessary to the strategic planning process.

## SUMMARY

Collaborative decision making is a basic ingredient in the process of successful middle level school restructuring. With its emphasis on collegial environments and involvement in significant decisions, collaboration reinforces the importance of each teacher, administrator, parent, and community member in the process of providing responsive programs for young adolescents.

Collaborative environments provide climates where faculty and staff can investigate, reflect, and improve learning situations. They make provision for parents and community members to be closely involved in the educational and decision-making process. Collaborative environments also make provision for the sharing of dreams, ideas, and expertise, a sharing that often results in higher quality decisions. In addition, involvement offers all groups a sense of efficacy, the power to make a difference in the direction and success of the school.

The importance of collaboration as presented in this chapter lies in its power to create environments where faculty, staff, parents, and community members can work cooperatively to promote appropriate learning opportunities for middle level students. Collaborative decision making provides the basis for the development and implementation of the strategic plan (Chapter 9), the organization of staff development (Chapter 10), and the development of procedures for school program assessment and evaluation (Chapter 11).

## REFERENCES

Aston, P., Webb, R., & Doda, N. (1982). *A study of teachers' source of efficacy—Final report, Vol. 1.* Gainesville, FL: The University of Florida.

Bahrenfuss, R. (1992). Four years later—How Greece, N.Y., uses site-based management. *Educational Leadership, 50*(1), 42-43.

Barth, R. (1986). The principal and the profession of teaching. *The Elementary School Journal, 86*(4), 471-492.

Bergman, A. (1992). Lessons for principals from site-based management. *Educational Leadership, 50*(1), 48-51.

Bird, T., & Little, J. (1986). How schools organize the teaching occupation. *The Elementary School Journal, 86*(4), 493-511.

Caldwell, S., & Wood, F. (1992). Breaking ground in restructuring. *Educational Leadership, 50*(1), 41-44.

Clark, S., & Clark, D. (1983, October). Staff development programs for middle level schools. *Schools in the middle: A report on trends and practices.* Reston, VA: National Association of Secondary School Principals.

Clark, S., & Clark, D. (1993). Middle level school reform: The rhetoric and the reality. *The Elementary School Journal, 93*(5), 447-460.

Dawson, J. (1984). *The principal's role in facilitating teacher participation. Mediating the influence of school context.* Philadelphia, PA: Research for Better Schools, Inc.

Flinders, D. (1988). Teacher isolation and the new reform. *Journal of Curriculum and Supervision, 5*(4), 17-29.

Harvey, T. (1990). *Checklist for change: A programatic approach to creating and controlling change.* Needham Heights, MA: Allyn and Bacon.

Howard, E., & Keefe, J. (1991). *The CASE-IMS school improvement process.* Reston, VA: National Association of Secondary School Principals.

Lindelow, J., Coursen, D., Mazzarella, J., Heynderickz, J., & Smith, S. (1989). Participative decision making. In S. Smith, & P. Piele (Eds.), *School leadership: Handbook for excellence* (pp. 152-167). Eugene, OR: ERIC Clearinghouse on Educational Management, University of Oregon.

Lindelow, J., & Heynderickz, J. (1989). School-based management. In S. Smith, & P. Piele (Eds.), *School leadership: Handbook for excellence* (pp. 109-134). Eugene, OR: ERIC Clearinghouse on Educational Management, University of Oregon.

Little, J. (1982). Norms of collegiality and experimentation: Workplace conditions of school success. *American Educational Research Journal, 19*(3), 325-240.

Lounsbury, J., & Clark, D. (1990). *Inside grade eight: From apathy to excitement.* Reston, VA: National Association of Secondary School Principals.

Marburger, C. (1985). *One school at a time. School based management: A process for change.* Columbia, MD: National Committee for Citizens in Education.

Purkey, S., & Smith, M. (1982). *Effective schools: A review.* Madison, WI: Wisconsin Center for Educational Research, University of Wisconsin.

Rosenholtz, S. (1985a). Effective schools: Interpreting the data. *American Journal of Education, 93,* 352-388.

Rosenholtz, S. (1985b). Political myths about educational reform: Lessons from research on teaching. *Phi Delta Kappan, 66*(5), 349-355.

Rosenholtz, S. (1989). *Teachers' workplace: The social organization of schools.* New York: Longman.

Sarason, S. 1982. *The culture of school and the problem of change.* Boston, MA: Allyn and Bacon.

Shedd, J. (1985). *From the front of the classroom: A study of the work of teachers.* Ithaca, NY: Educational Systems Division, Organizational Analysis and Practice.

Shedd, J., & Bacharach, S. (1991). *Tangled hierarchies: Teachers as professionals and the management of schools.* San Francisco, CA: Jossey-Bass Publishers.

Smith, S., & Scott, J. (1990). *The collaborative school: A work environment for effective instruction.* Eugene, OR: ERIC Clearinghouse on Educational Management/National Association of Secondary School Principals.

Valentine, J., Clark, D., Irvin, J., Keefe, J., & Melton, G. (1993). *Leadership in middle level education—Vol. 1: A national survey of middle level leaders and schools.* Reston, VA: National Association of Secondary School Principals.

# SECTION IV

Restructuring the Middle Level School:
Developing, Implementing, and
Evaluating the Strategic Plan

# 9

# Developing the Restructuring Plan

> "Strategic planners must have the
> courage to imagine the world they
> want their children to live in, then
> find practical ways to achieve their
> vision."
>
> Roger Kaufman
> Jerry Herman

Informed leadership is a crucial element in successful middle level school restructuring. Implementation of developmentally responsive programs, however, requires more than just informed leaders. It requires leaders who are (1) skilled in involving a variety of stakeholders (teachers, administrators, students, parents, and community members), (2) skilled in using group process, (3) skilled in collecting and using information, (4) skilled at building consensus, and (5) skilled in communicating the vision of effective middle level education. These are the kind of leaders who are required for the successful strategic long-range planning necessary for school restructuring.

The goal of this chapter is twofold: (1) to briefly examine strategic planning, its rationale and elements, and (2) to provide a "planning structure" that will assist middle level leaders in developing plans and procedures for the systematic implementation of change.

## STRATEGIC PLANNING

Strategic planning is an effective tool for bringing about change and school restructuring. While the goals of the plan for restructuring may be broadly or narrowly focused, Kaufman and Herman (1991) believe that strategic planning is most powerful when the planning results are concentrated on achieving the ideal vision at the individual, organizational, and societal levels. The model they have developed involves planners in the consideration of three levels: "the community and society to which learners go when they have completed school, the educational system itself, and individuals or small groups" (p. 4). Consideration of these three issues, called "scoping" by Kaufman and Herman, leads to the identification of the "ideal vision." Planners are then involved in data collection, and in the planning, implementation, and evaluation activities that provide practical strategies for achieving the identified vision.

The alternative futures approach, popular in the mid 1970s (Chase and Clark, 1974), has resurfaced in this decade as a viable form of strategic planning. Programs such as ED QUEST (Mecca and Adams, 1991), which incorporates the use of alternative futures, assists educational leaders in identifying trends and issues that will have an impact on their schools and districts. Common elements of alternative futures planning include clarifying or identifying the nature of the school, scanning the external environment (needs assessment), identifying and forecasting external changes, creating a model for the future (the ideal vision), developing and analyzing alternative futures or outcomes, developing/selecting appropriate goals, and developing and implementing procedures that will lead toward goal accomplishment (Chase and Clark, 1974; Clark and Clark, 1984; Clark, Clark and Thomas, 1979; Mecca and Adams, 1991).

Successful strategic planning must be reality based, data driven, and built on a strong foundation of theory and research on change. It must support collegial collaboration, professional development, and adult learning (Blum and Kneidek, 1971; Kaufman and Herman, 1991). School restructuring, based on effective strategic planning, must include the development of clear school goals, systematic communication between school and community, sufficient time for new program development (3-5 years), and principals and other school leaders who assume the role of change agents—"informing, motivating, and leading" (English and Hill, 1990).

The goal of strategic planning is, of course, to develop a systematic, gradual approach for bringing about the major changes required in school restructuring. With its focus on developing plans to achieve a "vision," strategic planning provides a process for clarification of mission, broadly based involvement, comprehensive assessment, site-based decision making, and the orderly implementation of change. In short, strategic planning at the middle level is a process that involves educators, students, parents, and community members in a careful examination of their school, its mission, its programs, and its strengths and weaknesses. Strategic planning provides an opportunity to study the special needs of young adolescents, assess community needs, identify trends and issues, develop a new "vision," and apply knowledge gained from research and experience to make the vision a reality.

## DEVELOPING A PLAN FOR RESTRUCTURING THE MIDDLE LEVEL SCHOOL

The structure for planning presented in the following section will include two major areas: (1) Developing a foundation for restructuring (program clarification, needs assessment, creation of the mission/vision/purposes, and identification of program goals) and (2) Developing the restructuring plan (analysis of program goals and development of operational objectives, organization of sequence for implementation of operational objectives, and development of activity lists for program implementation) (Figure 9-1).

**Figure 9-1**
The Strategic Planning Process

---

**Seven Stages of Planning**

Phase 1—Building a Foundation for Planning

Stage 1—Clarify Purpose
Stage 2—Collect and Analyze Information
Stage 3—Develop Mission Statement and General Goals
Stage 4—Determine Program Goals

Phase 2—Developing the Strategic Long-Range Plan

Stage 5—Analyze Program Goals/ Determine Operational Objectives
Stage 6—Sequence Implementation of Operational Objectives
Stage 7—Develop Yearly Activity Lists for Program Implementation

---

## PHASE I—DEVELOPING A FOUNDATION
## FOR RESTRUCTURING

This "structure" for restructuring builds on many of the issues identified in previous chapters. Within the parameters allowed by the school district, the decisions must be made at the building level. Involvement must come from all stakeholders (teachers, administrators, students, parents, and community members). Collaboration is crucial for success. Leadership must come from various stakeholder groups, and procedures must exist which provide leaders and members of their planning teams with time to reflect and make decisions as well as time for staff development and other preparation activities.

### Clarify Purpose

It is easy for middle level educators to get caught up in the day-to-day operations of schooling and lose sight of the school's reason for existence. As a result, the mission, the goals, the purposes of middle level education so important in formulating and maintaining responsive programs get lost in institutional bureaucracy. To recapture a sense of purposefulness and direction, the process of planning for restructuring must begin with a careful examination of current school practices, current rationale for the school, and a profile of what a student who has gone through the program *should look like*. Three major questions guide the process of clarification: Why are we doing what we are doing? Do we agree on the rationale for the existence of this school? What is the desired profile of our ultimate product? (Howell, 1981).

The process of answering these questions gives middle level educators a clearer picture of their school's functions and purposes. Clarification establishes a climate of inquiry that permeates the entire restructuring process. By initially establishing "what should and what could be," a focus is given which provides direction to the collection and analysis of information, to the determination of needs and appropriate responses to those needs, and to the development of the vision as represented by a statement of mission.

**Processes.** Organize into groups consisting of administrators, teachers, parents, students, and community members:

- Address the three clarification questions
    Why are we doing what we are doing?

> Do we agree on the rationale for the existence of this school?
>
> What is the desired profile of our ultimate product?

- Identify needed resources to answer questions
- Set timelines for answering questions and making recommendations
- Report preliminary information to all school constituencies with reference to the implications of answers to restructuring efforts (e.g., resources, needed information, time allocations, and staff development needs)

## Collect and Analyze Information

A major theme throughout this book has been the importance of information to support the decision-making process. Middle level restructuring decisions must be supported by accurate data. In Stage 2 procedures are organized and developed which lead to the collection of information which describes (1) the nature of the community (its demographics; its needs; its goals), (2) the nature of the young adolescent (general developmental characteristics—see Chapter 3, specific characteristics of enrolled students—for example, intellectual, physical, social, and emotional), (3) the nature of the school (its programs; its curriculum; its responsiveness to the needs of young adolescents), and (4) the knowledge base of educators, parents, and community members (early adolescent characteristics—Chapter 3; successful middle level programs—Chapters 4, 5, and 6) (Figure 9-2).

Middle level schools, to properly serve their communities, must have an understanding of the "contexts" outside of the school setting. Much of the information gathered by national and state demographers may be of great help in assisting school decision makers in understanding their communities. The following resources provide good information on national trends and issues:

- The Gallup Poll published each September in the *Phi Delta Kappan*. The reports of these annual polls provide excellent information on trends and issues in education and public attitudes toward American education.
- National reports by demographers such as Harold Hodgkinson's *All One System: Demographics of Education from Kindergarten Through Graduate School* (1985) and *The Same Client: Demographics of Education and Service Delivery*

**Figure 9-2**

Questions to Guide the Collection of Information

---

1. The nature of the community

   What are the specific demographics of this community that have an impact on this school? How do these demographics compare to national and state data?

   What do parents and community members see as the major purposes/goals of this school?

2. The nature of the young adolescents attending this school

   What are the specific needs of young adolescents in this community? In this school? (intellectual, physical, social, and emotional)

   How do these specific needs compare to those identified by national and state demographers?

3. The nature of this middle level school

   What are the strengths and weaknesses of this school? (opinions of teachers, students, administrators, parents, and community members)

   What recommendations should be made for school improvement? (teachers, students, administrators, parents, and community members)

4. The knowledge base of decision makers

   How knowledgeable are teachers, administrators, parents, and community members of the general characteristics of adolescent development and specific needs of the students in this school?

   Are teachers, administrators, parents, and community members knowledgeable about successful middle level programs?

---

(1989). These are both excellent resources for gaining a picture of major issues in our society and their relationship to education.

- The United Way of America's *What Lies Ahead: Countdown to the 21st Century* (1991) provides "the hard facts, the calculated projections, the informed opinions, and the educated guesses" (Brandt, 1991) about many important areas including racial and cultural diversity and environmental issues.

- *National Educational Longitudinal Study of 1988—A Profile of the American Eighth Grader* (Hafner, Ingels, Schneider, Stevenson, and Owings, 1990) provides an excellent overview of the status of young adolescents in America.

At the local level, planning teams can use a process called environmental scanning (Poole, 1991). This process calls for the gathering of information about the social, economic, political, and technical environment in which the middle level school operates. This information, which in most cases is available from local and state social service agencies, the local chamber of commerce, economic development agencies, realtor associations, and local corporations, gives guidance about the outside forces that may affect the school restructuring process.

If middle level schools are sincere about focusing on the developmental needs of their students, teachers, administrators, parents, and community members must have a thorough understanding of the general characteristics of young adolescents and of the specific needs of the students they serve. An overview of the general needs and characteristics was given in Chapter 3, but the information presented in the overview must be supplemented by specific information about the students enrolled in the school undergoing restructuring. Profiles should be developed that include data about academic achievement, special needs and problems (social, emotional, physical), self-concept, and attitudes toward teachers and the school. Other data important in determining specific needs are socioeconomic status, family status (for example, single parent family), and availability of adult supervision after school ("latchkey" kids).

Information such as academic achievement (as measured by standardized tests) is probably already available in each student's cumulative record. Numerous scales and instruments for measuring self-concept are available. The Search Institute's *Profiles of Student Life: Attitudes and Behaviors* is a particularly comprehensive measure of young adolescent behaviors, attitudes, and values (Blyth and Roehlkepartain, 1992). Teacher and parent observations, locally developed instruments, and student journals also provide insights into student self-concept. By systematically approaching the gathering of data about the students in their school with whatever methods are deemed appropriate, administrators, teachers, and parents can get a fairly clear picture of the socio/emotional, intellectual, and physical characteristics and needs of the children in their school. This information is vital in the development of the vision for the school.

Assessment procedures must include a thorough examination of the current school program. Leaders of the planning process must provide opportunities for their colleagues to identify strengths and weaknesses of the school. This process can be accomplished in numerous ways using formal instruments such as the *Comprehensive Assessment of School Environments* (Howard and Keefe, 1991) or the *Middle Grades Assessment Program* (Dorman, 1984) or locally developed procedures such as the Structured Interview which can also be used with small task groups (Figure 9-3).

In the process of determining school strengths and weaknesses, recommendations for school improvement must also be addressed. In identifying school weaknesses, every respondent or task group should also be asked at the same time to made a recommendation or suggestion for improvement for every "weakness" mentioned. These specific recommendations can then become part of the information used in developing the restructuring plan.

Through the process of program assessment, administrators, teachers, parents, and community members acquire a much more accurate picture of "what's working and what's not." This process, which identifies school strengths and school weaknesses, allows the various stakeholders to further clarify "what their school is all about" and to reflect about what the school's mission should really be. In assessing school programs, educators, parents, and community members are also forced to confront the school's shortcomings and to consider procedures to remedy them.

Assessing each individual's knowledge base in the area of early adolescent characteristics is not an easy task. Most frequently, data is gathered through classroom observations, discussions and interviews, and staff development experiences. Insights can also be gained as to administrator, teacher, parent, and community member knowledge about young adolescents by examining the responses to question No. 1 in the Structured Interview for both professional staff and parent/community members (Figure 9-3). Determining knowledge of middle level programs can be done through survey instruments such as *The Middle Level School* (Figure 9-4), a twenty-five item Likert scale instrument that determines program acceptability and degree of implementation (Clark and Valentine, 1981). The extent of knowledge of successful middle level programs can also be determined by examining the responses of teachers, administrators, and counselors to questions No. 5 and No. 6 in the Structured Interview (Figure 9-3) and parents' and community members' responses to question No. 5.

**Figure 9-3**
Structured Interview

*Form A: Professional Staff (Teachers, Administrators, Counselors)*

1.  What do you believe are the major needs of the young adolescents in this school?
    Intellectual
    Social
    Emotional
    Physical
2.  What do you believe should be the major purpose(s) of this school?
3.  What do you believe are the major strengths of this school?
4.  What do you believe are the major weaknesses of this school?
5.  What specific recommendations would you make for improving this school?
6.  What are some middle level school programs that you have seen, heard about, or read about that you think would be particularly appropriate for this school?
7.  What processes are you now using to anticipate future program or curricular needs?
8.  What major changes have you seen in this school in the last two years?
9.  What conditions do you see having significant influence on this school in the next five years?

*Form B: Parents/Community Members*

1.  How would you describe the typical student who attends this school? (Characteristics, needs, attitudes, behavior)
2.  What do you believe should be the major purposes of this school? (Goals, programs, curricular emphasis)
3.  What do you believe are the major strengths of this school?
4.  What do you believe are the major weaknesses of this school?
5.  What specific recommendations would you make for improving this school?
6.  What major changes have you seen in this school in the last two years?
7.  What conditions do you see having significant influence on this school in the next five years?

*Form C: Students*

1.  What do you really like about this school? (major strengths)
2.  If a new boy or girl moved to your neighborhood and asked you about this school, what would you tell him/her?
3.  What do you think needs to be improved?
4.  What specific suggestions would you make that would make this school better?
5.  What changes have occurred in this school since you first enrolled?
6.  In what ways does this school help you?
7.  What classes or subjects are most helpful?
8.  Who do you go to if you have a problem and want to get some help in solving it?

**Figure 9-4**
Middle Level Questionnaire*

*The Middle Level School*

Listed below are several goals and characteristics often used to describe middle level educational programs. Read each statement, then assess the statement in two ways. First, mark the degree to which the statement is *appropriate* (IDEAL) in your present educational setting. Then mark the degree to which the statement *is being implemented* (REAL) in your present educational setting.

| The Middle Level School Should | Appropriateness in Present Setting | | | | Current Level of Implementation | | | |
|---|---|---|---|---|---|---|---|---|
| | NA = Not Appropriate SA = Somewhat Appropriate A = Appropriate VA = Very Appropriate | | | | NI = No Implementation LI = Low Implementation AI = Adequate Implementation HI = High Implementation | | | |
| | NA | SA | A | VA | NI | LI | AI | HI |
| 1. Incorporate an interdisciplinary approach to the teaching of the basic skills courses in grades 6, 7, 8. | 1 | 2 | 3 | 4 | 1 | 2 | 3 | 4 |
| 2. Provide the opportunity for parents and students to select from programs representing a traditional subject-centered six- or seven-period day or a more nontraditional interdisciplinary approach. | 1 | 2 | 3 | 4 | 1 | 2 | 3 | 4 |
| 3. Provide learning processes which include practical approaches to individualizing the learning process through the utilization of small-group/large-group instruction and independent study. | 1 | 2 | 3 | 4 | 1 | 2 | 3 | 4 |
| 4. Provide a program centered around the developmental needs of the student rather than a traditional content-based program. | 1 | 2 | 3 | 4 | 1 | 2 | 3 | 4 |

*(continued)*

**Figure 9-4** (continued)

| The Middle Level School Should | NA | SA | A | VA | NI | LI | AI | HI |
|---|---|---|---|---|---|---|---|---|
| 5. Consider both the physical and emotional development of the students and thus provide differing types of extracurricular social programs for the students (parties, dances, etc.). | 1 | 2 | 3 | 4 | 1 | 2 | 3 | 4 |
| 6. Consider both the physical and emotional development of the students and thus provide athletic activities for the students (sports, intramurals, etc.) | 1 | 2 | 3 | 4 | 1 | 2 | 3 | 4 |
| 7. Provide a curriculum of basic skills in English, math, science, and the social sciences. | 1 | 2 | 3 | 4 | 1 | 2 | 3 | 4 |
| 8. Provide required reading program for all students at all grade levels. | 1 | 2 | 3 | 4 | 1 | 2 | 3 | 4 |
| 9. Provide a required exposure to exploratory courses in fine arts and practical arts. | 1 | 2 | 3 | 4 | 1 | 2 | 3 | 4 |
| 10. Provide a daily physical education program for all students which stresses conditioning activities and team and individual sports based upon the physical development level of the individual student. | 1 | 2 | 3 | 4 | 1 | 2 | 3 | 4 |
| 11. Provide a required health/sex education program for all students. | 1 | 2 | 3 | 4 | 1 | 2 | 3 | 4 |
| 12. Provide for the incorporation of values clarification, self-awareness, and group awareness into the basic curricular program. | 1 | 2 | 3 | 4 | 1 | 2 | 3 | 4 |
| 13. Provide opportunities for enrichment experiences for students. | 1 | 2 | 3 | 4 | 1 | 2 | 3 | 4 |
| 14. Provide opportunities for remediation experiences for the students. | 1 | 2 | 3 | 4 | 1 | 2 | 3 | 4 |
| 15. Provide a co-curricular program of mini-courses or special interest courses or programs offered during the school day on a regularly scheduled basis. (For example, once a week; twice a month.) | 1 | 2 | 3 | 4 | 1 | 2 | 3 | 4 |

(continued)

**Figure 9-4** *(continued)*

| The Middle Level School Should | NA | SA | A | VA | NI | LI | AI | HI |
|---|---|---|---|---|---|---|---|---|
| 16. Provide a time for school clubs or interest groups to meet during the school day on a regularly scheduled basis. | 1 | 2 | 3 | 4 | 1 | 2 | 3 | 4 |
| 17. Provide a teaching staff skilled in the ability to understand, relate to, and work with students of this age group. | 1 | 2 | 3 | 4 | 1 | 2 | 3 | 4 |
| 18. Provide appropriate planning times for members of the teaching staff, including common planning times for teaching teams. | 1 | 2 | 3 | 4 | 1 | 2 | 3 | 4 |
| 19. Provide a teacher-student guidance or advisory program which enables each student to relate and interact in a special way with his or her adviser (teacher). | 1 | 2 | 3 | 4 | 1 | 2 | 3 | 4 |
| 20. Provide a grade reporting system which assesses students based upon individual ability and related progress and incorporates parent contacts and conferences. | 1 | 2 | 3 | 4 | 1 | 2 | 3 | 4 |
| 21. Utilize a school-wide schedule which includes blocks of time within which teachers have the flexibility to group students in varied ways for specific instructional purposes. | 1 | 2 | 3 | 4 | 1 | 2 | 3 | 4 |
| 22. Utilize community involvement in the on-going school program by bringing community members and parents into the school and permitting students to explore the community from outside the school doors. | 1 | 2 | 3 | 4 | 1 | 2 | 3 | 4 |
| 23. Utilize multimaterials approaches to instruction, including both print and non-print learning materials. | 1 | 2 | 3 | 4 | 1 | 2 | 3 | 4 |
| 24. Provide learning experiences at appropriate cognitive development levels: concrete, formal, etc. | 1 | 2 | 3 | 4 | 1 | 2 | 3 | 4 |

* Clark, D. and Valentine, J. (1981). Middle Level School Programs: Making the Ideal a Reality. NASSP Schools in the Middle. Reston, VA: NASSP. Reprinted by permission.

Because of the difficulty in determining adequate information about the knowledge base of those involved in the restructuring process, many middle level leaders integrate the assessment process into staff development sessions which provide teachers, administrators, parents, and community members the opportunity to expand their knowledge base, share interests and concerns, and reflect on the implications of early adolescent characteristics and successful middle level programs on the creation of their "ideal" middle level school.

**Processes.** The following processes will be helpful in the collection and analysis of information (Stage 2):

*Nature of the Community* (Environmental Scanning)

- Obtain copies of reports that reflect national trends and issues.
- Obtain copies of reports reflecting state and local trends and issues.
- Analyze information from reports and identify trends and issues that impact now and/or will impact on the school in the next five years.

*Nature of the Young Adolescent*

- Obtain copies of books, journal articles, and reports dealing with early adolescent behavior (see Chapter 3 for references)
- Establish procedures necessary to develop student profiles (Self-concept, achievement, social behavior and attitudes, family status, economic status, special needs)

*Nature of the School Program* (see Chapters 4, 5, and 6)

- Determine school strengths and weaknesses
- Make specific recommendations for school improvement

*Knowledge Base of Decision Makers*

- Assess knowledge of early adolescent needs and characteristics
- Assess knowledge of appropriate middle level curriculum and successful middle level programs
- Establish staff development programs if knowledge base is inadequate

## Develop Mission Statement and General Goals

Using the processes begun in Stage 1 (clarification of purpose) and incorporating the wealth of information gathered during

Stage 2 (collection/analysis of information), planners formalize their vision for the school. Presented as a mission statement and elaborated by general goal statements, the vision should focus on broad educational and societal concerns. This vision must be commonly held and supported by all members of the School Leadership Council, and the ability of the council to articulate this commonly held vision is a vital step in the restructuring process.

The mission statement is a powerful tool for school restructuring. When properly written, it defines the direction in which the school intends to go. A mission statement "empowers everyone in the school to assume responsibility for the school's ultimate direction. It is, at once, a commitment, a promise, a guide for decision making, and a set of criteria by which to measure the school's progress toward its defined purposes" (Arth, Johnston, Lounsbury, Toepfer, and Melton, 1987).

Mission statements describe the reason for the existence of the school. Ideally they reflect a shared vision of the constituents of the school, and, most importantly, they represent a commitment by the teachers, administrators, parents, and community members (stakeholders) to a shared vision about the education of young adolescents. With commitment to the mission statement from stakeholders, it becomes a dominant force in planning, decision making, and evaluating (Arth et. al., 1987).

Well-written mission statements, which become the basis for goals, purposes, and objectives, should include the following components (Arth et. al., 1987; 7-9):

1. A statement of purpose
2. An indication of uniqueness
3. An explicit statement of commitment
4. A clear value position

Widespread involvement of stakeholders, which was important in Stages 1 and 2 of the restructuring process, is equally important in developing the mission statement and goals. Involvement leads to "buy in" and increases the likelihood of commitment. Involvement in writing the mission statement is facilitated by use of task groups composed of representatives from all constituencies who analyze data gathered during Stage 2 (demographics, characteristics of young adolescents, the structured interviews, knowledge bases, etc.) and develop mission statements which are shared with other task groups. Through a process of consensus a school mission statement is then created (Figure 9-5).

**Figure 9-5**
Mission Statement and General Goals

*Mission*

Recognizing the uniqueness of young adolescents, we the faculty, staff, students, parents, and community members of Desert Middle School share the mission of providing an environment which supports our commitment to promoting and fostering the academic success and personal development of each individual.

*General Goals*

1. To provide a positive, safe, and supportive environment for students and staff.
2. To meet the social, personal, and physical needs of young adolescents.
3. To maintain a high standard of achievement while meeting the intellectual needs of each student.
4. To encourage individual creativity.
5. To build positive relationships between students, parents, community, and school personnel.
6. To develop awareness of and appreciation for our different cultural heritages.
7. To provide a balanced curriculum which includes basic skills and opportunities for fine arts and vocational and physical education.
8. To develop in each student the ability to take responsibility for their own actions and to develop a responsible decision-making behavior.
9. To develop and maintain positive communication between home, school and community.

## Processes

*Task 1—Discussion of Mission and General Goal Statements*

- In task groups of six persons representing a cross-section of stakeholders:
    A. Discuss and identify the specific needs of the students who attend your school.
    B. Discuss and identify major school purposes, the strengths, the weaknesses, the recommendations for school improvement as reported on the structured interviews (Figure 9-3).
    C. Create an initial mission statement that includes a statement of purpose, an indication of uniqueness, an explicit statement of commitment, and a clear value position.

*Task 2—Reaching Consensus*

- Reconfigure task groups so that each new task group has one member from each of the Task 1 task groups.
  A.   Share written mission statements.
  B.   Rewrite group mission statement to include input from each task group member.
  C.   Select representative from group to meet with other representatives (Mission Statement Committee) to formulate a tentative draft of mission statement.

*Task 3—Finalizing the Mission Statement*

- In a meeting of the entire planning group—faculty, administrators, parents, community members:
  A.   Share mission statement
  B.   Discuss
  C.   Include final suggestions

*Task 4—Developing a Statement of General Goals*

- Using the Mission Statement as a basis for goals and purposes, reformulate task groups and develop goals. Use the same consensus process described in Tasks 1 through 3 (See Figure 9-5 for an example of a mission statement and purposes).

*Task 5—Examining the Implications of Mission Statement*
         *and General Goals for School Restructuring*

- In task groups, answer the following questions:

  A.   Does the new mission statement and general goals address early adolescent needs and characteristics?
  B.   Are the suggested purposes identified in the Structured Interview incorporated into the mission statement and general goals?
  C.   Are the strengths, weaknesses, and recommendations for improvement from the Structured Interview incorporated in the mission statement and general goals?
  D.   What current practices are supported by the new mission statement and purposes?
  E.   What changes in current practice will be needed to support the mission statement and purposes?

At this stage of the planning process, school purpose has been clarified, student needs have been identified, successful middle level programs have been studied and identified, and a mission statement and general goals have been written. The next stage, the final stage in **developing a foundation for restructuring**, is the identification of program goals.

## Determine Program Goals

Program goals differ from general goals in one very important way. While general goals offer broadly based statements of intent, program goals focus on the identification of specific programs or practices recommended for implementation.

The identification of program goals must be data based. That is, they must be driven by the information and decision making generated from the first three stages of this planning process. They also must be based upon a knowledge of the literature, research, and successful practice as described in the first six chapters of this book.

As in the case of the previous three stages, task groups should be organized for the purposes of determining program goals. The procedures described for writing the mission statement and general goals can also be used in effectively accomplishing the tasks in this stage.

Using the sample mission statement and general goals as presented in Figure 9-5 as a guide, program goals might be developed as follows:

**Program Goals**

1.  To incorporate into the school appropriate structures for supporting intellectual development:
    A.  Provide flexibility of instructional time through the use of large time blocks and interdisciplinary teams.
    B.  Provide for student mastery of objectives through the use of a continuous progress curriculum format.
    C.  Provide for individual learning styles through the use of various instructional strategies and learning resources.
    D.  Provide relevant learning experiences through the use of integrated curriculum.
2.  To incorporate into the school appropriate structures that support social, emotional, and physical development:

    A.    Provide for social support and development through the implementation of teacher advisory programs.

    B.    Provide curricular experiences that allow students to participate in exploratory and elective courses and activities.

    C.    Provide for a diversity of student interests by offering opportunities to become involved in a variety of activities.

    D.    Provide youth/community service programs that allow students to contribute to their school and community.

    E.    Provide programs that facilitate interaction with students and adults from different cultures.

3.    To incorporate into the school developmentally appropriate strategies for diagnosis and evaluation of student learning:

    A.    Provide for the diagnosis of learning styles.

    B.    Provide alternative means of evaluating student learning through the use of exhibitions, portfolios, and demonstrations.

    C.    Provide alternative means for reporting students' learning progress.

4.    To incorporate into the school programs which will involve greater numbers of constituents in the life of the school:

    A.    Provide for the redefinition of administrator and teacher roles to involve a greater number of teachers in leadership and decision making.

    B.    Provide opportunities for parents and community members to become more involved in the school as aides, tutors, coaches, and advisory committee members.

5.    To incorporate into the school appropriate programs for assessing and evaluating the success of the school:

    A.    Provide for more authentic procedures for evaluating administrator and teacher performance.

    B.    Provide for the systematic assessment of student, parent, and community members' satisfaction with their school.

    C.    Provide for the development of comprehensive

evaluative procedures that systematically and continuously assess the effectiveness of the school in "living up" to its mission and accomplishing its general goals.

These goals and subgoals, when formulated into specific objectives, provide the guidance necessary to develop the strategic long-range implementation plan.

Experience has shown that the completion of the four stages of Phase I—Developing a Foundation for Restructuring—takes approximately one year.

## PHASE II—DEVELOPING THE STRATEGIC LONG-RANGE PLAN

Now that the foundation for the long-range plan has been developed, the planning teams, the School Leadership Council, and others involved in the restructuring process have the responsibility to analyze the program goals, develop operational objectives, and determine the sequence for implementation of these objectives over an extended period. The analysis of program goals and development of operational objectives is achieved during Stage 5, sequencing of the operational objectives is performed during Stage 6, and the development of yearly activity lists for program development is the main task of Stage 7.

### Analyze Program Goals/ Determine Operational Objectives

Each of the program goals and subgoals determined in Stage 4 must be carefully analyzed by those involved in the planning process. Operational objectives which define the program goals in terms of specific strategies and outcomes are generated from this analysis. In this process each program goal and subgoal is represented by operational objectives written to specify a particular practice or strategy to be incorporated into the school during restructuring. The end result of this procedure is a listing of specific operational objectives which give direction to the restructuring process.

For example, the sample program subgoal 1A—"provide flexibility of instructional time through the use of large time blocks and interdisciplinary teams," might have the following operational objectives:

- **6th Grade**—Establish a four-period daily block of time for all sixth graders during which language arts/reading, social studies, mathematics, and science will be taught by one teacher.
- **7th Grade**—Establish a four-period daily block of time for all seventh graders in which an interdisciplinary team of four teachers will be responsible for instruction in the areas of language arts/reading, social studies, mathematics, and science.
- **8th Grade**—Establish a three-period daily block of time for all eighth graders in which an interdisciplinary team of three teachers will be responsible for instruction in the areas of language arts/reading, social studies, and science.

## Sequence Implementation of Operational Objectives

Once identified and written, operational objectives must be sequenced in a logical order over a three- to five-year time span. This assures a gradual and systematic approach to the implementation of the new program. This task is facilitated through the use of a grid. This grid, entitled a Chart of Objectives by Year of Implementation (Figure 9-6), lists the following seven components down the left margin:

- **Schedule** (time and group size)
- **Content** (scope and sequence)
- **Advisories/Activities** (guidance, youth service, clubs, student government, intramurals, and sports)
- **Methods/Strategies** (instructional processes/classroom management)
- **Resources** (print/nonprint media, equipment, and facilities)
- **Evaluation** (diagnosis/assessment of student learning styles, skills, knowledge, and attitudes; program evaluation)
- **Human Resources** (staffing ratios, teacher role, administrator role, parent/community involvement, and personnel evaluation)

Across the top of the chart are listed the years of implementation (e.g., Year 1, Year 2, Year 3, Year 4, Year 5). Planning teams, using this chart, make decisions as to the appropriate years for the implementation of operational objectives, and place them in the appropriate "cells." This process continues until all of the operational objectives have been sequenced. Figure 9-6

**Figure 9-6**
Chart of Objectives by Year of Implementation

| Components | Year 1 | Year 2 | Year 3 | Year 4 | Year 5 |
|---|---|---|---|---|---|
| **Schedule** (time and group size) | *6th Grade* - Schedule 1 teacher 4 period blocks; *7th Grade* - organize 4 member teams for 4 period block (language arts/reading, social studies, science, and mathematics) | *6th Grade* - Continue with 1 teacher 4 period blocks; *7th Grade* - Implement 4 teacher/4 period block (language arts/reading, social studies, science, and mathematics); *8th Grade* - Organize 3 member/3 period block (language arts/reading, social studies, and science) | *6th Grade* - Continue with single teacher 4 period blocks; *7th Grade* - Continue with 4 teacher/4 period blocks/teams; *8th Grade* - Implement 3 teacher/3 period blocks/ teams; Explore flexible scheduling | *6th Grade* - Continue with single teacher 4 period blocks, organize 2 teacher/4 period team; *7th Grade* - Continue with 4 teacher/4 period blocks/teams; *8th Grade* - Continue with 3 teacher/3 period blocks/teams; Plan and organize a flexible schedule | *6th Grade* - Continue with single teacher 4 period blocks, implement 2 teacher/4 period team; *7th Grade* - Continue with 4 teacher/4 period blocks/teams; *8th Grade* - Continue with 3 teacher/3 period blocks/teams; Implement new flexible schedule |
| **Content** (scope and sequence) | Review and revise core requirements, exploratory courses, and elective courses; *6th/7th Grade* - Develop and sequence objectives for language arts/reading and social studies | *6th/7th Grade* - Develop and sequence objectives for science and mathematics and develop thematic units which include the 4 core subjects; *8th Grade* - Develop and sequence objectives for language arts/reading and social studies | *6th/7th Grade* - Continue integration of content and the development of thematic units; *8th Grade* - Develop and sequence objectives for science and mathematics; Develop thematic units which include the 4 core subjects | Implement performance-based learning at all grade levels; continue the development of interdisciplinary units | Continue with performance-based learning; continue the development of interdisciplinary units; begin review and revision of all curriculum sequences and thematic (interdisciplinary) units |
| **Advisories/ Activities** (teacher advisories; clubs; student gov't; intramurals; youth service) | Explore and investigate appropriate models for teacher advisory programs; Review and revise scope of activities programs to include activities, eligibility, budget, and sponsors | Plan and organize teacher advisory program; Implement club and student government programs; Examine sports programs (interscholastic and intramural) | Implement teacher advisory program; Continue with club and student government programs; Implement a limited interscholastic program; Organize intramural program; Organize youth service program | Continue with teacher advisory program; Continue with club, student government programs, and interscholastic sports; Implement intramural program; Implement youth service program | Review and revise teacher advisory program; Continue with club, student government programs, interscholastic sports, and intramural programs; Continue with youth service program |

*(continued)*

Figure 9-6 *(continued)*

| Components | Year 1 | Year 2 | Year 3 | Year 4 | Year 5 |
|---|---|---|---|---|---|
| **Methods/ Strategies** (classroom processes) | *6th/7th Grade* - Identify appropriate strategies for interdisciplinary team teaching | *6th/7th Grade* - Continue to integrate new teaching strategies into classroom instruction; *8th Grade* - Identify appropriate strategies for interdisciplinary team teaching | Continue to integrate new teaching strategies into classroom instruction | Continue to integrate new teaching strategies into classroom instruction | Continue to integrate new teaching strategies into classroom instruction |
| **Resources** (print/nonprint media; equipment; facilities) | Determine resource materials, equipment, and facilities needs for interdisciplinary team teaching | Phase in equipment purchase and budget for facilities revision; Identify and/or develop materials which support the continuous progress sequences for language arts/reading and social studies | Continue with equipment acquisition and facilities revision; Identify and/or develop materials which support the continuous progress sequences for science and mathematics | Continue with equipment acquisition and facilities revision; Identify and/or develop materials which support interdisciplinary units (thematic units); Identify and/or develop materials which support all exploratory and elective courses | Continue with equipment acquisition and facilities revision; Develop schedule for reviewing and updating all resource materials and equipment for all subject areas |
| **Evaluation** (student diagnosis, assessment; school evaluation) | Assess student achievement, attitudes, self-concept, and learning styles; Review and organize authentic assessment procedures | Develop performance measures for language arts/reading and social studies incorporating authentic assessment procedures | Develop performance measures for science and mathematics incorporating authentic assessment procedures | Develop performance measures for all exploratory and elective courses incorporating authentic assessment procedures; Identify and design strategies for evaluating program effectiveness | Evaluate effectiveness of performance-based learning program, interdisciplinary teaming program, teacher advisory program, activity program, and the youth service program |
| **Human Resources** (staffing ratios, teacher/ administrator roles; evaluation; parent/ community involvement) | *6th Grade* - Determine teaching assignments for 4 period blocks; Review teacher evaluation procedures; Explore parent and community involvement programs | *7th Grade* - Determine teaching assignments for 4 member/4 period interdisciplinary teams; Implement parent involvement program; Initiate peer review teacher evaluation program | *8th Grade* - Determine teaching assignments for 3 member/3 period interdisciplinary teams; Implement community involvement program; Continue with peer review teacher evaluation program | Evaluate teacher use of alternative classroom strategies; Review effectiveness of parent involvement program | Review effectiveness of community involvement program |

shows an example of a completed chart. While this chart is not as comprehensive as most long-range plans, it is representative of the sequencing process that must take place in the implementation plan.

Relationships of the various operational objectives should also be noted. For instance, the implementation of a four period, four subject interdisciplinary team at the seventh grade (Column—Year 1; Row—Schedule) will also require that attention be given to instructional processes (Methods/Strategies); the development of interdisciplinary curriculum (Content); and to staffing ratios, teacher roles, and staff development (Personnel). The interrelationships of the various operational objectives must be carefully considered in the sequencing process. The sequencing process, when completed and recorded on the chart, provides a guide to gradual implementation of the various components of the restructuring plan.

## Develop Yearly Activity Lists for Program Implementation

The final stage in the strategic long-range planning process is the development of yearly activity lists. At this stage "the What? How? Who? When? Why? Where? are determined" (Kaufman and Herman, 1991; 8). Using the Chart of Objectives (Figure 9-6) as a guide, the operational objectives for each of the seven components are listed for each of the five years. To accomplish the list of operational objectives for Year 1 as sequenced on the Chart of Objectives, tasks must be identified, deadlines established, strategies determined, and responsibilities assigned. A completed Activity List for Year 1 (see Figure 9-7) gives an example of this planning process.

The importance of this final stage cannot be overemphasized. For many educators, a major pitfall in their restructuring efforts has been the failure to identify early in the planning process the tasks to be accomplished, the deadlines for task accomplishment, and persons responsible for task completion. Successful strategic long-range planning requires that "the task be clear, that those involved understand the parameters for planning and the timeline to be followed, and that decision-making responsibility be identified" (Williamson and Johnston, 1991; 53).

With the plan developed, leaders and planners begin the process of putting the plan to work. This includes implementing what has been planned, gathering data for formative evaluation, and incorporating necessary revisions.

**Figure 9-7**
Activities List for Year 1

*Objectives to be Accomplished by August 15, 1994*

1. At the sixth grade level organize and schedule four-period single teacher blocks (language arts/reading, social studies, science, and mathematics).
2. Review and revise school core requirements, and exploratory and elective courses.
3. At the sixth and seventh grade level develop and sequence objectives for language arts/reading and social studies.
4. Explore and investigate appropriate models for teacher advisory programs.
5. Review, revise and determine the scope of the school's activities program.
6. Identify appropriate instructional strategies for use in interdisciplinary teaching blocks.
7. Determine resource materials and equipment and facilities needed to support interdisciplinary teaming.
8. Determine appropriate procedures and assess student achievement, attitudes, self-concept, and learning styles.
9. Review and organize authentic assessment procedures.
10. Determine teaching assignments for sixth grade teachers.
11. Review teacher evaluation policies.
12. Explore parent and community involvement programs.

| Task | Completion Date | Strategy | Responsibility |
|------|------|------|------|
| *SCHEDULE* | | | |
| • Develop schedule that will accommodate four-period blocks of time | March 1, 1994 | Consultations with sixth and seventh grade teachers who will be working in the four-period blocks | Leadership Team Sub-committee on scheduling/Ass't principal |
| • Adopt schedule for 1994-1995 | April 1, 1994 | Faculty approval/consensus | Principal |
| *CONTENT* | | | |
| • Review and revise core requirements and exploratory and elective courses | February 1, 1994 | Faculty, parent, community recommendations | Leadership Team/Principal |
| • Develop and sequence objectives for language arts/reading and social studies | May 1, 1994 | Curriculum development workshops | Curriculum Committee/Ass't Principal |

*(continued)*

**Figure 9-7** *(continued)*

| Task | Completion Date | Strategy | Responsibility |
|---|---|---|---|
| *ADVISORIES/ACTIVITIES* | | | |
| • Explore and investigate appropriate models for teacher advisories | April 1, 1994 | Faculty, parent, community workshops/investigations | Guidance Committee/Counselor |
| • Review and revise scope of activities program | May 1. 1994 | Assessments - faculty, parents, community members | Assistant Principal |
| *METHODS/STRATEGIES* | | | |
| • Identify appropriate instructional strategies for use in interdisciplinary teaching blocks | April 15, 1994 | Sixth and Seventh Grade Teachers - workshops, school visitations, consultants, university courses | Leadership Team/Principal |
| *RESOURCES* | | | |
| • Determine resource materials, equipment, and facilities needs for interdisciplinary teaching | March 1, 1994 | Surveys, plant evaluation to identify suitable space for large and small group instruction, teacher advisory space | Resources Committee/Ass't Principal |
| *EVALUATION* | | | |
| • Determine appropriate strategies for assessing student achievement, attitudes, self-concept, and learning styles | December 1, 1993 | Investigation of appropriate evaluative methods (workshops, visitations, conferences, consultations); teachers, parents, community members' recommendations | Guidance Committee/Counselor |
| • Assess student achievement, attitudes, self-concept, and learning styles | April 15, 1994 | Collection and analysis of data | Guidance Committee/Counselor |
| • Review and organize authentic assessment procedures | July 15, 1994 | Faculty, parent, and community member investigation and recommendations | Guidance Committee/Counselor |
| *HUMAN RESOURCES* | | | |
| • Determine sixth grade teaching assignments | April 15, 1994 | Consultations with sixth grade teachers | Principal |
| • Review teacher evaluation policies | May 1, 1994 | Study of teacher evaluation (workshops, visitations, consultations) | Human Resources Committee/Principal |
| • Explore parent and community involvement programs | August 1, 1994 | Study of successful programs by faculty, parents, and community members; recommendations for program components | Parent/Community Involvement Committee |

## SUMMARY

Successful restructuring can take place only through careful planning, gradual program implementation, and effective leadership from the administrative staff and leadership teams. Involvement of administrators, teachers, students, parents and community members ensures that the concerns and needs of all constituents will be addressed in the planning process.

Gradual implementation provides for the systematic installation of new programs and the revision of existing programs. Gradual implementation also allows educators, parents, and community members to accommodate the demands of program change in smaller, more acceptable increments. Along with its focus on gradual incremental change, the strategic long-range plan with its sequence of operational objectives provides criteria for assessing progress. By comparing actual implementation accomplishments with those projected on the Chart of Objectives, planners can determine their progress and make necessary revisions.

The strategic long-range plan is a blueprint for school change. With its emphasis on collaboration, it provides a systematic process that allows administrators, teachers, students, parents, and community members the opportunity to become informed, active participants in the planning and restructuring of middle level schools more developmentally responsive to the needs of young adolescents.

## REFERENCES

Arth, A. A., Johnston, J. H., Lounsbury, J. H., Toepfer, C. F., & and Melton, G. E. (1987). *Developing a mission statement for the middle level school.* Reston, VA: National Association of Secondary School Principals.

Blum, R. E., & Kneidek, A. W. (1991). Strategic improvement that focuses on student achievement. *Educational Leadership, 48*(7), 17-21.

Blyth, D. A., & Roehlkepartain, E. C. (1992). Working together: A new study highlights what youth need from communities. *Search Institute Source, VIII*(2), 1-4.

Brandt, R. (1991). On strategic management: A conversation with George Wilkinson. *Educational Leadership, 48*(7), 22-25.

Chase, R. B., & Clark, D. C. (1974). Long range planning in school districts. *Educational Technology, 14*(10), 32-36.

Clark, D. C., Clark, S. N., & Thomas, V. (1979). Individualizing business education instruction at the four-year college level. In B. Wakin, & C. Petitjean (Eds.), *Alternative learning styles in business education: National Business Education Association Yearbook, No. 17* (pp. 68-82). Reston, VA: National Business Education Association.

Clark, D. C., & Valentine, J. W. (1981, June). Middle level educational programs: Making the ideal a reality. *NASSP Schools in the middle: A report on trends and practices.* Reston, VA: National Association of Secondary School Principals.

Clark, S. N., & Clark, D. C. (1984). Creating a responsive middle level school through systematic long-range planning. *NASSP Bulletin,* 68(473), 42-51.

Dorman, G. (1984). *Middle grades assessment program: User's manual.* Carrboro, NC: Center for Early Adolescence.

English, F., & Hill, J. (1990). *Restructuring: The principal and curriculum change.* Reston, VA: National Association of Secondary School Principals.

Hafner, A., Ingels, S., Schneider, B., Stevenson, D., & and Owings, D. (1990). *National educational longitudinal study of 1988: A profile of the American eighth grader.* Washington, D.C.: U. S. Department of Education, Office of Educational Research and Implementation.

Hodgkinson, H. (1985). *All one system: Demographics of education from kindergarten through graduate school.* Washington, D.C.: Institute for Educational Leadership.

Hodgkinson, H. (1989). *The same client: Demographics of education and service delivery.* Washington, D.C.: Institute for Educational Leadership.

Howard, E. R., & Keefe, J. W. (1991). *The CASE-IMS school improvement process.* Reston, VA: National Association of Secondary School Principals.

Howell, B. (1981). Profile of the principalship. *Educational Leadership,* 38(4), 333-336.

Kaufman, R., & Herman, J. (1991). Strategic planning for a better society. *Educational Leadership, 48*(7), 4-8.

Mecca, T. V., & Adams, C. F. (1991). An alternative futures approach to planning for school systems. *Educational Leadership, 48*(7), 12-16.

Phi Delta Kappa. Annual Gallup Poll. *Phi Delta Kappan.*

Poole, M. L. (1991). Environmental scanning is vital to strategic planning. *Educational Leadership, 48*(7), 40-41.

United Way of America. (1991). *What lies ahead: Countdown for the 21st century.* Alexandria, VA: United Way of America.

Williamson, R., & Johnston, J. H. (1991). *Planning for success: Successful implementation of middle level reorganization.* Reston, VA: National Association of Secondary School Principals.

# 10

## Organizing Staff Development to Facilitate School Restructuring

> "Part of what staff development has to do now is teach people how to re-create environments and how to think about structures and functions that are right for children."
>
> Myrna Cooper

Staff development which supports the restructuring process must have two major focal points: the creation of cultures and structures that lead to the ongoing improvement of the school (this focal point was the subject of Chapter 8) and the continuous emphasis on developing the skills and competencies necessary to improve classrooms and support new programs (the topic of this Chapter).

In its broadest conception staff development is the totality of educational experiences, activities, or processes that contribute toward an individual's being more competent and satisfied in an assigned professional role. For the purposes of this chapter staff development will be defined as the processes and experiences designed to improve teacher and administrator skills, attitudes, understandings, and performance in present and future roles (Dale, 1982; Fullan, 1990). While building skills and competencies for instructional improvement, successful staff development also assists teachers and administrators in acquiring the skills and attitudes necessary for the creation of collegial environments for inquiry, reflection, and decision making.

In this chapter assumptions which serve as the basis for staff development programs will be presented, implications for leadership will be explored, procedures for planning staff development programs will be identified, and approaches for successful implementation will be described.

## SOME ASSUMPTIONS ABOUT STAFF DEVELOPMENT

Drawing from the research and literature on staff development during the decade of the 1980s, the following assumptions are presented (Clark and Clark, 1983; Dale, 1982; Fullan, 1990; Joyce, 1990; Lieberman and Miller, 1991; McLaughlin, 1991; Wood, McQuarrie, and Thompson, 1982):

*The successful restructuring of middle level schools takes considerable time and requires a commitment to long-term staff development.* The complexity of change required by school restructuring and the comprehensiveness of the staff development program to support that change demands a strong commitment to the provision of time for planning, inservice, and implementation. The change process should be gradual and phased in over a period of several years with time being scheduled for teachers, administrators, parents, and community members to meet, collaborate, inquire, reflect, and develop the school's restructuring plan. Time must also be available for comprehensive staff development which provides the opportunity for the continuing expansion of the knowledge and skills required for formulating and implementing the restructuring plan.

*School restructuring and appropriate staff development should be site-based.* The focus of the staff development which supports school restructuring should be centered on each school, its particular needs, the goals of its restructuring plan, and the specific inservice needed to support the successful implementation of the restructuring plan. The school must be recognized as the center of change, not the target of change. As the center of change, the school can recognize and tap the knowledge, expertise, and talent that exists among teachers, administrators, parents, and community members and involve these constituency groups in study groups, program development, curriculum writing, classroom innovation, action research, and school evaluation.

*Staff development should focus on the improvement of quality of the total school program and individual class-*

*room instruction.* At the heart of any middle level school restructuring program is the improvement of the educational experiences of the students it serves. This is done in two ways. First, by developing and implementing programs such as interdisciplinary teaming and teacher advisory programs, structures are put into place that have the potential to improve self-concept, reduce anonymity, and increase involvement in learning. Second, by addressing the improvement of classroom instruction, emphasis can be placed on those strategies and methodologies that are most appropriate for the specific learning styles and needs of young adolescents. Staff development must be readily available to assist teachers and administrators in changing their attitudes and in acquiring the skills to effectively implement new programs and integrate new, more effective strategies in the classroom.

*School environments which are favorable to staff development influence and foster the success of teacher and administrator professional development.* Successful staff development is built on a school culture that supports, encourages, nurtures, and has high expectations for professional development. Cultures supportive of staff development are more likely to occur when teachers and administrators are given major decision-making responsibilities in determining the what, the how, and the when of their staff development experiences. Empowerment at the school site, along with a strong sense of efficacy, are powerful factors in creating cultures supportive of professional development.

*Educators are more responsive to change and more highly motivated to learn when they have some control over the change process and their learning and are free from threat.* In restructuring schools professional development must occur in safe environments, environments that make problem solving and inquiry possible through the creation of safe environments for teachers and administrators which allow them to examine current practice, to reflect, and to take risks.

*Teachers and administrators vary widely in their openness to change, in their competencies, and in their readiness to learn.* It must be recognized that educators in a given middle school differ greatly in their attitudes toward decision making and change. They also differ greatly in their understanding of young adolescents and their needs, their comprehension of group organization and processes, and their perceptions of leadership, supervision, and evaluation. Because of these individual differences, staff development must address teacher and administrator self-defined needs for personal and professional development, while at the same time striking a balance between these individual needs and school and district needs. Staff development must be subject specific, not generic; site specific, not district specific; and teacher/administrator specific, not faculty specific.

***All teachers and administrators need staff development throughout their professional careers.*** Learning is a life-long enterprise. The demands of middle level school restructuring require that teachers and administrators assume new and continuing roles as problem solvers, curriculum developers, action researchers, and change agents. These roles demand new skills and competencies, new expertise, and new knowledge. Restructuring has no beginning or ending; it must be considered an ongoing process that calls for the comparison of current practices with what is known and making decisions based upon that comparison. Just as restructuring is an ongoing process, so is the staff development program which supports it. Successful staff development in a restructuring middle level school must be continuous, relevant, involving, timely, and supportive of educators and their personal and professional needs.

## LEADERSHIP AND STAFF DEVELOPMENT

Effective leadership for staff development "can, does, and must come from a variety of different sources in different situations" (Fullan, 1990; 21). Leadership at the district level should perform three important tasks: manage multiple, diverse opportunities for professional development; create supportive norms and expectations for professional growth; and develop and nurture structures for communication, collegiality, and feedback (McLaughlin, 1991). At the building level, principals, department chairs, and team leaders have the primary responsibility for establishing the norms, values, and expectations that are critical to promoting and maintaining a culture that supports professional growth (Clark and Clark, 1983; McLaughlin, 1991).

In the middle level school, the importance of the principal in planning and implementing comprehensive staff development cannot be overemphasized. Principals are the prime movers in the schools; they are the enablers; and their attitudes toward staff development help establish the climate, culture, and norms necessary for success. While the importance of the principal in sustaining norms for long-term professional growth is supported by the research (McLaughlin, 1991), the principal alone cannot and does not create successful staff development programs. Leadership and decision making should be shared by those who will be participating in the staff development program, allowing them to be involved in decisions about goals and objectives, activities, and assessment.

A staff development steering committee is an effective strategy for facilitating involvement. The steering committee, composed of representatives from the various constituency groups (teachers, administrators, staff, parents, and community members) is responsible for coordinating all of the facets of the staff development program (Clark and Clark, 1983; Wood, Thompson, and Russell, 1981). This collaborative committee, in working with building and district administrators and outside consultants, facilitates the planning of the staff development program; ensures that individual needs and concerns and school and program concerns are considered; fosters open-ended communication; and coordinates all staff development activities.

## PHASE I—PLANNING THE STAFF DEVELOPMENT PROGRAM

With direction from the steering committee, the faculty is involved in generating the plan for staff development. The development of this plan should be formulated around the following questions:

1.   What are the characteristics of the adult learners (teachers, administrators, staff members) in this school?
2.   What skills and knowledge are required of teachers and administrators to be successful in implementing the restructuring plan?
3.   What are the goals and objectives of the staff development program?
4.   What is the current level of teacher and administrator skills and knowledge as compared to those required for program implementation?
5.   What inservice activities will be used to assist teachers and administrators in the acquisition of the new skills and knowledge necessary for success?

6. What procedures will be used to evaluate the activities in accomplishing the staff development goals and objectives?

7. What arrangements will be made to provide teachers and administrators with time to participate in staff development activities including school study, skill and knowledge acquisition, program planning, curriculum development, reflection, and evaluation?

During Phase I of the staff development model (see Figure 10-1), the emphasis is on the continuing development of skills necessary to be successful in the classroom and on the development of new skills and competencies that will be required for

**Figure 10-1**
Phase I - Planning the Staff Development Program

---

1. *Needs and characteristics of adult learners*
   Identification/Diagnosis
   Faculty and staff learning profiles

2. *Required skills and knowledge*
   Analysis of restructuring plan goals and objectives
   Listing of specific skills and knowledge needed

3. *Goals and objectives of the staff development program*
   Goals and objectives drawn from listing of specific skills and knowledge
      needed for restructuring
   Sequencing of goals and objectives

4. *Current levels of skill and knowledge*
   Assessment of teacher and administrator skill and knowledge levels
   Comparison of current skill and knowledge levels with those required for
      program implementation

5. *Methods/strategies/modes of inservice delivery*
   Determine most effective methods for inservice
   Provide a variety of methods to accommodate different learning
      characteristics and needs

6. *Evaluation of staff development program and process*
   Determine procedures for assessing the effectiveness of
      methods/strategies/modes
   Assess the staff development planning and implementation processes

7. *Staff development calendar and plan*
   Sequence all elements and processes
   Establish time frames for learning and collaboration
   Establish deadlines for implementation
   Assign responsibility for planning and implementation

---

the new programs identified in the restructuring plan. In this process a balance must be maintained between the characteristics and needs of adult learners (teachers and administrators) and the new skills and knowledge they will be required to learn in order to be successful in the programs identified for implementation in the restructuring plan (see "Chart of Objectives by Year of Implementation," Figure 9-6).

## Determine the Characteristics and Needs of Adult Learners

Effective staff development places teachers and site administrators at the center of the process. As active participants, reflective learners, and competent decision makers, they are empowered to plan and make the decisions that best serve them as individuals, while at the same time providing a continuing process for improving their schools and classrooms.

The continuing improvement of and development of new teacher skills and competencies in the classroom falls into four categories on which teachers must work simultaneously: (1) the capacity to manage classrooms, (2) the continuous acquisition of proven instructional strategies, (3) the continuous acquisition of instructional skills, and (4) the focus on desired educational goals and content (Fullan, 1990). These classroom improvement categories, when linked with school improvement categories (a shared purpose, norms of collegiality, norms of continuous improvement, and structures that represent organizational conditions necessary for significant school improvement), bring into focus the importance of school and classroom improvement as the dual purposes of school restructuring.

The centerpiece or linking mechanism that bridges classroom and school improvement in Fullan's (1990) model is the concept of "teacher as learner." Integrated into this concept are four aspects of the teacher as learner—technical skills which increase instructional certainty; reflective practice which enhances clarity, meaning, and coherence; inquiry which fosters investigation and exploration; and collaboration which enables one to receive and give ideas and assistance.

Central to the concept of teachers and administrators as learners is an understanding of how adults learn. Bents and Howey (1981), drawing from the work of Knowles (1978), suggest that: (1) adults are motivated to learn as they experience needs and interests that learning will satisfy, (2) adult orientation to learning is life centered, (3) experience is the richest resource for adult learning, (4) adults have a deep need to be self-directing, and (5) individual differences among people increase with age. These statements, which have broad-based endorsement and some empirical support, have major implications for staff development planning and implementation. Staff development, to be successful, must build on interests; must organize learning activities around life (school and classroom) situations; must use methodologies that revolve around the analysis of experience; must engage teachers and administrators in the process of mutual inquiry; and must make provision for differences in style, time, place, and pace of learning (Knowles, 1978).

An awareness of the disparities among professional educators in terms of the relative levels of knowledge, skill, and commitment required to implement specific restructuring programs is critical to the planning process (Fenwick, 1992). Determining these differences is helpful in designing individualized/personalized approaches that will enhance learning and lead to changes in what teachers and administrators value and in how they perform in their various professional roles.

For years educators have advocated individualized/personalized instruction for students. Personalizing the learning experiences for teachers and administrators is equally defensible. Information about teachers' and administrators' individual differences, such as when and how one learns most effectively, what learning modes and activities are preferred, and how self-directed teachers and administrators are in new learning experiences, is valuable in designing appropriate staff development activities. The assessment of adult learning styles is an effective method for determining this information. Gregoric's (1982) Style Delineator, for instance, is an effective, easy-to-use assessment of learning style. Many other instruments are also available that will give a rough estimate of preferences and provide guidance for organizing staff development experiences (see Keefe, 1987). In determining the adult learning characteristics and needs of their school, the steering committee is able to develop a listing of characteristics that will be valuable in guiding the decision-making process in the selection of appropriate learning experiences.

Keeping the learners (teachers and administrators) central to the planning process, understanding basic elements in adult learners, and considering individual differences among learners are crucial factors in designing staff development programs that maintain the balance between human needs and new program requirements.

## Identify Skills and Knowledge Required for Implementation of Restructuring Goals and Objectives

During the process of developing the restructuring plan, program goals were identified by teachers, administrators, parents, and community members (Stage 4—Chapter 9). These program goals were then analyzed, operational objectives were established (Stage 5), and these operational objectives were then sequenced for implementation over a five-year period of time (Stage 6— "Chart of Objectives by Year of Implementation," Figure 9-6). Each of the objectives on the "Chart of Objectives by Year of Implementation" needs to be analyzed to determine the specific skills and knowledge that will be required for the successful implementation of that program or objective. For instance, if a decision is made to initiate a computer assisted instruction program, there will be a need for teachers with some basic background and competencies in the use of computers and CAI. The implementation of teacher advisory programs requires teachers who value supporting young adolescents in informal situations and who possess special skills in human relations and communications. The introduction of cooperative learning requires teachers skilled in the development and sequencing of curricular materials and instructional activities, skilled at organizing students into flexible grouping patterns, and skilled at assessing learning using alternative assessment procedures.

Using the "Chart of Objectives by Year of Implementation," each new program identified for implementation at some stage during restructuring should be carefully analyzed to determine the specific skills and competencies requiring training and preparation. This process is most often accomplished by subcommittees of teachers, site-administrators, and central office staff development experts. Under the direction of the steering committee, these subcommittees analyze the program goals and operational objectives, determine staff development needs, and develop goals and objectives for the staff development program.

## Establish Staff Development Goals and Objectives

Goals should be broad statements of intent, while the objectives should be much more specific. For example, a goal and accompanying objectives for the preparation of seventh grade teachers for interdisciplinary teaming might be:

Goal—Establish an inservice program for preparing teachers and administrators in the skills necessary for successful interdisciplinary teaming.

Objectives—Members of each teaching team will demonstrate their ability to:
- Use time flexibly—by developing flexible schedules within the time block constraints
- Use flexible grouping—by developing procedures for placing students in temporary instructional groups for instruction which vary in size and period of time
- Sequence and integrate content—by sequencing their content and identifying areas for integration of their team's subject areas
- Use a variety of instructional techniques—by identifying techniques/strategies most suitable for instructing students in large group, small group, or directed (independent) study and by matching these techniques/strategies with content area concepts.

Through this collaborative process of establishing staff development goals and objectives, the specific skills, knowledge, and attitudes required for successful implementation are identified by the same group of people (teachers and administrators) who will be the beneficiaries of the staff development program the restructuring plan has set into motion.

## Assess Current Skills and Knowledge Level of Teachers and Administrators

When the learning characteristics of adult learners have been determined, the specific skills for restructuring identified, and the goals and objectives of the staff development program established, the skill and knowledge levels of the faculty in comparison to the levels identified in the staff development program goals must be determined. One of the most effective ways of determining needs is through the use of collaborative groups where teachers and administrators discuss the various skills that are needed and that should receive emphasis. These skills are recorded and at a later date prioritized and sequenced into the inservice schedule.

Another effective way to assess the need for assistance in skill development is to construct a survey that lists all of the various identified skills and for each skill ask each faculty member to circle one of the following choices: (1) very knowledgeable or skilled, (2) somewhat knowledgeable or skilled, (3) not knowledgeable or skilled. For the same listing of skills, each faculty member should also indicate one of the following choices: (1) desire inservice, (2) do not desire inservice. From the information gathered from this type of survey, data can be obtained that will report faculty level of expertise for each of the skills and identify faculty desire for inservice. This survey approach is also helpful in identifying faculty expertise, a resource that can be used when the staff development program is initiated.

Assessing attitudes toward middle level programs can be assessed by using *The Middle Level School* questionnaire (Clark and Valentine, 1981) described in Chapter 9. This instrument assesses the degree to which programs are valued individually and collectively by the faculty and the degree to which programs are presently implemented in the school. Structured interviews with teachers and administrators provide the most accurate and honest feedback about needs as respondents usually give more consideration to each question, taking time to clarify and reflect, than they do on a questionnaire (Wood, Thompson, and Russell, 1981).

The assessment of teacher and administrator needs is completed when a comprehensive listing of needed skills is developed. This listing of needs becomes the focus of the inservice activities.

## Determine Methods/Strategies/Modes of Delivery

The information about the knowledge and skill levels of teachers and administrators provides critical information about the content of staff development. It is, however, the data on preferred learning styles of the participants that provide the basis for identifying and planning the most appropriate and relevant staff development experiences.

Involvement in the planning process must continue to be a major emphasis. In making decisions about staff development activities, however, parents and community members do not play as active a role as they played in the development of the restructuring plan. Collaboration about staff development activities involves teachers and administrators in the process of decision making about their own professional growth, a process that brings about ownership and a sense of efficacy. In addition, the involvement of teachers and administrators in the decision-making process will more likely lead to relevant, site-specific, subject-specific, teacher-specific, and administrator-specific experiences.

In designing individual staff development experiences, staff development planners should include opportunities to build relationships and communication among participants and time when participants can interact freely and reflect and share what they are learning and discovering. Careful consideration should also be given to providing learning options which accommodate different learning needs and learning styles (Wood, Thompson, and Russell, 1981).

Staff development experiences can most appropriately be built around the concept of the school as a community of learners (Barth, 1990; Schaefer, 1967). The school as a community of learners (as described in Chapter 8) is best described as an organizational development approach to school improvement which incorporates school study and inquiry, reflection, curriculum analysis and design, and assessment. Knowledge and skill development comes about when participants are given the opportunity to inquire together, discuss practice, observe and critique each other, and formulate plans for school and classroom improvement. This knowledge and skill development is augmented by a variety of different strategies and/or modes including workshops, school visitations, independent/self-directed study, credential and/or graduate degree programs, and professional association professional development programs.

**Workshops.** Workshops, which include seminars and retreats, provide teachers and administrators opportunities to work with resource people (both internal and external) to focus on issues of middle level school improvement. Workshops usually have a specific focus that emphasizes skill development in a program or subject area. For instance, a workshop might focus on developing team planning skills while another might focus on skills and understandings needed to implement a "whole language" program.

In keeping with the holistic approach to middle level restructuring, workshops should be part of the continuing process of staff development, which includes involvement in planning, participatory learning experiences, and formative assessment. Part of the planning process for workshops and seminars is the determination of expertise or leadership for the sessions. This leadership can come from a variety of sources within the school (teachers and administrators) or from outside the school (district office resource people or consultants).

**Consultants.** In a majority of restructuring middle level schools outside consultants are involved in the staff development process (Keefe, Clark, Nickerson, and Valentine, 1983). In some cases these consultants may be national authorities who are brought in for one or two presentations. Their responsibility is to motivate and share their broad perspectives and experiences in working with successful middle level schools. In other cases, consultants may come from nearby universities or consortiums. Unlike the national consultants, their role is to work with the school faculty on a long-term basis as resource persons, facilitators, and change agents.

If consultants are going to be used, particularly long-term consultants, a selection process should be created that involves faculty and staff in identifying the specific roles the consultant is expected to play, the specific tasks he or she is expected to perform, and the personal and professional characteristics needed to be successful. When selecting a consultant the following questions should be given careful consideration:

1.  Does his or her philosophy of middle level education fundamentally agree with that held by the school and the district?
2.  Does he or she have the ability to inspire, motivate, and win the confidence of teachers, administrators, parents, community members, and school board members?
3.  Is he or she approachable?
4.  What successful experiences does he or she have in other middle level schools which are establishing similar programs?
5.  Is he or she willing to get involved personally in the program and make a long-term commitment to the school for a period of several years?

There is some debate as to how effective outside consultants are in assisting schools in making long-lasting change. While some outside consultants may unintentionally diminish staff development outcomes, good consultants can have a positive influence and assist school personnel in learning how to solve problems on their own. McLaughlin (1991) contends that it is not the "externalness" of the outside consultant that may inhibit effectiveness, but the way that he or she interacts with the local setting. By getting involved, by being accessible, by facilitating thinking, by motivating teachers and administrators to participate, and by emphasizing collaborative problem solving, consultants can make a significant impact on school improvement efforts.

Once selected, the consultant should become a part of the steering committee and participate fully in the planning process. As a continuing participant in the staff development program, the consultant assumes several roles: advisor, motivator, listener, change agent, and reinforcer.

In addition to the use of consultants, other human resources are readily available within the school. In middle level schools with collegial climates and norms that focus on school improvement, members of the faculty, parents, and community members are regularly called upon to serve as "in house experts" or leaders, sharing their knowledge and expertise in collaborative environments. This type of leadership provides a source of information that is readily available to both teachers and administrators. Staff development organized around collaborative approaches recognizes and promotes leadership among teachers, a leadership that is specialized and that is regularly and systematically available to colleague teachers (Griffin, 1991).

**School Visitations.** School visitations provide another good approach for teachers and administrators wishing to increase their awareness levels and to acquire new skills. The schools identified for visits should be carefully selected and should be successfully practicing those concepts and/or programs to be implemented. Opportunities for school visitations should be encouraged and facilitated for all teachers. Visitations to other schools are an especially valuable experience for teacher leaders and change agents as it gives them an opportunity to confirm and validate the work they are doing in their own school.

Visitations also provide excellent staff development opportunities. For example, teachers who will be involved in programs such as interdisciplinary teaming and teacher advisories, or with specific instructional techniques such as cooperative learning and hands-on activities, should be given the opportunity of observing the successful use of these programs and techniques. Evidence is mounting, according to Fenwick (1992), that the most effective way to engage teachers in using proven instructional strategies is by allowing them to observe others who are proficient and successful in using those strategies. School visitations provide a unique opportunity for those observations to take place.

Organizing a successful school visitation/observation experience requires careful planning. The steering committee should complete the following tasks:

1.   Identify middle level schools that are successfully using middle level programs and practices.
2.   Schedule a preliminary visit that allows two or three members of the steering committee to confirm the presence of programs/practices to be observed.
3.   Prior to the visitation, organize a meeting of all teachers and administrators who will be taking part in the visitation. During the meeting the following tasks should be completed:
     A.   Identify and list specific information to be obtained from the visit.
     B.   Determine responsibility for obtaining the desired information.
     C.   Develop a schedule that will provide each participant time to observe classrooms and meet with the teachers he or she observed.
4.   During the day of the visitation, in addition to the observation of programs and practices, participants should talk with teachers, administrators, and, if possible, parents. The emphasis of the discussion should focus on rationale, implementation strategies, successes, trouble-spots, and attitudes and impressions about the program.
5.   After the visitation, time should be scheduled for the participants to share insights, reflect on their experience, discuss implications for implementation, and to report back to the other members of the faculty and staff.

School visitations are also helpful in introducing the concept of middle level education to parents, community members, and school board members. By including representatives from these three constituency groups in the visitations of innovative middle level schools, much can be done to assist them in understanding the nature and organization of developmentally responsive schools for young adolescents.

The benefits of school visitation can be enhanced through participation in a network of other middle level schools involved in restructuring. These networks, often supported by state departments of education and/or universities (partnership programs), also provide excellent opportunities for schools to share resources and expertise and to develop support systems.

**Independent/Self-Directed Study.** Independent/self-directed study is another effective approach for assisting teachers and administrators in acquiring new knowledge and skills. This particular approach to staff development, which capitalizes on individual needs and interests, provides the opportunity to explore ideas, read extensively, inquire into practice, and critique one's own performance. Self-directed study is often organized around study groups who use strategies similar to those found in cooperative learning. For instance, a group of three or four teachers and administrators who have an interest in youth service programs might join together to study the feasibility of developing a program at their school. In the process of pursuing this idea, one participant could take on the responsibility of conducting a "search" for research on the topic, another participant would gather pertinent literature, a third person might be responsible for determining resources needed, while the fourth person would be responsible for conducting a feasibility study. Periodically they would share their knowledge with each other with the goal of developing recommendations about the possibilities of implementing a youth service program in the school. When the study group has completed its assignment, their recommendations are shared with the entire staff. As a result of this process of self-directed study, teachers and administrators have an opportunity to pursue a topic of interest, while at the same time building expertise that eventually may be helpful in the restructuring process. Even if the school decides not to organize a youth service program, the individual members of the group feel empowered and enriched by the interactions with each other.

**Endorsement/Credential and/or Graduate Degree Programs.** Special middle level endorsement/credential and/or graduate degree programs can also be used to effectively augment the staff development program. Almost three quarters of the states have some provision for a middle level endorsement or certificate, and courses which meet endorsement or certification requirements provide another option for building awareness about middle level education. In addition, many colleges and universities are now offering majors or specializations in middle level education in their masters and doctoral degree programs, thus affording teachers and administrators the opportunity to gain specific expertise in the education of young adolescents. In some cases, these programs are available on-site and customized to meet the particular needs of the faculty and staff of the school or district.

Extension courses on various aspects of middle level education also offer valuable assistance to middle level schools embarking on the restructuring process. These courses are advantageous because they can focus on specific needs while at the same time providing a forum for scholarly inquiry and reflection about practice. As mentioned earlier, middle level school/university partnerships can also provide support for restructuring and excellent opportunities for staff development.

**Professional Associations.** Professional associations can also supplement staff development efforts. In a recent study of middle level education (Valentine, Clark, Irvin, Keefe, and Melton, 1993), it was reported that a vast majority of principals, assistant principals, and teachers who were members of leadership teams not only held memberships in professional associations but participated in (with district support) professional growth activities offered by those associations. Associations such as the National Association of Secondary School Principals and the National Middle School Association can provide helpful resources for middle level educators. In addition, attending a national convention or a regional conference can provide excellent motivation for teachers and administrators who, in associating with other middle level educators, get caught up in the enthusiasm and excitement. The Association for Supervision and Curriculum Development, many of the content area associations (e.g., National Council of Teachers of Mathematics, National Council for Social Studies, etc.) also provide staff development opportunities such as conference sessions and materials related to curriculum improvement at the middle level.

By being aware of the various types of professional development available through professional associations, the steering committee can coordinate the participation of teachers, administrators, and, in some instances, parents and community members, in ways that will support the restructuring efforts by building awareness, expanding knowledge, and enhancing skill levels.

Numerous books and monographs have been written on middle level education, excellent journals are being published, and various media presentations (videotapes, audiotapes, sound filmstrips, films) are available. Good materials are also available from commercial publishers, state departments of education, and regional research and development laboratories.

Even with limited resources, there are a variety of ways that middle level schools can provide the specific staff development activities necessary to improve the school and classroom instruction. By being aware of all the available possibilities (district office resources, consultant expertise, exemplary programs for visitation, college/university support, and professional associations' professional growth activities), by being cognizant of readily available resources (teacher and administrator expertise, community services, and state department of education resources), and by organizing all of these resources to support the restructuring plan, the steering committee can structure a comprehensive staff development plan that facilitates involvement, provides for individual needs, and develops the necessary skills, knowledge, and attitudes.

## Determine Procedures for the Evaluation of the Staff Development Program

In planning the procedures for evaluating the staff development program, the steering committee must focus on two areas: the effectiveness of the processes used to plan and implement the staff development program and the effectiveness of the inservice activities in accomplishing goals and objectives.

The processes used in assessing needs, developing goals and objectives, determining strategies of delivery, and evaluation should undergo periodic review by the steering committee, with participation from the faculty and staff. The effectiveness of the decision-making process and the involvement of participants is particularly critical in building a culture which supports professional growth. The following questions provide guidance in evaluating the effectiveness of the processes used in planning the staff development program (Clark and Clark, 1983; Fenstermacher and Berliner, 1983; McLaughlin, 1991):

1.  Who participated in the planning of the staff development program? (central office personnel, teachers, administrators, parents, community members, consultants, university professors, county and state department of education staff?)

2.  In what ways were the various participants involved—making decisions, giving advice, providing resources?

3.  What was the extent of support received from district administration?

4.  To what extent was involvement in the planning process and participation in the inservice activities perceived as being worthwhile?

5.  To what extent were the planning process and inservice activities perceived as being consistent with the cultural norms of the school?

6.  To what extent did the staff development program provide for a variety of learning experiences, provide positive incentives, and provide continuing support for participants?

7.  To what extent were the goals and objectives of the staff development program and/or the specific inservice activities known to both the providers and the recipients?

Appropriate procedures, which are drawn from the staff development goals and objectives, must also be identified or developed to assess the effectiveness of the inservice activities. For instance, for the staff development goal, "Establish an inservice program for preparing teachers and administrators in the skills needed for successful interdisciplinary teaming," the steering committee and selected teachers and administrators need to determine what information they wish to know and what questions need to be asked. Based on the staff development objectives established for this interdisciplinary teaming goal, the following questions might be asked:

1.  What types of activities assist teachers in becoming skilled at developing flexible schedules?

2.  What types of activities assist teachers in becoming more comfortable with the use of temporary groups for instruction which vary in number of students and length of time?
3.  What types of activities assist teachers in the sequencing and integration of content?
4.  What types of activities assist teachers in the development of skills in using a variety of instructional techniques?

These questions could be answered by the use of individual questionnaires and group interviews with members of the teaching team. This process should be initiated immediately after the staff development activities have begun and should be continued throughout the restructuring process, with teachers and administrators actively participating in discussion, reflection, and problem solving. This process would include the evaluation of each workshop session, presentation, and visitation with an emphasis on the identification of new information learned and how it can be applied to the teachers' and administrators' immediate work situation.

In planning the evaluation of staff development activities, it is helpful to structure a systematic process that identifies the goals and objectives, lists inservice activities, identifies assessment procedures, assigns deadlines, and designates responsibility for overseeing the various steps for the evaluation. Again using the example of interdisciplinary teaming, Figure 10-2 shows a planning sheet for evaluating the success of the inservice activities in meeting the goals and objectives established for interdisciplinary teaming.

In addition, information should also be gathered which determines whether or not the staff development activities have influenced actual behavior of teachers and administrators. This topic will be addressed in Chapter 11.

## Establish Staff Development Calendar and Finalize Staff Development Plan

The scheduling of staff development meetings (presentations, workshops, discussion sessions, action research, planning, etc.) is always a concern. One approach is to include inservice in the weekly schedule of events. Many schools arrange schedules so that once a week the pupil school day is shortened, allowing

**Figure 10-2**
Staff Development Evaluation Planning Sheet

*Staff Development Goal*
Establish an inservice program for preparing teachers and administrators in the skills necessary for successful interdisciplinary teaming

*Questions (Based on Objectives)*
1. What types of activities assist teachers in becoming skilled at developing flexible schedules?
2. What types of activities assist teachers in becoming more comfortable with the use of temporary groups for instruction which vary in number of students and length of time?
3. What types of activities assist teachers in the sequencing and integration of content?
4. What types of activities assist teachers in the development of skills in using a variety of instructional techniques?

| Objective(s) | Inservice Activity | Assessment Procedures | Deadline | Responsibility |
|---|---|---|---|---|
|  |  |  |  |  |
|  |  |  |  |  |
|  |  |  |  |  |

teachers and administrators an extended period of time either in the morning before students arrive or at the end of the school day (early release of students). Other schools set aside several full days during the course of the school year that are specifically identified for staff development. Summer workshops for skill acquisition and curriculum development also offer staff development opportunities for teachers and administrators.

Summer workshops and a few days scheduled throughout the year are not sufficient for developing and sustaining the kinds of supportive professional development cultures necessary for comprehensive school improvement. Opportunities for teachers, administrators, parents, and community members must be provided on a continuing basis. For this reason, school leaders must regularly schedule time for learning, study, inquiry, and reflection.

When scheduling staff development activities, the steering committee must coordinate carefully with the Chart of Objectives by Year of Implementation (Figure 9-6). Staff development needs to provide the supportive activities and skills for teachers and administrators who are in the process of introducing these new programs and strategies into their school and classrooms. For instance, the restructuring plan (Figure 9-6) calls for a four teacher interdisciplinary team at the seventh grade level to be organized during the first year. The steering committee needs to respond with appropriate staff development experiences that will assist teachers in this team to acquire the skills and knowledge to be successful. Figure 10-3 provides an example of a staff development plan designed to prepare teachers and administrators for interdisciplinary teaming. This planning format contains the following elements: the Restructuring Plan Goal (in this case, Goal 1 and Goal 1A), the identification of the cell (Schedule) in the Chart of Objectives by Year of Implementation, the Year (1, 1994), and the Staff Development Goal. The staff development objective(s), the inservice activity, the time of year scheduled, specific planning tasks to be completed, deadlines for completion, and the responsibility for task accomplishment are listed in the grid.

For each of the other restructuring plan goals, the steering committee needs to develop similar staff development plans. These plans, when combined, become the comprehensive staff development program for restructuring.

The planning of a staff development program for restructuring is a complex process based on many factors. Most schools in their process of planning develop a document that augments the

**Figure 10-3**
Staff Development Plan

*Restructuring Plan Goal:* 1. To incorporate into the school appropriate structures for supporting intellectual development.
    A. Provide flexibility of instructional time through the use of large time blocks and interdisciplinary teams.

*Chart of Objectives Cell:*   *Schedule*     *Year:* 1

*Staff Development Goal:* Establish an inservice program for preparing teachers and administrators in the knowledge and skills necessary for successful interdisciplinary teaming.

| Objective(s) | Inservice Activity | When Scheduled | Tasks | Deadlines | Responsibility |
|---|---|---|---|---|---|
| Use time flexibly | Workshop on block time scheduling and grouping | Summer 1994 | Schedule time, obtain consultant, select participants, secure funding | 3/1/94 | Steering Committee |
| Use flexible grouping | Workshop on block time scheduling and grouping | Summer 1994 | Schedule time, obtain consultant, select participants, secure funding | 3/1/94 | Steering Committee |
| Sequence and integrate content | Workshop Four half days during the school year | Summer 1994 Oct., Jan., March, May | Schedule times, obtain consultant, select participants, secure funding | 3/1/94 | Steering Committee |
| Use a variety of instructional techniques | School visitations | Spring 1994 | Identify schools, schedule visitations, select participants | 11/1/93 | Principal |
| | Seminars | Spring 1994 | Identify topics for seminars, secure expertise, schedule, secure funding, select participants | 10/1/93 | Steering Committee |
| | Conferences | Fall 1993 & Spring 1994 | Identify appropriate conferences, select participants, secure funding | 9/1/93 | Steering Committee |

restructuring planning document. By concentrating specifically on the procedures and strategies appropriate for accomplishing the identified needs, goals, and objectives of staff development, a comprehensive plan can be produced. As described earlier, such a planning document contains the following elements:

1.  Procedures for identifying and profiling the needs and characteristics of the adult learners in the school
2.  Procedures for analyzing restructuring plan goals and identifying specific skills and knowledge necessary for successful program implementation
3.  Procedures for establishing staff development goals and objectives
4.  Procedures for diagnosing current level of faculty skill and knowledge
5.  Procedures for identifying and selecting the most appropriate methods/strategies/modes for inservice education
6.  Procedures for evaluating the effectiveness of the inservice activities (Figure 10-2) and the processes used in structuring the staff development plan
7.  Procedures for scheduling inservice experiences and staff development planning (Figure 10-3)

## PHASE II—IMPLEMENTING THE STAFF DEVELOPMENT PROGRAM

The implementation of the staff development program includes four components:

1.  Instruction of teachers and administrators—implementation of the inservice program
2.  Introduction of programs—the implementation of the various programs identified in the restructuring plan
3.  Follow-up support—the support services given to teachers and administrators as they implement the new programs
4.  Evaluation—the collection of data as specified in Phase I (staff development evaluation plan)

These four components provide for the systematic application of the planning procedures to the implementation of staff development and to the restructuring plan (Figure 10-4).

**Figure 10-4**

Phase II - Implementing the Staff Development Program

1. *Implementation of the staff development plan*
   Skill and knowledge development for teachers and administrators

2. *Implementation of the restructuring plan*
   Systematic initiation of the various programs identified in the restructuring plan

3. *Provision for follow-up support*
   Continuing services which provide support to teachers and administrators as they learn new skills and implement the restructuring plan

4. *Implementation of staff development evaluation plan*
   Initiate the collection of data as specified in the staff development evaluation plan

## Instruction of Teachers and Administrators

Using the staff development plan and the restructuring plan, the steering committee initiates the inservice activities. The process should be monitored closely with close attention given to meeting individual needs and providing for a variety of experiences. Time frames should be adjusted as needed, moving faster when warranted, and slowing the pace when necessary to allow more time for skill acquisition and reflection.

## Implementation of New Programs

As staff development progresses and new skills and understandings are acquired, the steering committee can begin to implement the programs as specified on the Chart of Objectives by Year of Implementation (Figure 9-6). Caution should be exercised and adequate time must be provided for each person to grow at a rate of speed that is comfortable. Changing the roles and responsibilities of administrators and teachers requires gradual steps toward specified competencies in comfortable, collegial, supportive climates with a realistic time span.

## Follow-up Support

Middle level school restructuring is an ongoing process. The staff development program, therefore, does not end when new programs are implemented. Once new skills and understandings are acquired, opportunities must be provided to practice these new skills in appropriate settings and to reflect with colleagues on progress. Specialized help, either from consultants or mentor teachers, should be available throughout the process. Discussions and problem solving meetings should be regularly scheduled to share successes, to discuss problems and frustrations, and to develop suitable corrective strategies. New staff development activities should be planned to provide additional support as needed.

## Evaluation of the Staff Development Program

During the implementation phase, the staff development evaluation plan must be activated. The data collected should be formative in nature and provide feedback so that necessary modifications can be made. Evaluation data on the inservice activities should reflect changes in teacher and administrator attitudes and in the ways they perform their various work related responsibilities. Evaluation must also focus on the extent to which the inservice experiences were successful in meeting the goals and objectives for the staff development program during the first phase of planning. Those goals and objectives that were not met need to receive additional attention.

Evaluation is an integral part of both the planning and implementation phases of staff development. Without a carefully conceived evaluation plan, it is impossible to gain the data necessary for determining accomplishments and shortcomings, or to continue the cycle of learning and relearning so important to the restructuring process.

## SUMMARY

Staff development must be a continuing process. If a middle level school wishes to remain a viable institution, the process of restructuring must be a continuous process, with all phases of the plan undergoing constant scrutiny and revision. In a never ending cycle, needs are assessed, new curricular programs are developed and implemented, new staff development programs are organized, new skills and understandings are learned and implemented, and progress is evaluated.

Middle level schools, because of the changing nature of their clientele, must be on an ever-moving cycle of self-renewal. A well-conceived staff development program involves participants in the decision-making process and facilitates a collaborative culture focused on school improvement. It is on this foundation that successful middle level school restructuring is organized.

# REFERENCES

Barth, R. S. (1990). *Improving schools from within.* San Francisco, CA: Jossey-Bass Publishers.

Bents, R. H., & Howey, K. R. (1981). Staff development—change in the individual. In B. Dillon-Peterson (Ed.), *Staff development/organization development* (pp. 11-36). Alexandria, VA: Association for Supervision and Curriculum Development.

Clark, D. C., & Clark, S. N. (1983, October). Staff development programs for middle level schools. *Schools in the middle: A report on trends and practices.* Reston, VA: National Association of Secondary School Principals.

Clark, D. C., & Valentine, J. W. (1981, June). Middle level programs: Making the ideal a reality. *Schools in the middle: A report on trends and practices.* Reston, VA: National Association of Secondary School Principals.

Cooper, M. (1991). Stretching the limits of our vision: Staff development and the transformation of schools. In A. Lieberman, & L. Miller (Eds.), *Staff development for education in the '90s: New demands, new realities, new perspectives* (pp. 83-91). New York: Teachers College Press.

Dale, L. (1982). What is staff development? *Educational Leadership, 40*(1), 31.

Fenstermacher, G., & Berliner, D. (1983). A conceptual framework for the analysis of staff development—A Rand note. In *NIE Contract 400-79-0050, N-2046-NIE.* Santa Monica, CA: Rand Corporation.

Fenwick, J. (1992). *Managing middle grade reform—an "America 2000" agenda.* San Diego, CA: Fenwick Associates, Inc.

Fullan, M. (1990). Staff development, innovation, and institutional development. In B. Joyce (Ed.), *Changing school culture through staff development. The 1990 yearbook of the Association for Supervision and Curriculum Development* (pp. 3-25). Alexandria, VA: Association for Supervision and Curriculum Development.

Gregoric, A. (1982). *An adult's guide to style.* Maynard, MA: Gabriel Systems, Inc.

Griffin, G. A. (1991). Interactive staff development: Using what we know. In A. Lieberman, & L. Miller (Eds.), *Staff development for education in the '90s: New demands, new realities, new perspectives* (pp. 243-258). New York: Teachers College Press.

Joyce, B. (1990). Prologue. In B. Joyce (Ed.), *Changing school culture through staff development. 1990 Yearbook of the Association for Supervision and Curriculum Development* (pp. xv-xviii). Alexandria, VA: Association for Supervision and Curriculum Development.

Keefe, J. W. (1987). *Learning style theory and practice.* Reston, VA: National Association of Secondary School Principals.

Keefe, J. W., Clark, D. C., Nickerson, N. C., & Valentine, J. W. (1983). *The middle level principalship—Volume II: The effective middle level principal.* Reston, VA: National Association of Secondary School Principals.

Knowles, M. (1978). *The adult learner: A neglected species.* Houston, TX: Gulf.

Lieberman, A., & Miller, L. (1991). Revisiting the social realities of teaching. In A. Lieberman, & L. Miller (Eds.), *Staff development for education in the '90s: New demands, new realities, new perspectives* (pp. 92-109). New York: Teachers College Press.

McLaughlin, M. W. (1991). Enabling professional development: What have we learned? In A. Lieberman, & L. Miller (Eds.), *Staff development for education in the '90s: New demands, new realities, new perspectives* (pp. 61-82). New York: Teachers College Press.

Schaefer, R. (1967). *The school as a center of inquiry.* New York: Harper & Row.

Valentine, J. W., Clark, D. C., Irvin, J. L., Keefe, J. W., & Melton, G. (1993). *Leadership in middle level education, Volume I: A national survey of middle level leaders and schools.* Reston, VA: National Association of Secondary School Principals.

Wood, F., McQuarrie, F., & Thompson, S. (1982). Practitioners and professors agree on effective staff development practices. *Educational Leadership, 40*(1), 28-31.

Wood, F., Thompson, S., Russell, F. (1981). Designing effective staff development programs. In B. Dillon-Peterson (Ed.), *Staff development/organization development* (pp. 59-91). Alexandria, VA: Association for Supervision and Curriculum Development.

# 11

## Evaluating Middle Level
## Programs and Practices

> ". . . the test of an evaluation system is simply this: Does it deliver feedback that is needed, when it is needed, to the persons or groups who need it?"
>
> Fred Wilhelms

Evaluation serves many important functions in the restructuring process. When well-conceived and well-planned, evaluation programs provide: (1) insights into how programs are operating, (2) information on the extent to which they are serving their constituents, (3) findings which identify strengths and weaknesses, and (4) data about cost effectiveness. Information generated from evaluations can also assist in decision making, in establishing priorities, and in allocating resources. In short, evaluation can be organized to provide information on the processes of program implementation or it can be designed to provide information on the outcomes of restructuring efforts. Whatever the purposes, evaluation must be an ongoing process in the restructuring middle level school.

This chapter will focus on the evaluation of middle level school programs and practices (evaluation of student progress was discussed in Chapter 4). Emphasis will be placed on the purposes of evaluation, on formative and summative evaluation, and on the design and implementation of evaluation programs. Four different approaches to evaluation will be described and examples will be given.

## PURPOSES AND FUNCTIONS OF EVALUATION

Quality middle level programs depend on quality decision making; the quality of decision making depends on the ability of the decision makers to identify alternatives and to make sound judgments about these alternatives; sound judgments are dependent on timely access to information relating to the alternatives; the availability of this information requires a systematic approach to providing it; and the processes necessary for supplying this information collectively comprise the evaluative process (Stufflebeam, 1968). Stufflebeam, in fact, believed that producing data for decision making was the sole justification for evaluation (Stufflebeam, 1971).

Providing feedback for decision making was also the focus of Wilhelms (1967) and his colleagues on the 1967 Association for Supervision and Curriculum Development Yearbook Committee. In *Evaluation as Feedback and Guide* they submit that evaluation systems must provide feedback that is needed, when it is needed, and to the persons who need it. In order to satisfy these requirements, evaluation must meet the following conditions: (1) it must facilitate self-evaluation, (2) it must encompass all of the objectives valued by the school, (3) it must facilitate learning and teaching, (4) it must produce appropriate records for a variety of uses, and (5) it must facilitate decision making on curriculum and educational policy (Wilhelms, 1967).

While a major purpose of evaluation continues to be to provide feedback for decision making, Herman, Morris, and Fitz-Gibbon (1987), drawing from the literature of the last 25 years, have identified several other purposes of evaluation. These purposes include: assessing student progress and the effectiveness of educational innovations (Bloom, Hastings, and Madaus, 1971; Popham, 1975); describing program processes and the value perspectives of key people (Stake, 1975); identifying effects, explaining effects, and generating generalizations about program effectiveness (Rossi and Freeman, 1985); assessing programs based on criteria apart from the program's own conceptual framework, especially to the extent to which real client needs are met (Scriven, 1972); and structuring evaluation to maximize the use of its findings by specific stakeholders and users (Patton, 1986).

Although the purposes of the various models of evaluation differ, many writers believe that in practice program evaluation should include several approaches, thus fostering a more eclectic approach to the process (Glatthorn, 1987; Herman, Morris, and Fitz-Gibbon, 1987). In spite of differences, most evaluative approaches have commonalities (Glatthorn, 1987; Stecher and Davis, 1987). For instance, Stecher and Davis (1987) suggest that all evaluation approaches share the common goal of providing accurate information that will assist educators in assessing and or enhancing their educational programs. Brandt (1981) in an analysis of the models of Popham, Stake, Scriven, Eisner, and Worthen, found the following commonalities: studying the context, determining client concerns, using qualitative methods, being sensitive to unintended effects, and developing different reports for different audiences. By recognizing the specific purposes of the various approaches to evaluation and being cognizant of their commonalities, the eclectic approach offers middle level educators the opportunity to draw from the strengths of several models.

## Formative and Summative Evaluation

Formative and summative evaluation play important roles in evaluating the middle level school. While focusing on very different aspects of the program, systematic use of both forms of evaluation can provide educators with valuable information on processes and outcomes.

**Formative evaluation**, with its emphasis on process, encompasses numerous aspects of school improvement such as the planning process, the monitoring of progress, and the quality of involvement. Formative evaluation has as its major function the gathering of information that will facilitate ongoing improvement and monitoring of progress, information that is used in the continuing revision process. The purpose of formative evaluation is improving the middle level program, not offering proof of its effectiveness.

Program monitoring, a key function of formative evaluation, commonly focuses on the following components: information related to the implementation plan, information related to classroom practices, information related to the improvement goal, and information related to staff concerns (Office of School Improvement, 1983).

Data collection procedures for formative evaluation usually includes questionnaires, surveys, interviews, discussions, and observations.

**Summative evaluation** has as its goal the collection and presentation of summary information about the school program. This information forms the basis for judgments about program effectiveness and success. The primary purpose of summative evaluation is to provide summary reports to the various school constituencies.

Summative evaluation commonly uses the following steps in describing program outcomes: reviewing information collected during the monitoring process and looking for trends and describing them; collecting information concerning student achievement/social behavior goals and faculty/staff accomplishments and attitudes; assessing opinions from those involved in the effort; preparing the final report. This final report describes the goals and the process that led to program development, highlighting the events associated with implementation, emphasizing progress that has been made toward the goals, and suggesting ways in which things could have been improved (Office of School Improvement, 1983).

Typically, summative evaluation uses more sophisticated evaluation approaches based upon research design and the use of quantitative data. Common practices in information gathering include pre and post testing, standardized measurements, and performance-based evaluation.

## Organization of Evaluation Programs

There are certain organizational components that are common to all approaches to evaluation. Using these components will assure middle level educators that their evaluations will be comprehensive and will generate the kinds of data needed for school improvement and reporting outcomes.

While there are numerous listings of organizational structures for evaluation, the following listing, drawn from several sources (Glatthorn, 1987; Herman, Morris, and Fitz-Gibbon, 1987; Newman, 1991; Stake, 1972; Stecher and Davis, 1987; Stufflebeam, 1968; Wilhelms, 1967) will serve as a comprehensive structure for middle level leaders. The list includes:

1.　Establish the goals and objectives of the evaluation (focus of evaluation; breadth and depth of evaluation; purposes of evaluation)
2.　Identify and select appropriate evaluation models, designs, and procedures (evaluative instruments; strategies)
3.　Identify and generate resources to support the evaluation plan (funding; personnel; time)

4. Collect data (determine time lines; identify responsibility; distribute materials)
5. Analyze information
6. Report information (appropriate reports for differing constituencies)
7. Administration of information (use of information for program change; documenting effectiveness; reflection)

These components are universal in their application and should be carefully considered in the development of appropriate evaluation structures. When formulated into questions, these components provide excellent guidelines for middle level leaders in the development of their evaluation programs.

1. What do we need to know and how are we going to use the information when we obtain it? (purpose)
2. How will we obtain the needed information in appropriate and affordable ways? (data collection)
3. How will we analyze the information? (data analysis)
4. How and to whom will we report the findings? (communication of information)

## MIDDLE LEVEL SCHOOL EVALUATION— FOUR EXAMPLES

There are a variety of approaches that can be used to evaluate middle level schools and four examples of approaches that might be used will be described in this section. They include evaluation programs that focus on: (1) early adolescent characteristics as the basis for appropriate middle level school organization, (2) the impact of program and practice on middle level students, (3) program and organizational structures of successful middle level schools, and (4) school environment and school improvement. These four approaches, which have been used by numerous middle level educators and are representative of good evaluative practice, can be effectively used for gathering information for school improvement (formative evaluation) and for reporting outcomes (summative evaluation).

### A Focus on Early Adolescent Characteristics

The *Middle Grades Assessment Program (MGAP)* was developed by the Center for Early Adolescence, University of North Carolina

(Dorman, 1984). Concerned about the lack of consensus about what appropriate schools for young adolescents should be, the Center established criteria for successful middle level schools which were founded in an extensive knowledge base about early adolescent needs and characteristics. These criteria were established to form a common ground about developmentally responsive middle level schools that would serve the needs of educators who need guidance upon which to make decisions about programs and practice, of parents who desire understandable information about quality programs, and of elected and appointed officials who need a framework for setting policy.

Developed so that both educators and lay people can have a common understanding about middle level schools, *MGAP* instruments (structured interviews and observations) are designed so that all stakeholders can participate in the evaluative process and, as a consequence, build a common perspective about the success of their schools. In other words, teachers, administrators, parents, and community members can "see and hear evidence that will lead to productive dialogue and informed conclusions about their schools" (Dorman, 1984; 1).

Structured around the need of young adolescents for (1) diversity, (2) opportunities for self-exploration and self-definition, (3) meaningful participation in school and community, (4) positive social interaction with peers and adults, (5) physical activity, (6) competence and achievement, and (7) structure and clear limits, *MGAP* is guided by the following principles:

1. Adolescence is a normal stage of human development.
2. The *Middle Grades Assessment Program* is based on the premise that the understanding of adolescence as a normal and exciting developmental stage should be the basis upon which decisions are made about middle level schooling.
3. The education of young adolescents is a joint venture shared by educators, elected and appointed policymakers, parents, and concerned citizens.
4. Parents, concerned citizens, and educators need to know how to have a positive effect on the educational system.
5. Effective advocacy is more often collaborative than adversarial (Dorman, 1984; 1-2).

**Purposes of MGAP.** The major purpose of the *Middle Grades Assessment Program* is to be a tool for assessment and decision making in schools for young adolescents. The information gathered in the evaluation process is intended to provide direction for school improvement. Information can also be used to reassure parents by providing indicators of school success, to provide feedback to educators about the school's strengths and weaknesses, and to inform policymakers.

**Data Collection Procedures.** *MGAP* is designed to involve a number of persons in the evaluation process. Ideally, the assessment team should consist of teachers, school staff members, parents, community members, and perhaps a school board member. This assessment team has the responsibility of coordinating all aspects of the evaluative process.

Data is gathered by using structured interviews and observation checklists. In addition to the principal, structured interviews have been developed for teachers, guidance counselors, students, parents, and support staff. Observation checklists are developed to focus on the observation of facilities, classroom instruction, the media center/library, student rules and expectations, and general environment.

Since widespread involvement in the assessment process is encouraged, *MGAP* has developed specialized training that includes the use of the interview and observation forms. Special attention is given to interviewing skills, listening skills, and observation skills. To get a more comprehensive picture of the school, it is encouraged that the interviews and observations be conducted on different days and at different times.

**Analysis of Data.** Each member of the assessment team is responsible for analyzing the results of his or her interviews and observations. *MGAP* provides "summarizing sheets" for this purpose. Each question on the structured interviews and each element on the observation sheets is coded into one of the following needs: (1) safety, (2) academic effectiveness, (3) diversity, (4) self-definition, (5) participation, (6) social interaction, (7) physical activity, (8) competence and achievement, and (9) structure and limits. On the Summarizing Sheet for Safety, for example, assessors individually examine their interview and observation forms reviewing the items identified for Safety (e.g., principal interview—question #14, teacher interview—question #11, student interview—question #5, etc.). Inconsistencies among the groups are noted and comments are recorded. The process continues until each of the nine Summarizing Sheets have been completed.

When the individual analysis has been completed, the assessment team meets and exchanges information, arrives at consensus, and decides how the findings will be reported.

**Reporting the Findings.** The nature of the report depends on the purposes of the evaluation. If the purpose is to provide information for policymakers, a formal report should be written. If the purpose is to facilitate program improvement, more informal reporting, such as oral reports at faculty meetings or informal written reports such as memos or occasional papers should be used. Reporting to parents could be done at parent meetings or by newsletters.

## A Focus on the Impact of Program and Practice on Students

The *Shadow Study* technique is a procedure that has been used by numerous middle level schools to determine the impact of school programs and classroom instruction on young adolescents. A shadow study is an adult following a middle level pupil (who is unaware of the shadow) for an entire day and recording all of the experiences, activities, and interactions of that pupil. Notations are usually recorded at five- to seven-minute intervals. In addition to its use in individual schools, this technique has also been used in two national studies of eighth grade (Lounsbury and Clark, 1990; Lounsbury and Marani, 1964), one sixth grade study (Lounsbury and Johnston, 1988), one seventh grade study (Lounsbury, Marani, and Compton, 1980), and one ninth grade study (Lounsbury and Johnston, 1985).

Classified as a quasi-ethnographic procedure, shadow studies enable evaluators and researchers to obtain realistic snapshots of the educational experiences of students during the actual school day. By focusing on randomly selected pupils and the minute-by-minute activities of those pupils, revealing pictures of educational processes are presented (Lounsbury and Johnston, 1988).

While the activities and actions of teachers are a part of the picture of a student's school day, looking at the day's events through the eyes of a student, a different and in many ways a more valid perspective is secured than when focusing on the teacher's activities. Lounsbury and Johnston suggest that:

When taken altogether and analyzed, these shadow studies
provide a dramatic picture of the real curriculum, the curriculum actually experienced by the individual pupil (1988; 122).

The shadow study technique, with its systematic observation of students throughout the school day and an end-of-the-
day student interview, is an excellent approach for determining
the school experiences of middle level students.

**Purposes of Shadow Studies.** The primary purpose of shadow
studies is to determine the impact of school programs on the
lives of young adolescents. Because shadow study observations
give an accurate picture of the relevancy of curriculum to students, their involvement in learning, and their interaction with
peers and adults, the information collected can be used as a
basis for school improvement or for school personnel to make
judgments about how well existing programs are functioning.
For instance, a school with a standard schedule might intro-
duce interdisciplinary teaming after their shadow study showed
student apathy toward the curriculum and lack of student
involvement in learning. On the other hand, a school with interdisciplinary teaming might renew their efforts to be more flexible
in their scheduling and to develop integrated units after the
shadow study indicated that teaming was having no visible
impact on time usage or content organization.

Another important purpose of shadow studies is to allow
teachers, administrators, parents, and community members to
experience a typical student day. By walking in a student's shoes
for a day, many adults become committed to making education
more active and exciting for students.

**Data Collection Procedures.** Data are gathered by adults who
follow randomly selected students throughout the entire day.
This includes the classroom, the halls, the cafeteria, and the
gym and shower room. Every five to seven minutes the observer
records the time of the observation, the specific behavior of the
student, the environment, and comments and impressions. At
the end of the day the observer interviews the student using a
structured interview.

When the purpose of the shadow study is to determine the
program impact for the purposes of preassessment for school
improvement, the shadow study observers are usually drawn
from the faculty, staff, and parent organization. The process of

gathering the data by the stakeholders of the school is essential in building ownership for restructuring. If the purpose of the shadow study is to evaluate the impact of specific programs such as teaming or teacher advisories, shadow study observers are often drawn from other school settings. These teachers and administrators are usually able to make more objective observations than those who are intimately involved with the school.

Shadow study observers do not require extensive preparation for their day of shadowing. A session of about 45 minutes the day before or the morning of the shadow study which acquaints the shadowers with observation techniques, procedures for recording observations on the form, and strategies for conducting the student interviews has been found to be adequate. Considerable time, however, will be required after the data have been gathered to allow observers to collate, analyze, and plan for the appropriate use of the information.

To get a representative picture of the school, students shadowed should represent a wide spectrum of the student body. In addition, the observations should take place over a period of a couple of weeks, avoiding Mondays and Fridays and any day before a holiday.

**Analysis of Data.** At the end of the day, when the shadow study has been completed and the interview conducted, each observer should reflect on his or her experience. These reflections should be summarized by preparing a statement of reactions and thoughts about the shadowing experience. These reactions should also represent personal impressions and reactions as well as a discussion of the implications of these impressions for the school.

When the individual summaries have been written, the observers should meet as a group and discuss their findings. Information should be examined for trends and indications of school strengths and weaknesses.

Some schools analyze their shadow study data using specific criteria or focused questions. For example, the following topics might form the basis for analysis:

Based on the information we gathered from the shadow studies, what conclusions can we draw about our school?

1. Curriculum content (subject matter)
2. Scheduling arrangements/curricular organization (departmentalization; block scheduling; teaming; self-contained)

3.   Instruction and teaching methods
4.   Teacher-student interaction
5.   Physical environment
6.   Advising and counseling
7.   Opportunities for social skill learning
8.   School climate (student and teacher attitudes)

The conclusions drawn from such a listing of topics might form the basis of the report and become part of future school improvement plans.

**Reporting the Findings.** The procedures used for reporting the findings to the faculty, parents, and community members should be determined by the participants of the shadow study. In many cases, the report tends to be informal and often takes place during faculty and parent meetings or as part of a staff development activity.

The report should include a review of the major shadow study findings, a review of individual observer opinions and impressions, the identification of strengths and areas in need of improvement or modification, and specific recommendations for school improvement. As part of the reporting process, teachers, administrators, parents, and community members should have the opportunity to discuss and react to the findings and seek clarification when needed.

The reporting process serves as a culminating point for the actual study and a beginning point for program modification and restructuring.

## A Focus on Program and Organizational Structure

*Turning Points: Preparing American Youth for the 21st Century* presents the recommendations of the Carnegie Task Force on Education of Young Adolescents (1989). While not a plan for evaluation, the eight recommendations (see Chapter 2) provide criteria for implementing developmentally responsive programs and organizational structures, criteria which can also serve as the basis for evaluation. The fact that the recommendations in *Turning Points* are based on research drawn from a variety of disciplines make them very defensible as a guide for implementation and evaluation purposes.

When using *Turning Points* as a model for school assessment, the critical question that every middle level teacher and administrator should ask is: How well does our school compare with the recommendations of the Carnegie Task Force? This question is best addressed by answering a series of questions based on each of the eight recommendations found in *Turning Points*.

For the purposes of school assessment, Clark and Clark (1990) have developed sample questions which provide focus to each of the *Turning Points* recommendations. These questions have been used by numerous middle level school educators to guide the assessment of their programs and organizational structures. For example, the focusing questions for Carnegie Recommendation #1—Creating a Community for Learning are:

1. Is our school a place where close, trusting relationships with adults and peers create a climate for personal growth and intellectual development?
2. What steps have we taken or could we take to create smaller learning environments?
3. Does every child in our school have at least one adult who will serve as an advocate and/or advisor?

Examples of focusing questions for all eight recommendations in *Turning Points* are shown in Figure 11-1.

While the use of the Carnegie recommendations and the focusing questions is not an evaluation system or strategy such as the *Middle Grades Assessment Program* or the Shadow Study, it offers the advantage of greater flexibility in the selection of data collection strategies and the use of multiple research designs. Although the eight recommendations of *Turning Points* provide comprehensive guidelines for middle level school improvement, most middle level schools will not be implementing all of the *Turning Points*' recommendations at the same time. Because of time constraints, school and community belief systems, and limited financial resources, those recommendations that are most appropriate to the needs and characteristics of the students should receive top priority for adoption and for evaluation. Those recommendations not implemented initially should be studied and considered for future adoption.

**Purposes of Evaluation.** The focusing questions developed by Clark and Clark (1990) are most frequently used for preassessment; that is, to collect information about the school in order to determine how closely it comes to meeting the recommendations established by the Carnegie Task Force. This data then becomes

*Examples of Focusing Questions*

Carnegie Recommendation #1: **Creating a Community for Learning**

Questions:

> Is our school a place where close, trusting relationships with adults and peers create a climate for personal growth and intellectual development?
>
> What steps have we taken or could we take to create smaller learning environments?
>
> Does every child in our school have at least one adult who will serve as an advocate and/or advisor?

Carnegie Recommendation #2: **Teaching a Core of Common Knowledge**

Questions:

> Are young adolescents in our school learning to think critically? Are they given opportunities to become actively involved in problem-solving activities?
>
> Is there emphasis in the curriculum on the development of healthful lifestyles?
>
> Are there opportunities for young adolescents to learn life skills through participation in school and community service?
>
> Is subject matter being integrated across the various subject disciplines?

Carnegie Recommendation #3: **Ensuring Success for All Students**

Questions:

> Do all young adolescents in our school have the opportunity to succeed in every aspect of the program regardless of previous achievement or the pace at which they learn?
>
> Do we group students for instruction? If so, have we examined the consequences of grouping practices on adolescent learners? Have we examined ways in which instruction can be improved by the removal of tracking practices?
>
> Are we currently using any form of flexible scheduling?
>
> Are there opportunities for students to learn at times other than the regularly scheduled class periods (before school, after school, at lunch)?
>
> Are there opportunities for students to participate in a variety of school and community activities where they can experience success, self-worth, and recognition?

Carnegie Recommendation #4: **Empowering Teachers and Administrators**

Questions:

> Are decisions concerning the school experiences of our students being made by the teachers and administrators in our school?

*(continued)*

**Figure 11-1** *(continued)*

Are teachers given responsibility on what should be taught and how it should be taught?

Do teachers and administrators participate regularly in the governance of the school?

Are teachers given opportunities to assume leadership positions with regard to teaching and learning?

Carnegie Recommendation #5: **Preparing Teachers for the Middle Grades**

Questions:

Are teachers in our school specially prepared to teach young adolescents?

Are teachers in our school required to have middle level certification? If not, do we have special criteria for selecting and hiring teachers who have received special preparation for teaching in middle level schools?

Do we make provisions to provide regular staff development for all persons in our school?

Carnegie Recommendation #6: **Improving Academic Performance Through Better Health and Fitness**

Questions:

Does our school provide a climate that promotes healthy lifestyles for faculty, staff, and students?

Are all students given access to health services when needed?

Is our school a model for healthy behavior? Are good health practices promoted and modeled by faculty and staff?

Is our school emotionally and physically safe for both students and adults?

Carnegie Recommendation #7: **Reengaging Families in the Education of Young Adolescents**

Questions:

Are families and faculty members in our school allied through trust and respect in efforts to ensure that all young adolescents will succeed?

Does our school regularly involve parents in meaningful roles in the governance of the school?

Does our school work actively to inform parents of the progress of their children?

Does our school actively engage parents' help in the learning process? Are opportunities given for parents to work in classrooms as tutors? Are parents given assistance in how to help their children learn at home?

Carnegie Recommendation #8: **Connecting Schools with Communities**

Questions:

Are community organizations working with us to share the responsibility for each young adolescent's success?

*(Continued)*

**Figure 11-1** *(continued)*

---

Are all students required to participate in a service project?

Does our school serve as a clearinghouse for special community services needed by students?

Does our school work cooperatively with other community agencies to promote middle level education?

Does our school actively solicit support from community businesses, service clubs, and foundations in the provision of resources for students and teachers?

---

Adapted from Clark, S. and Clark, D. (1990). Restructuring Middle Level Schools: Strategies for Using *Turning Points*. Reston, VA: NASSP.

the basis for discussion and for developing the school restructuring plan. In some cases, the focusing questions have also been used to assess the progress the school has made in implementing the Carnegie recommendations.

**Data Collection Procedures.** In designing data collection strategies which address the focusing questions, teachers and administrators should use a variety of techniques, techniques which include both quantitative and qualitative approaches. Surveys, questionnaires, interviews, discussions, and observation all are excellent sources of data.

To address the questions in a systematic manner, it is useful to develop a planning grid (strategic plan) that includes: listing of the Carnegie recommendation, listing of the focusing question to be answered, assessment strategy to be used, procedures for analysis, time lines, and person(s) responsible for monitoring the evaluation process. This process, which should include broad-based participation of faculty, staff, parents, and community members, assures that each focusing question will be addressed appropriately, with procedures that are acceptable, and that will generate data that are relevant and useful.

**Analysis of Data.** Data analysis is largely dependent upon the measurement strategies used to collect the information. For example, if questionnaires or surveys are used, analysis should provide information on means, modes, and medians. Discussions should focus on the analysis of trends, the development of consensus, and the organization of the data into formats that are understandable and useful.

**Reporting the Findings.** There are numerous strategies for presenting the findings of the evaluation. As with the other approaches previously described (*MGAP* and Shadow Studies), the findings can be presented in a formal report, as part of faculty or parent meetings, or as the focus of staff development. The following format has been found to be helpful in organizing the report:

1. Statement of purpose (goals/objectives)
2. Listing of each Carnegie recommendation and focusing questions
3. Description of assessment strategies, analysis procedures, and major findings for each focusing question
4. Summary of findings to include major findings, trends, and conclusions
5. Implications of findings for school improvement

## A Focus on School Environment and Improvement

*The Comprehensive Assessment of School Environments— Instructional Management System* (*CASE-IMS*) was developed by the National Association of Secondary School Principals' Task Force on School Environments (Howard and Keefe, 1991). The purpose was to provide a process by which middle level and high school educators could systematically evaluate school programs and develop comprehensive plans for school improvement. The *CASE-IMS* differs from the three previous approaches to middle level school evaluation in that it (1) relies on questionnaires as its prime source of input and (2) it incorporates the use of technology in the analysis of data and the development of the school improvement plan.

*CASE-IMS* is a management and planning system that provides instruments for assessing district and school variables, including district and community demographics, school input variables, climate variables, and student outcome variables. The *CASE-IMS* system includes the following components:

1. Instruments for assessing 34 input, mediating, and output variables of a school environment.
2. Computer software for scoring response sheets and interpreting data.
3. Procedures for predicting the effects of alternative paths of action on school outcomes.

4. Suggested interventions for positively affecting selected variables.
5. A step-by-step process for translating assessment information into significant school improvement projects (Howard and Keefe, 1991; vii).

Rigorously validated and field tested, *CASE-IMS* variables are keyed into an extensive bank of school improvement strategies that can assist middle level educators in school planning and decision making. Facilitating this process is a software program that supports a variety of planning and restructuring processes, including budgeting decisions; presentations to parents, community members, and policymakers; and the development of reports which report specific program outcomes.

*CASE-IMS* provides a comprehensive approach to school evaluation. When used in combination with the *CASE-IMS* eight-step school improvement process or the strategic planning process described in Chapter 9, *CASE-IMS* is a "state-of-the-art system for data-based, outcomes-based decision making" (Howard and Keefe, 1991; v).

**Purposes of CASE-IMS.** The *CASE-IMS* system is designed to assess 34 middle level and high school input, mediating, and output variables for the purpose of initiating and maintaining school improvement programs. Although secondary in purpose, the system can also generate data that is useful in developing reports on school effectiveness.

**Data Collection Procedures.** Data collection, which consists of two phases, is coordinated by the leadership team. This team, which also oversees the development of the restructuring plan as described in Chapter 9, collects baseline data and administers the seven assessment instruments.

The baseline data on the six outcome variables, which can be collected independently or as part of the assessment, include data from the Principal Questionnaire (total achievement, percentage of students receiving discipline referrals, percentage of students passing all courses, and percentage of students completing the school year); and data from the Student Report Form (student self-efficacy and student satisfaction).

The assessment instruments from the *CASE-IMS* system include:

- **School Climate Survey**—55 items which assess the perceptions of students, teachers, and parents regarding ten characteristics of the school
- **Teacher Satisfaction Survey**—56 items which measure teacher perceptions on nine dimensions of job satisfaction
- **Student Satisfaction Survey**—46 items which assess eight dimensions of student satisfaction with school (also part of baseline data)
- **Parent Satisfaction Survey**—58 items designed to determine parent satisfaction with nine dimensions of school operation and services
- **Principal Report Form**—98 items which collect data on school/community demographics, budget expenditures, curricular offerings, school change processes, the school leadership team, district practices, school and district goals, characteristics of the school student population, and achievement test data
- **Teacher Report Form**—23 items which collect data on teachers' perceptions of school/district goals, teacher autonomy, and teacher participation in decision making
- **Student Report Form**—8 items which collect data on student responses to Brookover Self-Concept of Ability scale (also part of the baseline data)

**Analysis of Data.** NCS and SCANTRON answer sheets are available. For those schools without optical scanning equipment, answers can be entered into the computer by a keyboard operator; commercial scoring is also available. When using only the climate and satisfaction instruments, the manual provides specific information on how to score the materials by hand.

**Reporting the Findings.** The comprehensiveness of the assessment process and the versatility of the software program enables the leadership team to generate reports for a variety of purposes. In reporting the findings of the assessment, *CASE-IMS* is designed to assist in two important tasks: (1) the identification of program strengths and problems and (2) the planning of school improvement projects. For the purposes of identifying program strengths and weaknesses, the program facilitates the:

- Comparison of mean scores across various groups (students and teachers; teachers and parents)
- Provision for comprehensive printouts of mean scores on selected variables for each group being compared

- Explanation of the significance of differences between mean scores for educators interested in statistical differences

School planning and improvement is facilitated in two specific ways:

- An "interventions command" which suggests a number of possible actions a school might take to improve its performance on the variables
- A "what if" analysis that will predict the effect of demographic trends and/or planned changes on student outcomes

Using the full potential of the *CASE-IMS* System, a final report might contain the following elements:

1. A summary of the Climate and Satisfaction data with comparisons to validated norms
2. A listing of those variables perceived by various stakeholder groups as being strengths and weaknesses
3. A list of potential interventions, as suggested by the *CASE-IMS* program, for each variable perceived to be a priority
4. "A summary of the 'What if' analysis indicating which input/output mediating variables, if positively affected by the interventions, would be most likely to affect each of the six outcome variables" (Howard and Keefe, 1991; 12)

## SUMMARY

Four examples of appropriate evaluation programs have been presented in this chapter: (1) *Middle Grades Assessment Program* (focus on middle level school criteria based on the needs of young adolescents), (2) *Shadow Studies* (focus on the impact of programs and practice on middle level students), (3) *Turning Points'* Recommendations (focus on program and organizational structure), and (4) *Comprehensive Assessment of School Environments—Instructional Management System* (focus on school environment and improvement). These examples address major issues and themes of importance to middle level school evaluation and improvement.

While each example is unique in its approach, all four place emphasis on evaluation as an ongoing process that provides information to support the continuing process of school improvement. All four approaches also place great importance on collaboration in the planning, in the collection of data, in the analysis, and in the reporting. Involvement of all stakeholders in the process is critical to the success of the evaluation program.

In the restructuring middle level school, evaluation must become an accepted part of the school culture, recognized for the support that it gives to the reflective and school renewal processes. Evaluation is an ongoing process which provides feedback on school strengths and weaknesses, provides for the continuing flow of data that informs decision making, and provides the support for comprehensive school improvement efforts.

## REFERENCES

Bloom, B. A., Hastings, J. T., & Madaus, G. F. (1971). *Handbook on formative and summative evaluation.* New York: McGraw Hill.

Brandt, R. S. (1981). *Applied strategies for curriculum evaluation.* Alexandria, VA: Association for Supervision and Curriculum Development.

Carnegie Task Force on Eduction of Young Adolescents. (1989). *Turning points: Preparing American youth for the 21st century.* Washington, D.C.: Carnegie Council on Adolescent Development.

Clark, S. N., & Clark, D. C. (1990, December). Restructuring middle schools: Strategies for using Turning Points. *Schools in the middle—Theory into practice.* Reston, VA: National Association of Secondary School Principals.

Dorman, G. (1984). *Middle grades assessment program—User's manual.* Carrboro, NC: Center for Early Adolescence, University of North Carolina.

Glatthorn, A. A. (1987). *Curriculum leadership.* Glenview, IL: Scott, Foresman & Company.

Herman, J. L., Morris, L. L., & Fitz-Gibbon, C. T. (1987). *Evaluator's handbook.* Newbury Park, CA: Sage.

Howard, E. R., & Keefe, J. W. (1991). *The CASE-IMS school improvement process.* Reston, VA: National Association of Secondary School Principals.

Lounsbury, J. H., & Clark, D. C. (1990). *Inside grade eight: From apathy to excitement.* Reston, VA: National Association of Secondary School Principals.

Lounsbury, J. H., & Johnston, J. H. (1985). *How fares the ninth grade?* Reston, VA: National Association of Secondary School Principals.

Lounsbury, J. H., & Johnston, J. H. (1988). *Life in the three sixth grades.* Reston, VA: National Association of Secondary School Principals.

Lounsbury, J. H., & Marani, J. (1964). *The junior high school we saw: One day in the eighth grade.* Alexandria, VA: Association for Supervision and Curriculum Development.

Lounsbury, J. H., Marani, J., & Compton, M. (1980). *The middle school in profile: A day in the seventh grade.* Columbus, OH: National Middle School Association.

Newman, W. (1991). Program evaluation. In J. W. Keefe, & J. M. Jenkins (Eds.), *Instructional leaders handbook, 2nd edition* (pp. 201-202). Reston, VA: National Association of Secondary School Principals.

Office of School Improvement. (1983). *School improvement handbook, workshop four: Evaluation/Communications.* Anchorage, AK: Alaska Department of Education.

Patton, M. Q. (1986). *Utilization-focused evaluation.* Newbury Park, CA: Sage.

Popham, W. J. (1975). *Educational evaluation.* Englewood Cliffs, N.J.: Prentice-Hall.

Rossi, A., & Freeman, H. E. (1985). *Evaluation: A systematic approach.* Newbury Park, CA: Sage.

Scriven, M. (1972). Pros and cons about goal-free evaluation. *Evaluation Comment, 3*(4), 1-4.

Stake, R. E. (1975). *Evaluating the arts education: A responsive approach.* Columbus, OH: Charles E. Merrill.

Stecher, B. M., & Davis, W. A. (1987). *How to focus evaluation.* Newbury Park, CA: Sage.

Stufflebeam, D. (1968, July 30). Toward a science of educational evaluation. *Educational Technology,* 5-12.

Stufflebeam, D. (1971). *Educational evaluation and decision making.* Itasca, IL: Peacock.

Wilhelms, F. T. (1967). *Evaluation as feedback and guide.* Washington, D.C.: Association for Supervision and Curriculum Development.

Worthen, B. (1968, August 15). Toward a taxonomy of evaluation designs. *Educational Technology,* 3-9.

# 12

## Responsive Middle Level Schools:
## The Continuing Challenge

> "Schools are social entities and, like
> the human spirit, require the chal-
> lenge of improvement not only to
> soar, but to maintain themselves."
> Joyce, Hersch, and McKibbin

This book reflects the insights we have gained in our continuing work with middle level schools since the early 1960s. As teachers, administrators, university professors, and consultants, we have had the unique opportunity of viewing middle level education from many perspectives. We have witnessed many of the programs described in this book as they emerged from promising ideas to programs and practices that are supported by the research. We have grown with the middle school concept and watched it become more accepted by educators and parents throughout the nation. Perhaps, most of all, we have been captivated by the excitement, the enthusiasm, and the potential middle level education has for making a difference in the lives of young adolescents.

In this book we describe a systematic approach for middle level school restructuring. This approach relies heavily on enlightened and visionary leadership and informed collaborative decision making. We provide a structure for involving all of the school constituencies in a comprehensive process of strategic planning and program implementation. We do, however, recognize that even in the most systematic of strategic plans there is always the unexpected, the human element, the serendipitous. It is in the schools where the vision is shared, the mission is clear, and the plan is comprehensive that teachers and administrators are able to use the unexpected as an opportunity to make something good happen for themselves and for their students.

## MAINTAINING THE CLIMATE OF CHANGE

The insights gained from our experiences, tempered by our own research and that of others, have led us to the conclusion that there are five factors which are crucial in maintaining a climate supportive of middle level school restructuring. These factors, which include restructuring as a process, visionary and shared leadership, confronting knowledge bases, creating a community of learners, and establishing a school climate of inquiry, are described in this section.

### Restructuring is a Process not a Product

It must be clearly understood that the processes described in this book are only a starting point in changing schools. Middle level school restructuring is a continuous process of diagnosis, goal setting, program development and implementation, and evaluation. Schools that are committed to developmental responsiveness are always in the process of restructuring or "becoming."

### The Importance of Visionary Leadership

Visionary leadership is the foundation on which middle level school restructuring is built. Most often this leadership comes from an administrator who has a passion for middle level education and has communicated a vision of what that school can be like to his or her staff. In other instances, teachers have assumed leadership positions and have been powerful forces in the process of change. These teachers assume various important roles in school governance and are given the autonomy to make decisions. Where the leadership comes from is not important. What is important is that visionary leadership exists to guide the restructuring process.

### The Importance of a Comprehensive Knowledge Base for Decision Making

We believe strongly that teachers, administrators, parents, and community members must be well informed in order to make

# SECTION V

Restructuring the Middle Level School:
Maintaining the Climate for Change

good decisions about their schools. For that reason, four chapters of this book concentrated on important issues dealing with early adolescent development; curriculum, instruction, and assessment; and successful middle level programs and practices. We are also cognizant that while many middle level educators possess an excellent knowledge of middle level issues that knowledge is not always reflected in the programs and practices of their schools.

We agree with Glickman (1991) when he suggests that educators must confront their own professional knowledge base as a guide for restructuring. Drawing from major research in the field of education, Glickman (1991) identifies "what we know" and suggests educators confront this knowledge. He believes that for years schools have been operated in ways that are not in the best interests of children. Educators have chosen, perhaps driven by their own belief systems or standards and values of the community, to ignore or at least "pretend ignorance" of the professional knowledge base. Learning this knowledge base and confronting it, Glickman suggests, is where school restructuring efforts must begin. He identifies eleven issues supported by research and practice that educators need to examine and consider in their efforts to improve their schools. Five of those issues that are particularly important to middle level educators are: (1) tracking, (2) retention in grade, (3) corporal punishment, (4) learning from real activities and experiences, and (5) measuring school worth based on the learning their students can display in authentic or real settings.

Many middle level educators have not confronted this knowledge. If they have, they have not acted on it. For example, tracking remains a common practice in middle level schools (Braddock, 1990; Lounsbury and Clark, 1990), and middle level classrooms for the most part feature passive learning (Lounsbury and Clark, 1990). In addition, middle level educators need to confront the specific knowledge base of middle level education. Why, for instance, when a growing body of research is reporting positive findings in support of interdisciplinary teaming and teacher advisories, are fewer than fifty percent of American middle level schools implementing these programs? The growing body of knowledge about developmentally appropriate programs and practice must be confronted by middle level educators and then used as a guide to school improvement.

## The Restructuring Middle Level School as a Community of Learners

Restructuring schools are places where everyone is involved in learning; learners are teachers and teachers are learners. There is an atmosphere of collegial inquiry which facilitates a constant search for better ways to learn and teach. Teachers become committed to their own professional development, they become researchers, they inquire about teaching, and they observe each other teach. Barth (1990) suggests that in a community of learners the school is a context for everyone's lifelong growth and that adult learning "is not only a means toward the end of student learning, but also an important objective in its own right" (pp. 46-47).

A community of learners, which includes teachers, administrators, parents, and community members, is built around the following assumptions (Barth, 1990):

1. Schools have the capacity to improve themselves. Those on the outside have a major responsibility for helping to change conditions on the inside.
2. Under the right conditions and purposes adults and students learn, and each energizes and contributes to the learning of the other.
3. The focus of school improvement is on the school culture, the quality of interpersonal relationships, and the nature and the quality of the learning experiences.
4. Improving the school is focused on determining and providing, from within and without, the necessary conditions which will promote and sustain learning among the adults and students who attend and work at the school.

Principals in restructuring middle level schools play a crucial role in creating learning environments in their schools. As active learners, they experience, display, model, and celebrate what is hoped and expected of teachers and students. In these schools, principals establish the environment that enables teachers, parents, and community members, as a community of learners, to actively engage in confronting their knowledge base, in inquiring and reflecting about programs and practice, and in clarifying goals and purposes. These processes enhance the learning process and lead to a continuing environment of school improvement.

## The Restructuring Middle Level School as a Center of Inquiry

In the early years of our work with middle level school improvement we became interested in the work of Robert Schaefer (1967) and his concept of the "school as a center of inquiry." Although developed more than twenty-five years ago, Schaefer's concept of school inquiry still has great relevance for middle level school restructuring. His idea of teachers and administrators actively engaged in learning about their school forms the basis of action research. Action research is defined by Holly (1991) as collaborative inquiry conducted within the context of collegial support. Among other things, action research is an appropriate vehicle for teachers to undertake collaborative and systematic investigations into instructional practice. It links teachers with vital sources of knowledge, it provides opportunities for intellectual stimulation outside the school, it enhances the professional development experiences, it supports continual teacher learning which enables students to become continuing learners, and it encourages teachers to investigate the organizational aspects of their schools as they relate to learning (Holly, 1991; Schaefer, 1967).

In middle level schools, action research provides numerous opportunities for teachers and administrators to become engaged in the study of their schools. It supplies the structure for answering the specific programmatic and instructional questions about current school practices. Action research also provides those closest to the issues and problems with a vehicle for inquiry and reflection.

Action research is a powerful tool in middle level school restructuring. Not only does it facilitate the continuing process of school improvement but it actively engages teachers in collaborative efforts which are focused on addressing and solving the major issues of their school. Continuous inquiry and reflection are cornerstones of middle level schools who maintain supportive climates for ongoing school improvement. Action research provides an excellent structure for facilitating that inquiry and reflection.

## SUMMARY

Almost a century old, middle level schools, much like the young adolescents they serve, are still seeking their identity. In spite of the richness of the literature describing appropriate programs and the verification of responsive practice by the research, far too many middle level schools still fail to incorporate programs and practices that are developmentally responsive.

While some middle level schools are making significant progress toward developmental responsiveness, much needs to be done. Those schools that have implemented appropriate programs must continue their efforts to improve by making sure that these programs are functioning as intended and by pursuing new ways to help all young adolescents be successful. Middle level schools that have not yet implemented programs which have been identified as being developmentally responsive must begin to take the necessary steps to develop and implement appropriate organizational and learning arrangements.

Lounsbury and Clark (1990) state that the sign in front of middle level schools should read "work in progress" or "under construction." What will it take to make this "work in progress" successful? We believe there are four factors that will sustain the process of change:

1. Middle level educators must look to themselves for the answers. Within each school community there is considerable expertise to solve the problems that exist. In spite of many constraints, successful middle level schools find ways to solve problems, implement new programs, improve school climate, and provide professional development. These schools' success comes from a group of people who believe they can make a difference.

2. Middle level educators must reduce the sense of isolation that exists in their schools. They must find ways for teachers, administrators, parents, and community members to collaborate, to share expertise, and to participate in decision making.

3. Middle level educators must actively seek alliances, networks, and partnerships. Building partnerships with community agencies and colleges and universities enhances the opportunities to expand services to teachers and students and their families. Participating in networks with other middle level schools facilitates the sharing of ideas and expertise.

4. Middle level educators must recognize that parents are powerful allies in the education of young ado-

lescents. Steps must be taken to establish structures that will involve parents in the everyday life of the school.

For many young people middle level schools will be their last best chance to avoid a diminished future (Carnegie Task Force on Education of Young Adolescents, 1989). Will middle level educators rise to the challenge of creating environments where all students can be successful? We have confidence that middle level educators are up to the challenge and that the middle level schools of the 21st century will be places where young adolescents can prosper and flourish.

## REFERENCES

Barth, R. (1990). *Improving schools from within: Teachers, parents, and principals can make a difference.* San Francisco, CA: Jossey-Bass.

Braddock, J. H., II. (1990). Tracking in the middle grades: National patterns of grouping for instruction. *Phi Delta Kappan, 71*(6), 445-449.

Carnegie Task Force on the Education of Young Adolescents. (1989). *Turning points: Preparing American youth for the 21st century.* Washington, D. C.: Carnegie Council on Adolescent Development.

Glickman, C. (1991). Pretending not to know what we know. *Educational Leadership, 48*(8), 4-11.

Holly, P. (1991). Action research: The missing link in the creation of schools as centers of inquiry. In A. Lieberman, & L. Miller (Eds.), *Staff development for education in the '90s, 2nd edition* (pp. 133-157). New York: Teachers College Press.

Joyce, B., Hersch, R., & McKibbin, M. (1983). *The structure of school improvement.* New York: Longman.

Lounsbury, J. H., & Clark, D. C. (1990). *Inside grade eight: From apathy to excitement.* Reston, VA: National Association of Secondary School Principals.

Schaefer, R. (1967). *The school as a center of inquiry.* New York: Harper & Row.

# NAME INDEX

299

# SUBJECT INDEX